BLOODY BRITAIN

A history of *murder*,
mayhem and *massacre*

First published 2002
Reprinted 2008

Researched and written by: Mike Ivory (South-west England), Hilary Weston (South-east England), Michael Nation (London), Nia Williams (Central England, Wales), Chris Bagshaw (Northern England), David Kinnaird (Edinburgh), Hugh Taylor (Scotland).

Produced by AA Publishing

Mapping produced by the Mapping Services Department of The Automobile Association.

Published by AA Publishing (a trading name of Automobile Association Developments Limited, whose registered office is Fanum House, Basing View, Hampshire RG21 4EA; registered number 1878835).

A03923

ISBN 978 0 7495 5165 0

A CIP catalogue record for this book is available from the British Library.

Visit AA Publishing at www.theAA.com/travel

Printed in Slovenia by MKT Print

BLOODY BRITAIN

A history of *murder*, *mayhem* and *massacre*

Foreword by
Tony Robinson

SOUTH-WEST ENGLAND

10–41

LONDON

42–61

SOUTH-EAST ENGLAND

62–93

CENTRAL ENGLAND

94–125

CONTENTS

WALES
126–153

NORTHERN ENGLAND
154–185

EDINBURGH
186–205

SCOTLAND
206–237

FOREWORD

by Tony Robinson

'Sweet Fanny Adams!' That was the nearest my mother ever came to uttering a profanity. Ours was a respectable family. We lived in a respectable house in a respectable neighbourhood and, behind their closed doors, our neighbours were doubtless as respectable as we were. But how much undiscovered horror was being played out on the other side of their lace curtains? How much wife-beating, rape, poisoning and torture? 'Sweet Fanny Adams!' my mother would have replied.

Yet the manner of her denial offers evidence that her complacency may have been misplaced. Pick almost any spot on the map of Britain and, at some time in the past, a brutal crime will have been committed there, more often than not by a relative, friend or neighbour of the victim. Our respectability is a futile attempt at warding off the demons. It is the taut web we weave around ourselves in order to prevent base desires from engulfing us in a fervour of violent and lustful gratification. But all too often that web can be broken. At any time, and in any place.

My mother used sweet Fanny's name lightly, on the misguided assumption that she was uttering only a playful euphemism for a four-letter expletive, but Fanny Adams was a real live person – or at least she was until she was brutally murdered. What county is more respectable than Hampshire? What place more charming than Alton? Yet it was here that little Fanny, just eight years old, went out to play, and was later found murdered a short distance from her home. But not quite all of her was found. A leg was discovered, and her mutilated torso lay near by. Her head was found resting on two hop-poles at the foot of a hedge. But, to this day, despite the most comprehensive of searches, how much more of her has been recovered? – Sweet Fanny Adams!

The dark forces that engulfed Fanny can be summoned at will. In Reading, on the banks of the gently flowing Thames, Amelia Dyer slaughtered the illegitimate babies of compromised servant girls and cast them into the deep.

At Coombe, a small village which offers charming views across the Berkshire Downs, George Brougham murdered his wife by thrusting her head into a hive of furious wasps. So many thwarted people, so much tragedy!

But these tawdry acts of domestic horror pale into nothingness compared with the violence perpetrated by whole communities. Respectable Christians in Edinburgh tortured, strangled and burnt those accused of witchcraft. In 1190 the good people of York burnt alive their Jewish fellow-citizens in the castle keep. In the 16th century the air around the Kentish town of Amersham stank from the roasting flesh of Lollards blazing at the stake.

Of course horror isn't always planned. Sometimes it appears unbidden as the consequence of the slightest mishap. A woman stumbles, someone falls and 111 Londoners are trampled to death in Bethnal Green tube station. It can take place on the sunniest of afternoons in the most pleasant of locations. In 1845 a spellbound crowd on the Great Yarmouth Suspension Bridge watched Nelson the Clown sail up the River Bure in a wash-tub drawn by four geese, little knowing that within minutes a chain would snap, they would be cast into the river and 130 merry sight-seers would never see another day.

Horror can be tinged with black comedy, as in the tale of Redhand the Camarthenshire gang-leader, who thrust his arm through an old woman's larder window to steal her food, only to discover when he withdrew it, that his hand had been severed by her carving knife. And in the last resort our primeval desires can cast off every last vestige of respectability as in the tale of the Beans, a family of incestuous cannibals who lived on the road to Ballantrae, and stalked unsuspecting travellers whose limbs they hung on hooks or salted in barrels.

Our island is a theatre of blood. As you wend your way through Britain's byways searching for the spot were the heretic's fingernails were torn out, the saint was beheaded, or the unfaithful wife beaten to a pulp, have a pleasant and respectable day.

But take heed. Those with whom you travel are doubtless respectable too, but the web can break at any time, and in any place.

Tony Robinson

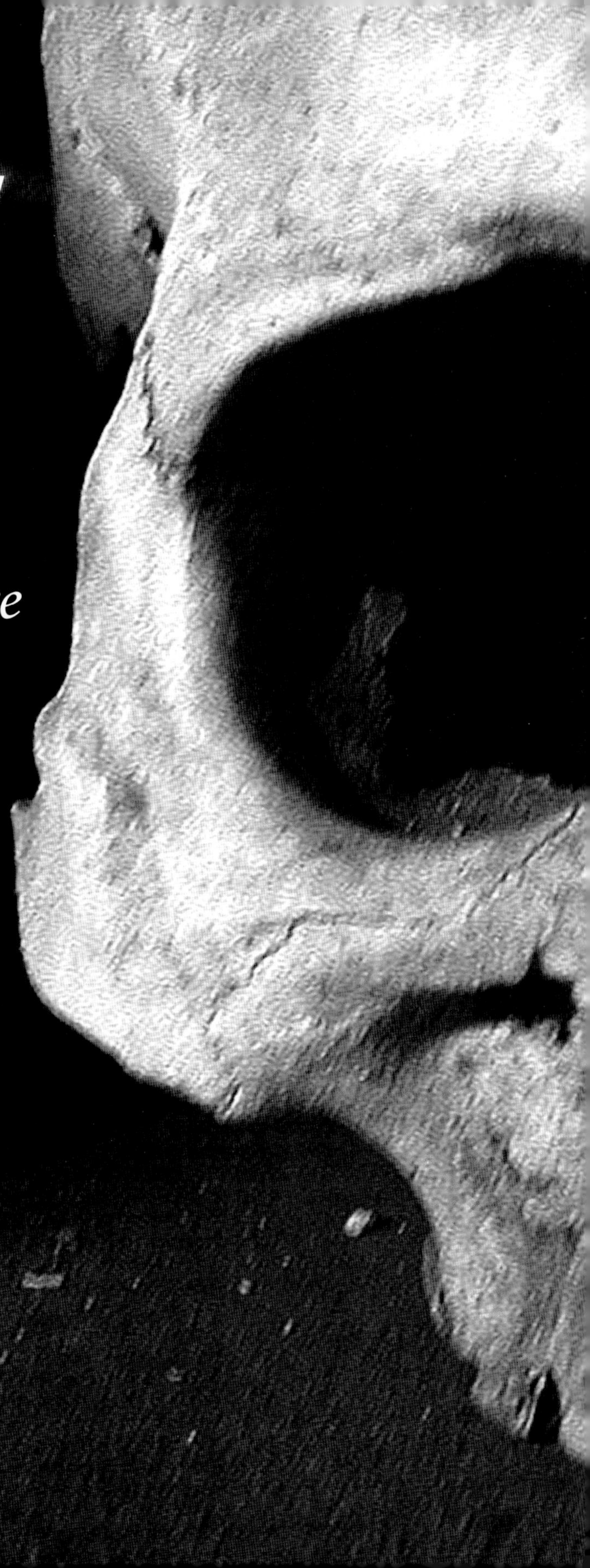

BLOODY BRITAIN

A history of *murder*, *mayhem* and *massacre*

How did Mrs Blunden come to be buried alive in Basingstoke in 1674?

What made Chelmsford such a hot hotbed of witchcraft?

Who placed 17 miniature coffins in a cave in Edinburgh?

What ghastly crime did Thomas Wells of Bognor Regis commit to earn the penalty of being pressed to death?

How did Oswestry's Weeping Cross get its name?

And what was the appalling secret vice of the Bean family of Ballantrae?

INTRODUCTION

In every part of Britain, in some place at some time a bloody event has taken place – notorious murders, bloodthirsty retribution and punishment, outbreaks of plague and pestilence are the stuff of absorbing history and horrified fascination. Where did it happen? In what village or town or at what lonely crossroads did these villainous deeds and ghastly events take place?

From place to place in each area of the country this book charts the history of Britain's bloody, tragic and horrific past. Terrible stories of pain and conflict and human suffering that defy belief make compulsive reading. Some are the stuff of notoriety and known to us all, some are known only in local legend but all illustrate the enduring nature of man's cruelty to man or the terrifying power of fate to inflict tragedy on humankind.

Piracy and torture, murderous battles, ritual burnings and much more are the stuff of Britain's rich, colourful and often dreadful past – how full our history is of such events is clearly illustrated in the unputdownable pages that follow. Read and feel your flesh begin to creep…

SOUTH-WEST ENGLAND

Rebellion and revolt against the centralising tendencies of the English Crown often had their origin in the West Country, particularly in Celtic Cornwall, and were characteristically put down with the utmost ruthlessness. In 1496, 15,000 Cornishmen marched on London, only to be bloodily defeated at Blackheath by Henry VII's army of German mercenaries.

Pretenders to the Throne

Queen Margaret landed at Weymouth with her son, the Prince of Wales, in 1471. They planned to wrest the crown from their Yorkist rival Edward IV, but were soundly defeated at the Battle of Tewkesbury. The pretender Perkin Warbeck set off from Cornwall some 26 years later to claim the throne, but fled the field and abandoned his supporters before getting much further than Exeter.

In 1549, during the Reformation, Devon and Cornwall passionately resisted the imposition of newfangled ways of conducting church services. What became known as the Prayer Book Rebellion was mercilessly suppressed in a campaign of terror, with the mass slaughter of prisoners of war and exemplary executions.

During the Civil War the towns and cities of the south-west suffered many a siege, their populations decimated by sickness and starvation. The last Royalist post in England to hold out against Parliament was Cornwall's Pendennis Castle, which finally surrendered in 1646, its defenders exhausted by epidemics and haggard through lack of food. Then, in 1685, the Duke of Monmouth, another pretender to the English throne, made the West Country his base. After his defeat at the Battle of Sedgemoor, the region was subjected to a reign of terror hardly equalled in English history, as the notorious Judge Jeffreys presided over the Bloody Assizes and handed out hundreds of death sentences.

Piracy

With its innumerable bays and inlets, the long coastline of the south-west was impossible to police effectively. It was therefore easy for pretenders to the throne to land here unopposed, while invaders and pirates from France, Spain and even North Africa were often able to raid ports and

Slave graves, Bristol; the slave trade, on which much of the city's wealth was based, reached its peak in the late 18th century.

fishing villages with impunity, killing, sacking, burning, and occasionally carrying off slaves and hostages. The West Country produced its own race of pirates, many of them in league with local landowners in pursuit of profitable plunder. Sometimes though, a pirate would overstep the mark, and end up dangling from a gibbet on the beach as a grim example to others.

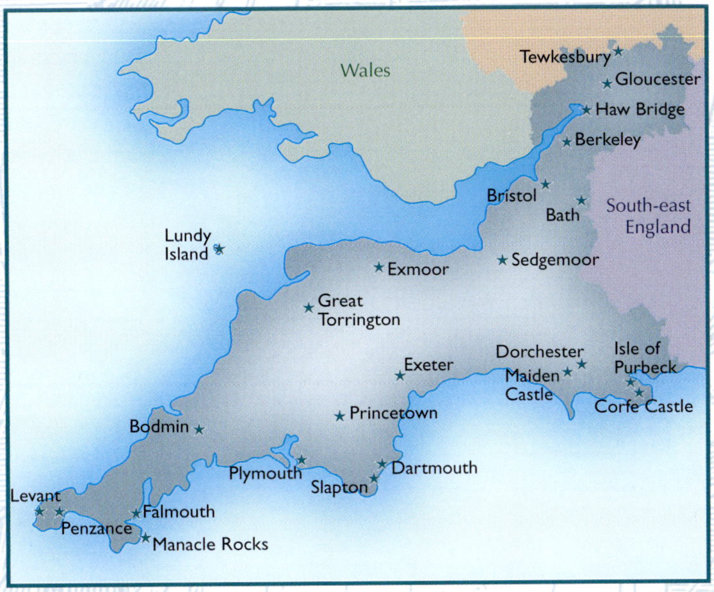

Smuggling and wrecking

Those other characteristic West Country activities of smuggling and wrecking offered easier if less spectacular pickings than piracy, and frequently involved whole communities. The innumerable wrecks claimed by the rugged coastline may have cost countless lives, but were regarded by the local populace as gifts from Heaven. In the rush to pillage the cargoes of stranded vessels, human charity was frequently forgotten, with shipwrecked sailors left to drown or stripped of their possessions.

Such heartlessness was never excusable, but is perhaps understandable in the context of the harsh life led by many West Country folk. Cornwall in particular was an inhospitable place for many of its inhabitants. Even when its famous tin-mining industry was at its height, conditions were unforgiving, and death and injury commonplace. The tragedy at Levant in 1919, when 32 died, was only the worst of many disasters.

Protest and riot

What is still a largely rural region had its share of agricultural disturbances in the early 19th century, when appalling living conditions in the countryside led to widespread protest, the most notorious case being that of the Tolpuddle Martyrs, transported to Australia for daring to join together in an early form of trade union.

However, some of the worst riots in British history took place in Bristol, when military action was required to subdue the mob violence and over 250 people were killed. Plymouth, the region's next largest city and its greatest naval port, was where Frenchmen captured in the Napoleonic Wars were confined in vile conditions in rotting prison ships. Their situation eventually became too unbearable even for their captors, leading to the construction of what became one of Britain's most forbidding prisons at Princetown high up on the lonely wastes of Dartmoor, the scene of much mayhem and riot.

In the early months of World War II, the West Country seemed far away from the scene of conflict, and it was a terrible shock to their inhabitants when its cities were subjected to some of the country's most devastating aerial bombardments. Hundreds of lives were lost as the centres of Bristol and Plymouth were obliterated in the Blitz of 1940–41. Then, in April 1942, medieval Exeter and Georgian Bath were viciously attacked in the course of the vengeful 'Baedeker Raids', conceived by the Nazis as a way of punishing Britain for the RAF's destruction of Germany's historic cities.

Elegant Roman sculpture at the baths

Bath SOMERSET

With its refined social rituals centred on 'taking the waters', Bath traditionally prided itself on its elegant architecture and fine ways. However it also had some of the foulest slums in England, and some of its citizens were capable of behaviour that was far from genteel.

> **“ George Montagu declared 'They may say what they will, but it does one ten times more good to leave Bath than to come to it! ”**

The battle of Lansdown Hill Every year, the great sheep and cattle fair held on Lansdown Hill, on the outskirts of Bath, was the scene of much merrymaking, with hundreds of stalls, sideshows, swings and amusements. Respectable dealers and farmers were prepared to pay for their entertainment in a law-abiding manner, but as day turned to evening they would make their way home, to be replaced by a motley crowd of ruffianly city-dwellers, who sometimes had other ideas. Fights were common, and drunkenness rampant, but few were prepared for the mass invasion that took place on the occasion of the 1839 fair.

Around ten o'clock, as night set in, the stallholders started to close their booths. At this point, a great roar arose from down the hill; a brutal mob came swarming up from the slums of the city, high on drink and intent on destruction. Led by a grossly overweight and foul-mouthed red-head rejoicing in the name of Carroty Kate (denizen of a malodorous den known as Bull Paunch Alley), they set about wrecking the fair.

First to be attacked were the drinking-booths; their owners were battered into insensibility and bottles and barrels drained of their contents, firing the looters into an even more ferocious frenzy. The booths were torn down and trampled on, then the other showmen who had not made good their escape were assaulted, their possessions stolen, their precious stalls smashed to smithereens, and their wagons broken up and set on fire.

The riot lasted until dawn. As the troublemakers began to stumble back towards the city, they got into another fight, this time with the police, who up until now had proved ineffectual. The showmen were to have their revenge.

Capturing Kate and those of her accomplices who had not fled, they lashed the men together and hauled them through the muddy water of a pond, then tied them one by one to a wagon wheel and thrashed them. Spared a ducking, Carroty Kate was given a good caning, and left the scene still cursing, to lick her wounds in her lurking place in Bull Paunch Alley.

LOCATION: 15 MILES EAST OF BRISTOL

SQUALOR AT THE SPA

The healing properties of Bath's famous waters are supposed to have been discovered by pigs. Banished from the royal court because he had fallen victim to leprosy, the Ancient British prince Bladud eked out a living as a swineherd, passing on his disease to his charges, who like him developed disgusting sores and swellings. One day the porkers rushed headlong into a patch of marshy ground and wallowed in the muddy waters. When they emerged, all trace of their affliction had gone. Gingerly, the prince immersed himself in the foul-smelling slime, and found that he too was cured.

In later centuries, following Bladud's example, thousands came in search of a cure for their ailments – Romans afflicted by arthritis brought on by Britain's damp climate, medieval people with the pox, then elegant 18th century folk drawn as much by the city's glittering social life as by the beneficial qualities of its springs. Local doctors claimed cures for every imaginable affliction, including 'chorea, green sickness, gout, sciatica, ulcers, uterine diseases and septic wounds', while the relief of constipation, that 'most obstinate costiveness attended with exquisite pain in the bowels' or 'hardnesse and binding of the Bellye' seems to have attracted a disproportionate amount of attention.

Rubbish and worse

When you consider the condition of the waters, it is amazing that any cures were effected at all. The frolicsome goings-on of the Middle Ages, when men and women bathed naked together, may have ended but even in the 18th century little account seems to have been taken of the most elementary rules of hygiene. All kinds of rubbish was dumped in the waters, including dead dogs and cats. Most spa guests would have made little effort to wash before lowering their bodies into the shared bath. There were no limits on the amount of time spent in the bath, and few bothered to climb out in order to relieve themselves.

A graphic depiction appears in Smollett's novel *The Expedition of Humphrey Clinker* (1771). When his eponymous hero visits the King's Bath, the first thing he sees is a child, covered in scrofulous ulcers, being carried among the bathers. He then speculates on the relationship between the water being bathed in and that being consumed in the nearby pump room, suspecting that the patients are probably swallowing the 'scourings of the bathers', a mixture of 'sweat, dirt and dandruff, and abominable discharges of various kinds'. Sickened by these thoughts, he repairs to another set of baths, but, noting the strange taste and smell of the waters here, discovers that they were probably strained through the 'rotten bones and carcasses' of the adjacent burial ground.

...the patients were probably swallowing the 'scourings of the bathers', a mixture of 'sweat, dirt and dandruff, and abominable discharges of various kinds'.

Berkeley GLOUCESTERSHIRE

Unspeakably assassinated Neglectful of his kingly duties, Edward II (1284–1327) preferred to amuse himself in the company of handsome young friends like Piers Gaveston and Hugh Despenser. Such unconventional behaviour outraged traditionally minded earls and barons, already annoyed by Edward's habits of favouritism. They conspired to get Gaveston sent into exile, then had him executed, while Despenser died a horrible death in Hereford – castrated, disembowelled and then beheaded, all in front of a jeering mob.

In 1327 Edward himself was arrested and imprisoned in Berkeley Castle, near Gloucester, where at first he was treated well by its owner, Thomas, Lord Berkeley. But Berkeley was soon elbowed aside by the ruthless figures of Sir John Maltravers and Sir Thomas de Gournay, who planned with other conspirators to kill the king. Since their orders were to leave no mark on the monarch's body, they tried to starve him to death, then to asphyxiate him by leaving rotting carcasses beneath the floorboards of his room. When these stratagems failed, a red-hot poker was inserted into the rectum of the wretched Edward, whose dying screams echoed all over the little town. The official version of this terrible event was that the King had died of a sudden seizure, but the corpse's agonised features told a different tale. Unloved by his subjects in life, Edward was revered in death, his tomb in Gloucester Cathedral becoming a popular place of pilgrimage.

LOCATION: 20 MILES SOUTH OF GLOUCESTER VIA A38

Bodmin CORNWALL

The Mayor's last supper Appointed in the aftermath of the 'Prayer Book Rebellion' of 1549 to terrorise the Cornish and suppress their tendency to revolt, Sir Anthony Kingston went about his task with relish, ruthlessness and a particularly cruel and twisted sense of humour.

Edward II's tomb in Gloucester Cathedral

Bodmin's mayor had played a minor part in the rebellion, so when Kingston invited himself to dinner, the Mayor took this as a sign that his misdemeanours had been forgiven and prepared a lavish spread. On his arrival, Kingston asked for a gallows to be made ready, as there was unfinished business to attend to. Dinner was a convivial occasion. Then, when the last toast had been drunk, Sir Anthony took his host aside and enquired about the strength of the scaffold. The Mayor assured his visitor that it was solidly built and would serve its purpose excellently. 'Then climb up to it, for it is for you', chortled his callous guest.

Execution specials The County Assizes at Bodmin were the scene of many a harsh sentence in the days when the death penalty punished a host of trivial offences, and Bodmin prison was the scene of a series of public executions.

Between 1785 and 1835, no fewer than 40 offenders were hanged outside its walls; while some were murderers, others had done no more than steal a sheep or set fire to a haystack. Among them was John Hoskins, condemned to death (despite his denials) for his part in a riot in which a miller had been beaten and some of his grain stolen. On the gallows in 1796, Hoskins harangued the crowd that had come to watch his demise, made sure the rope fitted tightly round his neck, and sang a hymn before he died. The last person to be hanged for a crime other than murder was William Hocking, who stood on the scaffold in 1834 convicted of 'bestiality', the precise nature of which remained unreported.

In 1840 the Wadebridge-to-Wenford Bridge Railway built a branch line to Bodmin, and until the last public hanging in 1862, the company laid on special trains whenever an execution took place. The railway line ran past the walls of the jail, offering a grandstand view for the thousand or more passengers brought there in open coal trucks which had been cleaned up for the occasion. Thousands more would settle on the slopes that formed a natural amphitheatre around the prison.

An execution meant good business for Bodmin as countryfolk crowded in, bringing rich pickings for pubs and prostitutes, shops and stallholders, thieves, pickpockets and balladmongers. Carrying a pole with a picture of the murder on one side and the hanging on the other, Old Jack Perry hawked leaflets purporting to be the murderer's last speech and confession. To complete the entertainment, sideshows were set up where, for a penny, spectators could see a re-enactment of the murder.

Infanticide Naturally enough, the hanging of perpetrators of particularly gruesome murders drew the biggest crowds. Plenty came to the execution of young Elizabeth Commins in 1821. Orphan Elizabeth had been placed in service, where she was taken advantage of and became pregnant. With no-one to turn to, she kept her shameful condition secret, and then, when her pains started, she hid in a cowshed, where she gave birth to a baby boy. Terrified that the infant's wailing would give her away, she dashed his head against the wall. Utterly contrite, she was found sitting on the floor of the cowshed, staring at what she had done. The court showed the distraught mother no mercy, and she was hanged and her body delivered for dissection.

Just deserts Public satisfaction was widespread when notorious killers got what were seen as their just deserts. When Matthew Weeks cut the throat of his 18-year-old sweetheart, Charlotte Dymond, in a fit of jealous rage, all Cornwall was outraged, and he was hanged here in 1844. Even more horrifying was the beating to death of the kindly and popular local merchant Neville Norway by the Lightfoot brothers, William and James. Their hanging, in April 1849, was attended by a vindictive crowd of 25,000. When one spectator, overcome by the imminent execution, seemed about to faint, he was revived with a blow to the jaw by his neighbour, who declared 'Fancy faintin' to see blaggards like they 'anged!'

LOCATION: ON A30

Bristol

Carnage at College Green On 28 September 1764, a revoltingly brutal murder took place in the pleasant setting of the city's College Green, close to the cathedral and the Church of St Augustine. The perpetrator was Edward Higgins, a seasoned criminal who was eventually caught after a series of further attacks and robberies. His victims were Frances Ruscombe and her maid, Mary Champneys. Higgins had cut Frances' throat and beaten her around the head with such violence that she lost an eye and fragments of her skull penetrated her brain. A terrible blow split Mary's head apart and almost severed it from her body. At his trial, Higgins protested innocence of the crime, but finally admitted his guilt on the eve of his execution in 1767.

Riot and destruction For years, everyone crossing Bristol Bridge had had to pay a toll. Bitterly resented by the poorer members of society, the fee was due to be abolished in 1793, but at the last minute was re-imposed. Outraged, the populace ripped the gates of the bridge from their hinges and made a bonfire of them. New gates were put in place but were burnt in their turn. The authorities read the Riot Act and brought in the Herefordshire militia. In two days of rioting, missiles were thrown, muskets fired, and the militia made a charge with fixed bayonets. In all, 12 people were killed, a high price to pay for the privilege of crossing a bridge without paying.

Reform Bill riot A riot in 1831 had a more weighty cause. The great Reform Bill had raised the common people's hopes by seeming to promise them increased representation in Parliament. But the bill was heartily opposed by vested interests, most flagrantly represented in Bristol by the gross and insensitive Sir Charles Weatherell. On Saturday 29 October, as Sir Charles came to the city to open the Assizes at the Mansion House, he was booed, hissed, and pelted with mud and stones. Not content with demonstrating their disapproval in this way, the crowd then stormed the Mansion House, partly wrecking it and gobbling up the civic banquet laid out in honour of Sir Charles, who meanwhile had escaped over the rooftops.

On Sunday morning the attack was renewed, despite the presence of soldiers. After the Mansion House had been set on fire and the contents of its wine cellar consumed in the streets, the growing mob surged through the city, releasing prisoners from the jails, attacking public buildings and gutting the graceful residences on Queen Square. On the third day, as rumours circulated of crowds of looters heading towards the city from the surrounding countryside, more troops were called in. Order was rapidly and violently restored, at a cost of 250 killed or seriously wounded.

Surgeon Smith and Horwood's skin

Fair-skinned John Horwood was devastated when his 19-year-old sweetheart Eliza rejected his advances. The young man threatened to burn her house down, then sought consolation in the ale-house. Emerging into the dusk, he caught sight of Eliza fetching water from the brook, and, still smouldering with anger, threw a stone at her. Despite having downed several pints of cheap porter, his aim was accurate, and Eliza ran home bleeding from a head wound. Her mother's bread and milk poultice relieved the pain, but her skull was fractured, and within days the ill-used girl was dead.

Harwood was arrested and brought to trial, where one of the chief witnesses was surgeon Richard Smith, notorious for his ghoulish public dissections. Smith was much taken with the lad's physique and fresh complexion, and relished the prospect of getting his hands on what he knew would make a 'good corpse'. The law took its course. Harwood was hanged, and his body spirited away in a cab by Smith. What the enthusiastic surgeon referred to as the corpse's 'smooth pelt' was stripped off, tanned in a tub, stretched out to dry, then fashioned into a splendid binding for all the papers relating to the trial.

What the enthusiastic surgeon referred to as the corpse's 'smooth pelt' was stripped off, tanned in a tub, stretched out to dry, then fashioned into a splendid binding for all the papers relating to the trial.

The dizzying height of the Avon suspension bridge has tempted scores to jump to their deaths

BRISTOL (CONTD.)

Suspension bridge suicides Brunel's daringly engineered suspension bridge has spanned the Avon Gorge since 1864. In that time it has become notorious for suicides, with more than a thousand unfortunates having climbed its railings and leapt to their deaths in the river below. Not all the stories end unhappily, however. One dark night in 1896, a father threw his two daughters, aged three and twelve, from the bridge. Amazingly, they survived almost uninjured, and were rescued from the water by boatmen.

An even more extraordinary escape was that of pretty 22-year old Sarah Ann Henley, in 1885. Jilted by her railway porter sweetheart, she caught the horse-bus from the city centre, climbed the zigzag path to the bridge, paid the toll and launched herself into space. Instead of plunging to her doom, she was borne up by her voluminous skirts which acted like a parachute. Drifting gently down, she made a soft landing in the slime of the riverbank. Bystanders hauled her out, and the mud-bespattered beauty was rushed to hospital by cab, the mean-spirited driver having extorted a £10 fee for damage to his upholstery. Sarah made a full recovery, was eventually married (though not to her porter), and lived to the ripe old age of 84.

The Bristol Blitz In the early stages of World War II, many people in the West Country felt their distance from the Continent made them reasonably safe from attack by German bombers. With a medieval core crammed with highly inflammable timber buildings, and impotant aircraft factories around the city, however, Bristol was vulnerble to attack.

The bombers duly came, not once but many times, beginning on the night of 24 November 1940, when incendiaries and high-explosive bombs turned the city centre into an 'inferno hotter than Hell itself'. Streets turned into rivers of fire, molten lead poured from church roofs, and the air was filled with smoke, ash, sparks and burning debris. The roar of the fires was interrupted by the crash of collapsing buildings, among them one of England's finest Elizabethan edifices, the timber-framed, high-gabled St Peter's Hospital. By morning, the heart of what had been one of the country's finest historic cities lay in smouldering ruin and hundreds of Bristolians had been killed or wounded.

LOCATION: 6 MILES SOUTH OF M4 JUNCTION 19

Corfe Castle DORSET

A wicked stepmother and a saint

The gaunt ruins of Corfe Castle perched on their hilltop are one of the most evocative images of England's Middle Ages. In AD 879 it was the residence of Queen Elfrida, stepmother of the teenage King Edward. Elfrida had previously plotted to put her own son, Ethelred (the Unready), on the throne. When Edward called here in the course of a hunting trip, she spied her chance. As the King rode up on his horse, she slyly offered him a cup of mead. All unsuspecting, the

Wartime devastation in the heart of Bristol

young man bent over to drink, and as he did so, one of the Queen's retainers plunged a dagger into his side. Spurring on his steed, Edward made off, but fell from the saddle and was dragged along with one foot still in the stirrup, leaving a ghastly trail of blood before expiring, half-buried in a bog. His corpse was eventually recovered, buried at Wareham, then transferred to Shaftesbury. Miracles were reported from the places associated with the assassination, and within a few years Edward was known as a saint and martyr.
LOCATION: 8 MILES NORTH OF SWANAGE ON A351

Dartmouth DEVON

The French frustrated At the conclusion of the Hundred Years War in 1389, enmity still existed between the West Country and the coastal population of Brittany and Normandy. In August 1403, in response to constant raids by men from Devon harbours, a powerful force was assembled by the aristocratic Guillaume du Châtel from St-Malo. Sailing into Plymouth Sound, the Frenchmen disembarked and battled their way into the lower part of the town of Dartmouth, then spent the night in an orgy of killing, burning and pillaging. As they withdrew the following morning, du Châtel's men were assailed by the arrows of the English bowmen, and many of them perished before reaching their ships.

Far from deterring the English, the French attack drew a swift response; in November a fleet of ships from Plymouth, Dartmouth and Bristol destroyed 40 French vessels and laid waste a large area of the Breton coast. Du Châtel could only reply in kind, but when his boats attempted an assault on Dartmouth the following April, they failed to break the chain stretched across the harbour. A land attack also failed, du Châtel's heavily armed knights being cut down in great number by common English bowmen. A French chronicler bewailed this triumph of peasants over nobles, declaring 'The crows have pecked the eagles.'
LOCATION: 22 MILES SOUTH OF NEWTON ABBOT

Dorchester DORSET

Saintly martyrs Born in Cornwall, John Cornelius trained in France and Rome as a Catholic priest, then returned to England to join the struggle against Protestantism. In 1594 he was arrested together with three associates at Chideock Castle and taken to London, where despite being tortured, he refused to recant or implicate anyone else. Returned to Dorchester, he and his colleagues were condemned to death. Stepping up to the gallows, he kissed the rope and prayed for the executioners and for the welfare of Queen Elizabeth. Once the hangman had done his work, Cornelius's body was quartered and his head nailed to the gibbet. He and his fellows are commemorated in Dorchester by a poignant statue on Gallows Hill, the work of the sculptress Elizabeth Frink.

Secular martyrs In 1833, six labourers from the Dorset village of Tolpuddle met to swear a secret oath of brotherhood and to form a branch of the Agricultural Labourers' Friendly Society. Their aim was a simple one: to persuade landowners to pay more than the starvation wages which were then the norm, but the rural establishment determined to make an example of them. The six were arrested, brought to Dorchester, and charged with making a clandestine and unlawful oath. The prosecution painted a lurid picture of the oath-taking ceremony and the judge himself accused the men of sedition and treason, directing the jury – made up of those very tight-fisted landowners who stood to lose out if the men gained their objective – to find them guilty. The sentence was the cruel one of transportation to Australia. The condemned men were shackled, incarcerated for a while in prison hulks, then sent off on the five-month voyage to Tasmania. However, the obvious injustice of the verdict and the severity of the sentence aroused public indignation, and the 'Tolpuddle Martyrs' were eventually pardoned. By 1839 they were back in England, but all but one of them turned their backs on the country which had treated them so harshly and set off across the ocean once more, this time voluntarily, their destination Canada.

Maumbury Rings These substantial earthworks are the remains of Dorchester's Roman amphitheatre, a place where gladiators and wild beasts once fought. Long after the Romans had gone, the earthworks once again served as

Figures of the Dorchester martyrs by Dame Elizabeth Frink (1930–93)

the setting for gruesome entertainment: public executions. An enthusiastic crowd attended that of Mary Channing in 1705. As a girl, Mary had been forced to wed a dullard of a grocer, a man for whom she felt no affection. Lost in a loveless marriage, she fed her husband poison. She was tried, condemned to death, and dragged to the Rings, still screaming her innocence. A crowd of 10,000 looked on as Mary was strangled and her body set on fire.

LOCATION: ON A35

Exeter DEVON

The man they couldn't hang Elderly spinster Emma Keyse, a former maid to Queen Victoria, demonstrated a seeming kindness when she took on 19-year-old John Lee as footman, despite his having served a six-month prison sentence for theft. But Emma was a stingy employer, and John was far from being a reformed character. When she docked his wages for some minor misdemeanour, he turned on her, battering her about the head and slitting her throat so deeply that the back bone showed. His trial at Exeter was straightforward enough, and the sentence – death by hanging – was never in doubt. On 4 December 1884, the convicted murderer stood on the gallows trapdoor with the hood covering his head and the rope around his neck. The hangman pulled his lever – but the trapdoor failed to open. He tried again, with the same result. Further frantic attempts were made and still the trapdoor stayed firmly shut. Having survived this ordeal, John Lee had his sentence commuted to life imprisonment.

Demonstrators at a London rally in 1834 showed their support for the Tolpuddle Martyrs

EXETER (CONTD.)

A vicar hanged from his own church tower The Prayer Book Rebellion of 1549 was brought to a bloody end when the mercenaries of Lord Russell's army made short work of the ill-armed Cornishmen besieging Exeter. Hundreds fell in battle and hundreds more were butchered after they had been captured. But perhaps the most horrid fate was that meted out to Robert Walsh, the Protestant vicar of Exeter's Church of St Thomas, which lay just outside the city walls.

A Cornishman, much loved by his parishioners, Walsh sympathised with the rebels and their attachment to Catholic tradition. Although he had stopped them firing red-hot shot into the town to set it ablaze, this earned him no credit once the rebellion had been crushed: he was accused of Popish sympathies. A scaffold was set atop the church tower, and Walsh, dressed in 'Romish vestments', was hauled up to it by a rope tied around his waist, then hanged in chains high above the churchyard. Decorated with 'Popyshe trash' such as a holy water bucket and a bell, his corpse was tarred and left to dangle.

It was removed four years later, when Queen Mary took the throne and restored the 'Old Religion'.

King Cholera As cholera spread through the West Country in the summer of 1832, the respectable citizens of Exeter prayed their city might be spared its ravages. But away from the pious precincts of the cathedral and the fine Georgian houses of the middle classes, the town was in a disgusting state. As many as 15 families might be crammed into the filthy rooms of a single crumbling house, while pigs grunted in backyard sties, chickens scrabbled in cellars, and refuse, dung heaps and slaughterhouse effluent befouled the streets. The water supply and sanitation were quite inadequate 'for the daily usages of the population'.

When the cholera struck, it struck with a vengeance, killing 400 people in the space of a few weeks. Futile measures like spreading lime and attempting to smoke out the disease by placing burning tar barrels in the streets had no effect. As people huddled in their houses, the town was uncannily still, the silence broken only by the tolling of the funeral bell and the clip-clop of the single horse pulling the wagon that bore the corpses. A drunkard who mocked the macabre spectacle as he emerged from a pub was struck down before he could reach home. Within hours he was aboard the same hearse on his final journey.

Having first
body in a
feared disc
cast i

Tragedy at the Theatre Royal
On 5 September 1887, at the gala opening performance of Exeter's splendid new Theatre Royal, stage machinery failed to work and actors fluffed their lines, drawing hoots and jeers from the gallery. Within minutes, their merry mockery turned to cries of pain and terror. Behind the half-lowered curtain, a gaslight had set fire to some canvas scenery; the flames and smoke spread slowly at first, and actors and stage-hands were able to leave through the stage door while the people in the stalls and circle made a more or less

orderly exit. But for the 200 or so people in the gallery, escape was not so easy. Their exit was obstructed by a half-door barrier; and as the crowd jostled and fought their way towards it, the flames burst through the stage curtain, and a cloud of smoke billowed out, filling the theatre. Within instants the whole interior was an inferno. Such was the intensity of the fire that corpses were burned beyond recognition, and the exact number of those who perished has never been established.

LOCATION: JUST WEST OF M5 JUNCTION 30

buried his daughter's field, Burgess had overy, dug it up and down the shaft.

Exmoor SOMERSET

Preserved as a national park, Exmoor is regarded as one of England's most precious and welcoming landscapes. But come to these wind-swept uplands on a bleak winter's day and you'll understand why the area seems to have suffered more than its fair share of gruesome murders…

Little Anna Burgess When William Burgess told his Simonsbath landlady that his eight-year-old daughter, Anna, had gone to live with her grandmother at Porlock, she had no reason to disbelieve the widower's tale. He had found it difficult to make ends meet after the death of his wife, and had already sent his other two children away to work on a farm. But when the landlady discovered some half-burnt child's clothing, her suspicions were aroused.

By the time it emerged that Anna had never reached her grandmother's home, Burgess had fled, though he was soon found and arrested. For weeks he languished in jail, protesting his innocence, and since no body had been found, it seemed that he would have to be released. Then a mysterious blue light was seen flickering over the shaft of old mine workings known as Wheal Eliza. Local people were convinced that a sinister secret must lie in its depths. The mine was drained and little Anna's corpse was found, wrapped in a tarpaulin. Having murdered his daughter and buried her body in a field, Burgess had feared discovery, dug it up again and cast it down the shaft. He was publicly hanged at Taunton on 4 January 1859.

The wild, open spaces of Exmoor provided a fertile ground for grisly crime

EXMOOR (CONT)

Mollie Phillips On 8 September 1929, young Mollie Phillips set out from the farm where she worked to visit her aunt in the next village, reassuring her employer that she would be back in the evening in time to feed the chickens. She never returned. Her disappearance caused a great stir; search parties beat their way through woods and across the moorland, ponds were drained and rivers dragged, but no trace of Mollie could be found. Then, well over a year later, a farmer made a grisly discovery; protruding from boggy ground high up on the moors near Dunkery Beacon was a skull, together with other parts of a human skeleton, all that was left of poor Mollie. The case was a national sensation, with great resentment felt locally that no culprit was ever traced.

The Reverend Edward Trat The charming village of Old Cleeve close to the coast near Minehead was the unlikely setting for a particularly horrible murder at the beginning of the 17th century. As the village curate, Edward Trat had made enemies of his less salubrious parishioners by denouncing their behaviour from the pulpit. Several of them banded together and swore to silence him. One day, as the curate was riding his horse around the parish, his foes sprang from the ditch where they had been lying in wait, dragged him from the saddle and stabbed him to death. Trat's body was taken to his house. There it was dismembered, the intestines stuffed into a pot, the head cut off and partly burnt, the arms, legs and torso boiled in a vat. But the evil-doers were caught, and on 25 July 1604, four of them were hanged for the crime at Stonegallows, near Taunton.
LOCATION: NORTH DEVON

Falmouth CORNWALL

Pendennis Castle Dominating the headland that projects into Falmouth harbour, Pendennis Castle was built by Henry VIII to defend the Cornish coast from a French attack. But the stronghold's most dramatic moments came in 1646, towards the end of the Civil War, when a Royalist force of Cornishmen led by the redoubtable 80-year-old Colonel John Arundell of Trerice defied a Parliamentary siege for several months.

Life under siege was hard. The defenders – more than a thousand of them, including numerous women and children – had plenty of ammunition, but little in the way of provisions. As the weeks wore on, horses were eaten, then dogs. Weakened by starvation, people fell victim to all kinds of illnesses, then were further decimated by an outbreak of plague. Surrender seemed the only option, especially when honourable terms were offered. Even then, diehard defenders plottted to send the fortress and all inside it sky-high by blowing up the magazine, and were only stopped in the nick of time. Those Royalists still able to stand summoned their last energies and marched out with drums beating and flags flying, leaving behind them several hundred sick and dying.

The custom of the sea When the German vessel *Moctezuma* landed three terribly emaciated seamen at Falmouth on 6 September 1884, a dreadful story was revealed. Making no attempt to conceal what had happened, Captain Tom Dudley of the yacht *Mignonette* and his two crewmen had invoked the age-old but never codified 'custom of the sea' to justify their survival after the sinking of their ship. To save themselves from certain starvation, they had killed and eaten their cabin-boy.

The 31-ton *Mignonette* had set sail from England on 5 July 1884, bound for Sydney. Off the coast of Africa the vessel was caught in a storm, and broke up under the impact of a freak wave. The four men barely managed to scramble into the ship's dinghy before the yacht sank. With no provisions or water and no shelter from the fierce equatorial sun, the sailors seemed doomed to die from thirst, starvation and exposure. The capture of a turtle reprieved them for a few days, but once they had eaten the last of its rancid flesh, their demise appeared inevitable. It was then that Tom Dudley took his fateful decision. Against strict instructions, the desperate cabin-boy Richard Parker had drunk sea-water: he was delirious and obviously about to die. Mindful of the 'custom of the sea' which permitted cannibalism in situations as extreme as this, Dudley killed the lad by stabbing him in the throat. His blood was collected in a metal bowl and passed round before it congealed. Drinking it instantly gave his shipmates renewed vitality. The corpse was swiftly butchered. Heart and liver were devoured straight away, while head, feet, intestines and genitals were thrown overboard to the sharks. Dried, the rest of Parker's flesh kept the three men alive until they were finally picked up by the *Moctezuma*.

The men were arrested and charged with murder. Dudley and one of his crew were sentenced to death, but such was the public outcry, they were soon reprieved.

LOCATION: 12 MILES SOUTH OF TRURO

Gloucester GLOUCESTERSHIRE

The city's whores humiliated Gloucester's image in the early 16th century was not one of which the city fathers were proud. All over England the town was spoken of as an 'abominable and vicious' place because of its 'excessive number of common strumpets and bawds'. In an attempt to remedy the situation, the council set up a pillory in the marketplace for these ladies of the night. Before being taken there, the unfortunate prostitutes were forced to wear a striped paper hat and carry a sign announcing their trade while they were paraded around the town in a cart. Once in the pillory, unless they were very lucky, they would be bombarded by all the idlers in town with anything that came to hand – stones, filth, rotten eggs and decaying vegetables, even dead dogs and cats!

A slow-burning bishop John Hooper was a fundamentalist of his time, an ardent Protestant who fell foul of Church authority more than once for his refusal to moderate his extreme views. He served one prison sentence for refusing to don the prescribed vestments, denouncing them as 'the livery of the harlot of Babylon' and 'the rags of Popery'. He was released, and did much good work

A slow-burning suffered terrible for the wood of to be relit more

The botched burning of Bishop John Hooper

as a conscientious Bishop of Gloucester, but with the renewed ascendancy of Catholicism under Queen Mary, he found himself once more behind bars. Accused of being 'a false and detestable heretic' and of having 'infected the city with his pernicious doctrine', Bishop Hooper was condemned to death by burning at the stake. The sentence was carried out where his statue now stands in St Mary's Square, on 9 February 1555. The poor bishop suffered terrible agonies for nearly an hour, for the wood of his pyre was damp and had to be relit more than once. But perhaps he was better off than a later Gloucester martyr, this time a Catholic. In 1586, the Blessed John Sandys was cut down from the scaffold still conscious, and had sufficient strength to wrestle with the executioner who nevertheless proceeded to disembowel him with a rusty knife.

LOCATION: ON A40, 10 MILES SOUTH-WEST OF CHELTENHAM

bishop – The poor bishop agonies for nearly an hour, his pyre was damp and had than once.

Great Torrington DEVON

A right royal explosion During the Civil War a Royalist army found the parish church of this hilltop town the most convenient place to store their ammunition and gunpowder – all 50 barrels of it. In February 1646, Great Torrington was attacked by a powerful Parliamentary force under the command of Sir Thomas Fairfax and the Royalists were driven out. Now the church became a prison as around 200 of the defeated soldiers were herded inside. As the Parliamentarians carried out their final mopping-up operations, there was a terrible explosion which showered stones, timber and other building materials all over the town. The prisoners and their guards were annihilated; the church and everyone inside had been blown sky-high when the gunpowder exploded. Fairfax himself narrowly escaped death from falling debris. Suspicion fell on the imprisoned Royalists, diehards among whom may well have preferred death and destruction to whatever fate awaited them at the hands of their enemies.

LOCATION: 7 MILES EAST OF BIDEFORD VIA A386

Haw Bridge GLOUCESTERSHIRE

The torso in the Severn Gossip was rife in the 1930s when Cheltenham resident Mrs Sullivan discovered the body of her son, Brian, in his bedroom, having apparently committed suicide by gassing himself. As well as being a gigolo in London's West End, Brian had also, so rumour had it, honed his skills as an abortionist and blackmailer. Letters found by the police showed that he and a neighbour, a Captain William Butt, had been homosexual lovers. Subsequent enquiries at the Captain's residence revealed that he had not been home for many weeks. A few days later at nearby Haw bridge a human torso was hauled from the River Severn. Divers searching the riverbed recovered an arm, a leg, then a second arm. Crowds of up to 5,000 watched in ghoulish anticipation for the head to be dredged up, but were disappointed.

Without the head there could be no positive identification, though the torso and its severed limbs could well have been those of Captain Butt. The popular consensus was that he met his horrible end because of a lovers' quarrel, and that a remorseful Brian Sullivan then killed himself.

LOCATION: 9 MILES SOUTH OF GLOUCESTER VIA A38 AND MINOR ROAD

The Levant Mine, scene of one of Cornwall's worst mining disasters

Levant CORNWALL

With its buildings clinging to the clifftop not far from Land's End, the Levant tin-mine seems to typify the romance and austere beauty of this most ancient Cornish industry. Levant's underground galleries extended far out from the shoreline, and as they worked the miners could hear the Atlantic breakers pounding above their heads. With no need for the ventilation essential in explosion-prone coal-mines, the air in the shafts was thick with dust and fumes and the heat oppressive. Miners had to clamber hundreds of feet down a ladder into the depths of the earth before they could even start work, then scale it again at the end of their exhausting shift, a process that added up to two hours to the working day.

The man-engine In 1857, this particular burden was eased with the installation of a strange contraption known as a 'man-engine'. Two parallel timber rods with little platforms just big enough for a man to stand on attached at 12ft intervals were set into the shaft. The rods were activated by a steam engine on the surface, which moved them 12ft up and down with a reciprocal motion, bringing opposing platforms momentarily in line with one another. All a miner had to do was to keep on stepping from one platform to the other to be borne effortlessly up (or down).

Mayhem in the mine For decades, the man-engine worked well, but in the early afternoon of 20 October 1919 disaster struck. Every platform was occupied with a miner coming off the morning shift when the cap attaching the rod to the beam of the steam-engine snapped. The upper portion of the rod fell hundreds of feet down the shaft, carrying its load of 30 men with it. The miners below clung desperately to the side of the shaft as, with a terrible roar, an avalanche of shattered timber, stonework and other debris crashed past them into the abyss. The search for survivors was hindered by the blocked shaft, and the last body was only recovered five days later. In all, this worst of Cornish mining disasters claimed 32 lives.

LOCATION: 8 MILES WEST OF PENZANCE VIA A3071 AND MINOR ROADS

Lundy Island DEVON

The lawless island A natural fortress some 3 miles long and half a mile wide, windswept, treeless Lundy is defended by granite cliffs rising sheer from the turbulent waters of the Bristol Channel. If you make the day trip here by boat from Bideford or Ilfracombe, it's easy to see why the island was for long the lurking-place of those who preferred to remain beyond the reach of the law, among them renegade aristocrats, pirates and privateers, smugglers, slavers and swindlers.

In the Middle Ages, the hot-blooded and fiercely independent De Marisco family ruled Lundy, defying the authority of the king until one of their number overstepped the mark and became implicated in an assassination attempt on

Steep cliffs form a natural defence on the island of Lundy

Henry III. Captured, he was tied to a horse's tail and dragged to the Tower of London, where he was hung, drawn and quartered. Pieces of his body were displayed around the kingdom as a gruesome warning to other potential regicides.

Pirates and looters After the demise of the De Mariscos, the island was used as a base by cut-throats from France, Spain and North Africa, who found it ideal for preying on ships passing to and from Bristol and other ports. Even when more settled times ensued, the island's farmers and their animals were not safe from bloody attack. On one occasion a Spanish man o'war sailed in, its crew storming ashore to burn houses and carry off not only the island's young women, but (more importantly in the inhabitants' eyes), its young sheep.

Years later, what seemed to be a shipload of friendly Dutchmen put ashore, asking for food and medicine for their sick captain. This the islanders gave, but the captain nevertheless expired, and it was agreed that he should be given a proper funeral. The coffin was borne in solemn state to the church, whereupon the 'Dutchmen' asked if they could conduct their ceremony in private. The islanders again agreed, but once they had gone, the coffin was opened. It contained, not a corpse but weapons, which were at once put to use by the 'mourners'. Far from being amiable Hollanders, they were fierce Frenchmen bent on loot and slaughter. The raiders cut down those islanders who opposed them, and stole everything that could be moved, including the clothes of the survivors. Some cattle were taken aboard, the rest cruelly hamstrung, and goats and sheep hurled over the cliffs on to the rocks below.

LOCATION: 23 MILES NORTH-WEST OF ILFRACOMBE

Maiden Castle DORSET

Crushing the Celts Maiden Castle was one of the most formidable fortifications of prehistoric Europe, and today its great earthern ramparts still dominate the cornfields all around. The hilltop was first occupied by Neolithic people. At the time of the Roman invasion of Britain in AD 43 it was one of the strongholds of the Iron Age people known as the Belgae, who were bitterly opposed to the Roman assault on their homeland. The fort stood directly in the path of the Second Augustan Legion, who were marching westward around AD 45 to complete their conquest of southern England. As they forded the River Frome where the town of Dorchester now stands, the legionaries must have looked up with dread at the seemingly impregnable series of ditches and banks and heavily defended gateways which they had been ordered to attack.

Ancient bones from Maiden Castle reveal the grim details of a fierce battle

Roman discipline and battle technique were to subdue even this well-defended stronghold. A barrage of iron bolts (ballistae) prepared the way for the foot-soldiers, who hacked and sliced their way into the fortress. The fighting seems to have been fiercest around the eastern gateway, where the invaders, infuriated by the obstinacy of the resistance, cut down men and women, old and young alike. Opposition overcome, the Romans then set about systematically wrecking the defences and burning down buildings, before moving on the following day. The anxious survivors crept out and hastily buried their dead close to where they had fallen, no doubt shuddering at the terrible wounds inflicted by bolt and broadsword; one unfortunate had received no fewer than nine cuts to the head, each one vicious enough to have killed him. And a skeleton on display in the Dorchester museum still has the fatal ballista bolt lodged in its spine.

LOCATION: 2 MILES SOUTH OF DORCHESTER VIA MINOR ROAD

Manacle Rocks CORNWALL

The wreck of the *Mohegan* Of all the perils presented by the rugged Cornish coast, the Manacle Rocks are perhaps the most insidious, a razor-sharp reef extending a mile-and-a-half out to sea, east of the Lizard peninsula. Almost submerged at high tide, they have destroyed more

than 100 ships and claimed at least 1000 lives. Their most illustrious victim was the *Mohegan*, a luxury liner bound for New York on what was only her second voyage.

Ill-starred from the start, the *Mohegan* suffered delays in completion because of a shipyard strike. Then, pressed into service too quickly, she developed severe leaks on her maiden voyage and had to be laid up while these were made good. Nevertheless, the mood among her 60 first class passengers was cheerful as she sailed from Tilbury on 13 October 1898. As well it might be, with nearly 100 crew under the command of Captain Griffiths to attend to their needs.

The captain's competence was not in question, but for some reason, despite clear night-time conditions, he deviated from his course and steered his ship straight on to the Manacles, tearing a great gash below the waterline in her starboard side. The stricken vessel sank within minutes, tipping passengers and crew into the sea where most of them drowned before help could arrive, even though watchers on the shore had seen her heading for her doom and alerted the authorities. A few clung desperately to the rigging and were saved, and two women passengers were found alive in the water beneath an upturned lifeboat, though the child with them had perished from the cold.

A total of 106 lives were lost in the disaster, including all the officers and a stowaway. Many were buried in a mass grave at St Keverne's Church overlooking the site of the tragedy. Three months after the wreck, Captain Griffiths' headless body was washed up in far-off Caernarvon Bay.

LOCATION: 12 MILES SOUTH OF HELSTON OFF MANACLE POINT

Shipping hazard: the rocks of the Lizard

WRECKS AND WRECKING

Jutting out into the Atlantic, the long south-western peninsula of England has always claimed more than its fair share of shipwrecks, frequently with loss of life. But the doom of ships and the death of seamen often brought benefits for the local population, many of whom lived harsh and poverty-stricken lives and were glad to salvage whatever they could from a ship cast up on their shore.

Stories, many of them untrue, tell of vessels deliberately lured onto the rocks by unscrupulous wreckers, but what is certain is that wrecked vessels – and sometimes their crews – were frequently and systematically stripped of anything at all of value, and that news of a wreck, far from being greeted with sorrow, was a cause of rejoicing in all sections of the community. Parson Troutbeck of St Mary's in the Scilly Isles is on record as pleading 'We pray Thee, O Lord, not that wrecks should happen, but that if wrecks should happen, Thou wilt guide them into the Scilly Islands'. On learning that a ship had been forced ashore between Prawle and Pear Tree Point, his counterpart at Portlemouth is supposed to have abandoned his sermon and led his congregation to the beach, ignoring the cries of the drowning crew in order to plunder the cargo.

Plunder for all

A well-stocked wreck might yield provisions for the larder, gear of all kinds for fishing boats,

A well-provisioned wreck could be a lifeline to isolated coastal communities

canvas for clothes, rum to make merry, and timber for building; at one time, most of the houses on the Lizard peninsula were made from material taken from wrecked ships. Attempts by customs officers to regulate the pillage met with little success. Vastly outnumbered by crowds of plunderers, who might number thousands, they were often too intimidated to discharge their duties effectively, and sometimes went in real fear of their lives. Inured to hardship in their working lives, tin-miners seem to have been particularly brutal, not hesitating to attack half-dead survivors for their possessions or strip corpses of rings and clothing. On one occasion a gang of 'tinners' even carried off the clothes of shipwrecked sailors that had been washed and hung out to dry by kindly villagers!

Sailor's burial

Before the 19th century, a drowned sailor washed ashore was not entitled to a Christian burial, and bodies were often simply buried in the sand, where they might be dug up by rooting pigs or hungry dogs. In an attempt to avoid this horrible fate, some mariners would wear an earring, in the hope that it would be sufficient reward for whoever found them to ensure they had a decent burial.

A dangerous trade

'Going a-wrecking' had its own dangers. A brig beached at Porthleven in 1817 immediately drew the attention of a 'lawless multitude', who descended on it armed with pickaxes, hatchets and crowbars, plus an array of pails, pots, jars and kettles in which to carry off its cargo of wine. In the drunken melee, fighting broke out, a young boy was drowned, and two of the plunderers fell by the wayside on the way home and perished from intoxication and exposure.

Penzance CORNWALL

The Spanish storm In the years following the defeat and wrecking of the Armada invasion fleet, relations between England and Spain were strained. In July 1595, fired up with thoughts of revenge on the unspeakable English and their vile heresy of Protestantism, a force of four galleys carrying 400 pikemen landed to the south of the little Cornish fishing port of Mousehole, at a place now named Point Spaniard. While the warships bombarded the village with their cannon, the soldiers fought their way through the streets, setting 200 houses on fire and putting the inhabitants to flight. Only the squire stood his ground, killing several Spaniards before he was cut down by a cannon ball. (For many years afterwards the ball stayed lodged in the stonework of his house, as a grim reminder.) The invaders then marched on the church at Paul, just inland, which they referred to in their report as a *mezquita* (mosque), such was their belief in the un-Christian ways of the English.

The Spaniards' next stop was Newlyn, and then Penzance, where another local notable, Sir Francis Godolphin, stood in the market place valiantly attempting to organise resistance. His efforts were in vain, for the townsfolk fled, leaving him alone in the square apart from his faithful retainers. Once possessed of the town, the Spaniards set it ablaze, too, burning down a total of 400 buildings. Well aware that a superior English force might arrive at any minute from Plymouth, the raiders set sail for home once more.

LOCATION: ON A30, 18 MILES SOUTH-WEST OF REDRUTH

Rotting ships made fetid prisons, rife with disease

Plymouth DEVON

Plymouth's prison hulks Britain's victories in the battles of the Napoleonic Wars brought a rich haul of French prisoners, and by 1814 there were 17,000 of them incarcerated around the country. The more fortunate (and wealthy) among them, if able to draw on private funds and prepared to be paroled, could lead an almost normal existence in the country towns to which they were directed. The least lucky were housed in the prison hulks which disfigured the otherwise pleasant landscape of the Hamoaze inlet, to the west of Plymouth. Stripped of their superstructure, these once proud warships resembled nothing so much as gigantic, blackened coffins, and for those crammed into them they were little more than a living hell.

Regarding its own sailors as vicious animals only able to respond to the most brutal discipline (see Naval Punishments, page 37), the Royal Navy could hardly be expected to coddle its captured enemies. Those guarding the French prisoners of war were drawn from the dregs of British society, while the command of a hulk was regarded as a golden opportunity to turn a pretty profit.

Commanders would conspire with the contractors supplying food to swindle the prisoners out of their rations, meagre enough anyway. Half-starved, clad in coarse, rarely renewed clothing, breathing air contaminated by overcrowding or poisoned by the foul exhalations from the mud of the estuary, the prisoners suffered every kind of illness and disease. Desperate for some variation in the diet of weevil-ridden biscuit and oak-textured salt beef, and spying the stoutly-built Danish hound of a visiting dignitary, one prisoner swiftly butchered the unfortunate dog, turning it into 'two legs of mutton, several ratatouilles, and any number of bifteks'. Puzzled by the disappearance of his pet, the visitor left, only to catch sight of its pelt prominently nailed to the mast.

Escape attempts from the hulks were frequent, and sometimes spectacularly successful. One group sawed their way through the side of their vessel and swam ashore, while another bold band sprang overboard, took possession of an ammunition ship, and sailed off merrily to France. But another would-be escapee was unable to extricate himself from the stinking mud into which he had fallen. No attempt was made to rescue him; instead, he was left to die, and his corpse remained as a deterrent to others.

An incendiary for everyone For its size, Plymouth suffered more from bombing in World War II than any other British city. By 1945, as well as any number of high explosive bombs, more than a quarter of a million incendiaries had been dropped on the town – that is, more than one for every man, woman and child living there. Hundreds were killed and maimed in the carnage, and some 20,000 buildings destroyed or severely damaged.

That Plymouth would be a prime target could hardly have been in doubt. It had the country's most important naval dockyard, and was a significant base for escorts protecting the vital Atlantic convoys. Yet in the summer of 1940 the city was ill-prepared for the awful fate about to befall it. The complacency and insularity bred by its position in the far west of England and the inertia of the 'Phoney War' persisted, even though the fall of France meant that German bombers now had bases just across the English Channel. Amazingly, even as the Luftwaffe was preparing its assault, people were still being evacuated to Plymouth from other places in Britain which were thought to be more vulnerable to attack from the air.

The first raids came in July 1940, but Plymouth's agony really began later in the year and lasted into 1941, reaching a peak of intensity at the end of March. Wave after wave of bombers devastated the city centre, destroying shops, banks, houses, pubs, churches and the 19th-century Gothic guildhall. Melted glass made pools on the pavement, and streets turned into rivers of boiling, bubbling asphalt. Hospitals were not spared, and 14 new-born babies were killed in one raid.

Plymouth's misery was increased by the widespread looting which took place in the aftermath of the bombing, at a time when the forces of law and order were stretched to the full. When heavy bombing resumed in 1943 and 1944, Plymouth was better prepared and there were fewer casualties and less damage.

BARBARY PIRATES

The English Channel was always infested by pirates, but in the early years of the 17th century, legitimate trade was almost brought to a standstill by a new breed of pirate: corsairs, who operated from the coast of North Africa.

Commonly referred to as 'Turks', they sailed aboard fine vessels of up to 400 tons, mounting 20 guns, and with a complement of dozens of men-at-arms. Preying on people as well as the contents of ships' holds, they sometimes came boldly ashore to snatch men, women and children to sell as slaves in the markets of the Maghreb. At one time it was reckoned that there were some 25,000 Christian slaves in Algiers alone. *Renegados* was the name given to those who avoided slavery by converting to Islam and adopting their captors' ways. One such was the Devon man Henry Chandler, who captained a pirate boat crewed by other renegados like Mustapha (formerly William Winter), Isfar (Richard Clark), and Mamme (John Browne), as well as by slaves like Plymouth skipper John Rawlins. A clever ruse enabled Rawlins to capture the vessel; the 'Turks' were thrown overboard while Chandler was delivered to the Exeter hangman.

The dramatic capture of a Barbary pirate vessel

Princetown DEVON

Dartmoor prison To reach this grimmest of British prisons, high up on a bleak and windswept moor you drive along roads built by the forced labour of its first occupants, Frenchmen captured during the Napoleonic wars. As British victories multiplied, the rotting hulks in Plymouth Sound in which these unfortunates were first incarcerated could not house their ever-increasing numbers. Dartmoor was built to relieve the pressure, and by 1814, some 9,000 French prisoners-of-war were crowded behind the bars of its austere brick buildings, along with more than 1000 American prisoners taken during the war of 1812.

The horrors of the hulks may have been left behind, but conditions in the crowded, unheated prison were not much better. The unglazed windows offered little protection against Dartmoor's harsh climate, with its driving rain, dense fogs and frequent snowfall which could cut the area off for weeks on end. Sickness and disease were common; typhus raged, and in 1809, 500 prisoners succumbed to the ravages of measles.

Strict social segregation prevailed among the French; at the top of the scale were the 'Lordes', officers with private means enabling them to live something like a civilised life; at the bottom were the 'Romans', described as the 'scum and sweepings of seaport towns', who lived in filth and squalor, spent their time fighting and gambling, and were known to eat rats alive.

But it was the Americans who, when their repatriation was delayed, were involved in the bloodiest episode in the prison's history. Their protests were met with gunfire; nine men died and dozens were wounded. An international inquiry

Strict social segregation prevailed among the French; at the top of the scale were the 'Lordes', officers with private means enabling them to live something like a civilised life; at the bottom were the 'Romans', described as the 'scum and sweepings of seaport towns', who lived in filth and squalor, spent their time fighting and gambling, and were known to eat rats alive.

Far right: the recruiting methods of the dreaded Press Gang were simple and brutal

found the use of firearms inexcusable, and the 'Dartmoor Massacre' is still remembered in the United States today.

LOCATION: 8 MILES FROM TAVISTOCK VIA B3357

Purbeck, Isle of DORSET

Purbeck pirates In the late 16th century the coast around the Isle of Purbeck was a notorious nest of pirates, many of them financed and protected by consortia of local landowners who took their share of the spoils. However, they failed to save John Piers of Padstow, who made the mistake of preying on English ships as well as French-owned vessels. Another black mark against Piers was that he had 'an olde mother noted to be a Wytche' to whom 'he hath conveyed all such goodes and spoiles as he hath wickedlie gotten at the Seas'.

Watched by a vast crowd from all over Purbeck, Piers was strung up on a gibbet specially set up on the shore of Studland Bay, and his body was left to swing. But in the dead of night, a band of fellow pirates stole in, cut down the corpse, and spirited it away to sea.

Pirate torturer Another pirate, Stephen Heynes, was noted for his merciless treatment of captured crews, and is supposed to have introduced the technique of setting light to matches jammed under his victims' fingernails in order to make them reveal the whereabouts of their valuables. One of his worst atrocities was perpetrated on the skipper of a ship from Danzig, Gregorius Neumann. Shot in the leg and stabbed in the shoulder, the wretched captain was then tortured by having a rope round his neck twisted and tightened until his blood spurted and the rope broke. The treatment was repeated, then repeated again. Astonishingly, Neumann lived, to be put ashore at Swanage, while his stolen cargo was sold on deck in the bay. But on his next voyage, the heartless Stephen Heynes was swept overboard and drowned.

LOCATION: SOUTH OF WAREHAM

NAVAL PUNISHMENTS

Always severe, discipline aboard the ships of the Royal Navy was enforced with almost unbelievable brutality in what became known as the 'flogging decade' of the 1790s. In order to fight the French, the navy had been vastly expanded, with many of its new recruits **pressed** from the ranks of the riff-raff to be found in any harbour town. The only way to keep this unpromising human material in line, so the thinking went, was to fill it with fear. The favourite instrument of pain and terror was the cruel **cat o'nine tails**, each 'tail' of cord with a trio of knots designed to lift the flesh off the back of the offender. Pieces of metal might be inserted in the knots for extra effect, or the 'cat' might be pickled in salt to ensure a painful afterglow.

Keel-hauling – being dragged from one side of the ship to the other under the keel – was even more of an ordeal than it sounds, since the exposed skin of the naked victim would be ripped open by the barnacles covering the bottom of the boat, if he didn't drown first. **Running the gauntlet** was a frequent punishment, its agony prolonged by making the offender march, not run, between the two lines of shipmates forced to deal him a heavy blow on pain of suffering the same punishment themselves. Worst of all though was **flogging round the fleet**. To the beat of a drum and the shrilling of a fife, the prisoner would be towed from ship to ship and ceremoniously beaten into near-insensibility before the assembled crews.

JUDGE JEFFREYS AND THE BLOODY ASSIZE

Lord Chief Justice George Jeffreys (1645–89) was a zealot and a bully noted for extracting the kind of verdict required by his political masters. He was just the man to terrorise the rebellious folk of the West Country into keeping their heads down after daring to support the challenge to royal power led by the Duke of Monmouth in the summer of 1685.

Even before Jeffreys arrived to carry out the orders given him by King James II, the scene had been set by the leaders of the royal army, flushed with their triumph at Sedgemoor. The commander himself, Lord Feversham, had one batch of 22 prisoners, summarily hanged from a tree in the village of Bussex, without pretence of a trial or court-martial. His subordinate, Colonel Kirke, who had learnt cruel ways while on garrison duty in Tangier, drove other rebels, some of them wounded, along the road from Bridgwater to Taunton. As the exhausted men arrived in the county town, they were strung up, their death agonies mocked by the shrilling of fifes and the pounding of drums in time to their last twitchings. Cut down from the gibbets, they were slashed open, their hearts removed and burned, their bodies quartered, boiled in pitch, then distributed around the county to be displayed prominently.

These savage deeds were committed in the immediate aftermath of battle by men whose blood was up, who regarded their opponents as ignoble traitors and were determined to avenge their own casualties. But with the arrival of the Lord Chief Justice on the scene, there followed a series of more ordered atrocities. Beginning at Winchester on 25 August, Judge Jeffreys progressed around the county towns of the West. The citizens of Salisbury got off lightly with fines and whippings, but at Dorchester Jeffreys tried the accused in batches, condemning a total of 300 to death, nearly 100 of them in a single day.

By the end of his month's tour of duty, Jeffreys had sentenced no fewer than 333 to death, and more than 800 to transportation. His instructions to town and village councils around the region still make chilling reading. They were ordered: 'to erect a gallows in the most public place; to provide a sufficient number of faggots to burn the bowels of the said Traitors; to provide a furnace

Sedgemoor SOMERSET

The Battle of Sedgemoor In 1685 the Duke of Monmouth, one of Charles II's illegitimate offspring, reckoned the time was ripe to grab the crown from his unpopular uncle, James II. Landing at Lyme Regis, he headed for Taunton, where many rallied to his banner.

But Monmouth's men, armed with farm implements and mounted on carthorses, were to prove no match for James's professional army. Attempting an attack in utmost stealth on the night of Sunday 5 July, the Duke's force crept across the soggy fields of Sedgemoor, only to lose the essential element of surprise when the enemy was alerted by a pistol shot – perhaps fired by a traitor. Terrified by the crash of cannon, the carthorse cavalry fled in uncontrollable panic, mowing down the foot-soldiers coming up behind them. When battle was joined, billhooks, scythes and home-made pikes were poor protection against keenly sharpened swords and well-aimed muskets. By dawn, Monmouth knew his cause was utterly lost. He fled, but was soon captured, cowering and half-starved in a field of peas. His subsequent execution was a horribly botched affair (see page 58).

LOCATION: BATTLEFIELD SITE AT WESTONZOYLAND, 3 MILES EAST OF BRIDGWATER

or cauldron to boil their heads and quarters, tar to tar them with, and spears and poles to fix and place their heads and quarters'. The Judge did his job well; the boiled and tarred body parts of the 'said Traitors' were displayed in towns and villages all round the region, and the West Country never rose again.

Reporting to King James on 28 September at Windsor Castle, Jeffreys was rewarded with the Great Seal of the office of Lord Chancellor.

Judge Jeffreys fell from grace after the exile of James II, and died, a prisoner in the Tower of London, in 1689.

Slapton DEVON

D-Day rehearsal disaster Parts of southern Devon were cleared of their inhabitants during World War II to make way for Allied troops preparing for the D-Day invasion of France. Backed by a shallow lagoon, Slapton Sands bore a strong resemblance to Omaha Beach on the far side of the English Channel and was an almost perfect place to rehearse some of the Normandy landings.

On the night of 27–28 April 1944, a convoy of landing-craft carrying hundreds of US troops and their equipment was making for Slapton when it was attacked by a flotilla of German E-boats that had somehow managed to avoid Royal Navy patrols. Two landing-craft were torpedoed and sank almost immediately and a third was badly damaged. Hundreds of soldiers found themselves in the water, and, weighed down by their heavy equipment, many of them drowned.

In order to keep the impending invasion under wraps, the bodies washed up on the beaches were hastily collected and buried in secret and the whole incident was hushed up. Only at a much later date was a memorial erected to those who had lost their lives.

LOCATION: 13 MILES FROM PAIGNTON VIA A379 AND DARTMOUTH FERRY

Tewkesbury GLOUCESTERSHIRE

Death through obstinacy Among the 'remarkable and interesting incidents' recorded in the Black Book kept by the Corporation of Tewkesbury is the horrible fate suffered in 1216 by a Jewish member of the community. This poor fellow fell into the town's public latrine (or was he pushed?), and, because it was Saturday, the Jewish Sabbath, he refused all offers of help to haul him out, expecting to be saved on the following day.

But the hard-hearted lord of the manor, Richard de Clare, resolving that the unfortunate Jew should observe the Christian Sabbath 'with the same solemnity he had done his own', gave orders that Sunday should pass without any assistance being provided. By sundown, according to the account in the Black Book, 'this ceremonious Israelite' had 'expired in filth and stench'.

The Battle of Tewkesbury From the battlements of Tewkesbury Abbey tower on the morning of 4 May 1471, ex-Queen Margaret watched with horror as the Lancastrian army was cut to pieces and her own son, the Prince of Wales, slain on the field of battle. This, one of the most decisive battles of the Wars of the Roses, put an end to Margaret's attempt to regain the power she had exercised during the reign of her weak and naïve husband, Henry VI, now deposed and a prisoner in the Tower of London. The way was open for the loose-living but competent Yorkist Edward IV to consolidate his rule over the kingdom.

Edward had already smashed the army of Margaret's ally, Warwick 'the Kingmaker', at the Battle of Barnet on 14 April – on the very same day that Margaret and her followers had landed at Weymouth from exile in France. The Lancastrians headed northward, hoping to find support in the counties of northern England, but always with Edward close on their heels. From Bristol they trudged to Berkeley, then to Gloucester, where the town's gate was slammed in their face. Desperately weary, they plodded on to Tewkesbury, through 'foul country, all stony ways, with no refreshment'. Here they camped for the night on a low hill, separated from town and abbey by water-meadows and the Swilgate Brook. Roused at dawn by the approach of Edward's army, they executed an ill-planned charge which quickly degenerated into chaos. The Yorkists showed no mercy to their demoralised opponents.

Many, including the Prince of Wales, were killed on the field of battle, while others died as they fled, floundering in the waters of the Swilgate Brook or jostling to cross the narrow bridges across the muddy and increasingly blood-stained stream. The field where hundreds fell is still known as Bloody Meadow.

To complete Edward's ascendancy, a final killing had to be carried out, that of the miserable Henry VI; he was executed in the Tower, and his body put on display in St Paul's Cathedral.

Class and cholera The cholera outbreak of 1831–32 caused great consternation in Tewkesbury. Around 100 inhabitants of this small town perished, most of them from the 'humbler classes'.

While attributing their heightened susceptibility to this 'singularly painful and fatal disease' to the 'intemperance, filthy habits and dissolution' of their fellow citizens, their betters strove to counter the outbreak by distributing religious tracts and pious exhortations, whitewashing affected dwellings, and providing free meals of nutritious beef soup. Respectable opinion was particularly horrified at the way in which one Maria Huntley, 'a common prostitute', spent her last hours, 'clad in meretricious finery, and parading the streets in a state of intoxication' before finally succumbing.

LOCATION: 11 MILES NORTH OF GLOUCESTER VIA A38

DEATH ON THE BATTLEFIELD

Before the development of antibiotic drugs and modern surgical procedures, it was probably better to be killed outright on the field of battle than merely suffer wounds. Medieval military surgeons were drawn from the ranks of peacetime barbers, and might treat wounds with substances such as shoemakers' wax, the rust of old kettles, or the grease used to lubricate horses' hooves. The introduction of firearms in the late Middle Ages complicated their task. Spears, swords and arrows made wounds which were relatively clean and with a clearly defined track. If they failed to penetrate vital organs, the victim had a reasonable chance of survival. But musket-ball and cannon tended to cause widespread contusions, which became a breeding ground for gangrene and tetanus. Gunpowder itself was considered poisonous, and to eliminate it wounds were cauterised with a red-hot iron, burning charcoal or boiling oil. Alternatively, the gunpowder might be removed by pushing a metal instrument into the wound and working it back and forth before applying a plug moistened with bacon or ox-grease. Not surprisingly, death from shock was a common phenomenon.

...musket-ball and cannon tended to cause widespread contusions, which became a breeding ground for gangrene and tetanus...

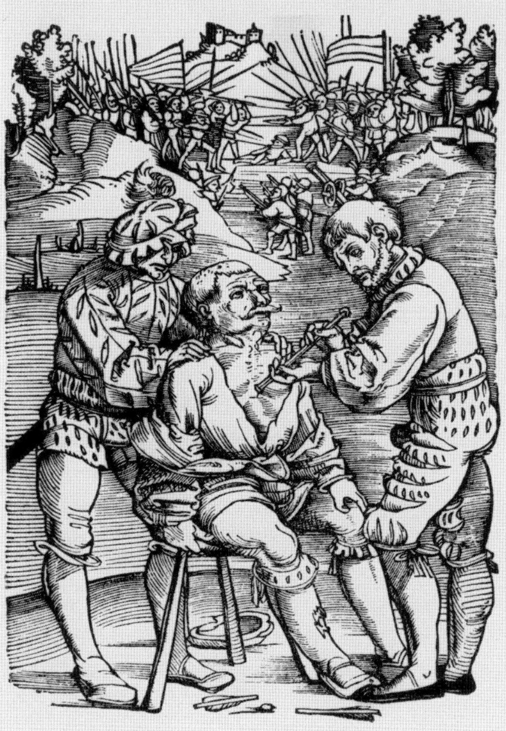

Surgery was primitive, and with little understanding of the processes of infection, recovery was doubtful

LONDON

It is the link with the ancient past and its savage ways that characterises Bloody London. London, or something like London, has existed for a long time. Six thousand years ago there were villages on what are now the runways at Heathrow airport and on Hampstead Heath. The prehistoric warriors who fought there for territory, lived on in the clashes when Boudicca fought the Romans, and in the 17th- and 18th-century gangs that strutted along, ready to slash passers-by with their swords. More sinister still were the sacrifices that took place on the London Stone, which still exists in the heart of the City.

Until the 20th century, London dwarfed all other cities in the world. Modern-day mega metropolises such as Tokyo or Mexico City, where it is possible to travel for hours along dreary roads through concrete buildings, past tens of millions of strangers, now attract a similar level of wonder and fear. But if alienation or fear of terrorism are seen as the greatest dangers of the modern city, London was until only recently a place of much more immediate physical danger.

Plague ridden

The plague regularly slaughtered the citizens of London. There was no cure for the deadly disease and no way of stopping it, for medicine could do little against such infectious diseases when no-one knew what caused them and how they spread.

Almost worse than fear of the disease itself was the impossibility of escape. During the Great Plague of 1665 sufferers and their families were locked up in their houses with a guard at the door. Those who managed to escape the city were turned back, imprisoned, or hounded away from places of safety.

During the Great Plague a quarter of the population of London died a terrible death. The fear and hopelessness of those expecting to die and watching death around them was perhaps the worst aspect of the horror.

London's prisons

While plague and poverty could imprison a person in the city as effectively as any crime could send a highwayman to the gallows, London contained more real prisons than the rest of the country put together. Bridewell, Newgate, the Tower, they all had an appetite for more – more prisoners, more executions, more tortures.

Bedlam, the popular name for the Hospital of St Mary of Bethlehem, was a prison for the insane and the place itself seemed to be London's emblem for the madness that splits the human personality. It was modelled on the Tuileries in Paris and from the outside it looked like a gorgeous palace, but inside it was a dark prison where semi-naked men and women lay chained to the wall.

Then and now

The mis-match between the sedate contemporary appearance of certain sites and the horror stories which lie in their past is often startling. Tyburn, where hundreds were hanged each month, is only two minutes from Selfridges department store to the east and the Dorchester hotel and the gambling-clubs of Mayfair to the south. The spectacular glass city that has grown up in the Docklands still has a new and gaudy look to it, but remember that the luxury apartments of Wapping overlook the site on the River Thames where pirates were hanged and their bodies suspended in cages until they rotted. Parts of London just outside the city walls were built on the huge plague pits filled with victims in the Middle Ages and the 17th century.

The streets of Whitechapel where Jack the Ripper murdered his victims in 1888 are much altered, but some of the scenes remain. George Yard and Mitre Square are unchanged; they are still bleak.

At the time society shuddered at the conditions of the East End, thinking of it much as they thought of far-off colonies in Africa and India. Social problems, we now believe, all have a solution. Money, education and welfare will make things better, but the nightmarish figures who have haunted London's streets murdering and maiming cannot be bought off or explained away. They come out of the shadows, kill, and them walk back into them again, like Jack the Ripper did.

Jack the Ripper recalled in a pub sign

Visitors queue to relish the horrors of the Tower of London

The Devil's pay

For example, there is a mad, melodramatic story set in Elizabethan times of a great ball given by Sir Christopher Hatton at his mansion in Clerkenwell. Lady Hatton had sold her soul to the Devil, however, and Beelzebub chose that very night to exact payment.

As the party was in full swing, a sinister black-robed figure strode into the ballroom, took Lady Hatton by the hand and led her outside. Suddenly there was a terrific crash of thunder followed by a dreadful scream. The guests rushed outside. There was nothing to see except, freshly torn out of her body, Lady Hatton's heart, bleeding on the ground. Nonsense, of course, but anyone can go and see the place, anyone can stand there if they want. It's called Bleeding Heart Yard.

Bankside SE1

Bear Gardens The Bear Gardens at Bankside lay near the Globe, Shakespeare's theatre, and rows of brothels, or stew-houses. Modelled after the Coliseum in Rome, these pleasure gardens offered a variety of entertainments: swordsmen, wrestlers, jugglers, all sorts. But what the crowds came especially to see was animals tormented by dogs. Bulls and bears were set upon by packs of mastiffs. The dogs were often killed, torn by the bear's fearsome teeth and claws or gored by the bull and tossed in the air, sometimes landing in the crowd itself. A particularly brutal event recorded in the early 1600s involved tormenting a chained bear who was blinded and then flogged by six men who stood in a circle around it. Unable to see or escape, the bear lashed out at the men, sometimes striking one, sometimes grabbing a whip and breaking it.

The crowd at Bankside came hoping to see death. Once, when a horse defeated the packs of dogs that had attacked it, the crowd demanded that more dogs be brought on. More dogs came and the horse still fought them off. Finally, men with swords came into the ring and the horse, which in Roman days would have earned the right to live, was hacked to death.

LOCATION: SOUTHWARK STATION

Bedlam (Bishopsgate) EC2

And so to Bedlam The hospital of St Mary of Bethlehem was founded in Bishopsgate Ward by Simon Fitz Mary in 1246 to house the mentally ill. It was moved to Moorfields in 1673, to Southwark in 1807, then to Beckenham in Surrey in 1930. In its early years it provided a ghastly public spectacle, which was to make its familiar, shortened name – Bedlam – synonymous with a confused hell.

Up to 1770, the public could come and gawp at the inmates from the two viewing galleries. They would see patients who were manacled inside cages, some crying or screaming, others silent until provoked into roars by the taunts of the spectators. In the public galleries prostitutes looked for customers, hoping that men would be excited by the contortions of the unfortunate inmates.

Patients inside cag screaming provoked taunts o

Until the 19th century the common treatment for mental patients was whipping and chaining. They were kept in manacles and stocks, locked in rows against the walls, some wearing loose shifts, others naked under blankets. Some had their mouths held open by an iron key to stop them screaming. One inmate, James Norris, was imprisoned in a special harness. An iron ring around his neck connected him by a chain to the wall, while iron bars around his chest pinioned his arms to his side. He could move only a few inches along his bed. After 10 years of this, Norris was released in 1814. He died soon after, as if his body gave way without its cage.

LOCATION: LIVERPOOL STREET STATION

were manacled
es, some crying or
others silent until
into roars by the
f the spectators.

50 Berkeley Square W1

Haunted house In the late 19th century this house was haunted by ghosts, echoing screams, and the sound of footsteps. One night, a maid sleeping in an upper room was heard screaming. They discovered her rigid with fear, but no-one ever found out why; she never spoke again. The house soon stood empty, for people did not dare to live there. One night two sailors broke in, looking for a place to sleep. Once upstairs, they heard footsteps thumping closer and closer, then a hideous, dripping mass began to fill the room from all the walls. One man escaped and fetched a policeman. Outside the house they found the mutilated corpse of the other man, impaled on the railings after he had jumped from the window.

LOCATION: GREEN PARK STATION

Bethnal Green Underground Station E2

Wartime crush At its height, the Blitz meant total blackness, the screeching of bombs, and a fearful crush inside the public shelters. On the night of 3 March 1942 the alarm sounded and people surged into Bethnal Green underground station – up to 10,000 souls seeking protection. Suddenly, anti-aircraft fire exploded nearby and the crowd at the entrance surged forward. A woman stumbled, others fell on top of her, and soon the stairs were jammed with screaming bodies. The crowd outside in the dark panicked and pushed forward even harder. Those at the bottom of the stairs were crushed. The final death toll was 111 people.

LOCATION: ROMAN ROAD E1

Borough High Street SE1

When quicklime failed On 11 September 1875 a police constable in the Hen and Chickens pub saw the surprising denoument of a peculiar story. Henry Wainwright murdered his mistress, Harriet Lane, and buried her body, covered in quicklime, in a warehouse in Whitechapel. But Wainwright lost his money and had to sell the warehouse. Fearful of discovery, he dug Harriet up and was horrified to find that her body had been preserved by the quicklime, and was not the skeleton he had expected. Wainwright's brother owned the Hen and Chickens in Borough High Street, so Harriet was chopped up, and wrapped neatly in two bundles to be taken there. Wainwright asked his employee, Stokes, to help carry the parcels and went off to fetch a cab. The body was rotting by now and starting to smell, so Stokes looked inside. Wainwright managed to escape in his cab but Stokes gave chase. When the murderer took the parcels into the pub, Stokes was ahead of him, with a constable waiting...

LOCATION: BOROUGH STATION

Bridewell Palace, unwelcome home to the destitute of London

Bridewell Palace EC4

Workhouse life Bridewell Palace used to stand on a site stretching from the Thames to present-day Fleet Street. In 1552 it became one of the first workhouses – places where the destitute were housed under a grim regime. Petty criminals, prostitutes and the homeless were all thrown in together.

The inmates were expected to work at whatever was needed; some were sent out in gangs to clean the sewers. If there was no work, there were always the treadmills, even a special one for amputees, where the unfortunate inmates walked endlessly round and round inside a wheel that turned as they walked, like a hamster in its cage. Inmates were routinely flogged on arrival, twelve lashes for adults and six for children, and a Bridewell Flogging became one of the sights of London. A gallery was built to hold the onlookers, especially those who enjoyed seeing half-naked prostitutes being whipped.

LOCATION: BLACKFRIARS STATION

Bruton Street W1

A servant problem In 1758 Sarah Metyard, who kept a milliner's shop, and her daughter, also called Sarah, cruelly mistreated their servants. When one of them, Anne Naylor, particularly enraged the pair, they fastened her hands together, tied her to a doorknob so that she could not stand or lie properly, and left her to starve to death.

At first, mother and daughter concealed the body in a box in the attic, but they soon had to dispose of the rotting corpse. A sewer ran by Chick Lane (now covered by Farringdon Street station), and the two Sarahs attempted to float the dismembered corpse down this. Frustratingly, the body pieces would not move, so the women buried them in the mud and filth that surrounded the gratings. Their crime was discovered when young Sarah confessed to a friend. Both women were hanged at Tyburn.

LOCATION: GREEN PARK STATION

Cannon Street EC4

The London Stone Set in the wall of the Bank of China in Cannon Street, the London Stone reaches back to London's mythical past. It is believed to be a cornerstone from the Roman governor's palace, dating from about AD 200.

Some writers have suggested that the London Stone was used by the judiciary to settle debts and disputes, but the visionary poet William Blake (1757–1827) thought it had a much more sinister purpose. For him, it was the place where human sacrifices were carried out by the Druids. Victims would be slit open, still alive, on the stone and their blood offered to the spirits.

The murder of Sarah Millsom

Cannon Street provides another mystery. One evening in April 1866, Sarah Millsom was sitting with a friend when the doorbell rang and she went to answer. After a while the friend became worried and went down to look.

She found Sarah lying dead on the floor, with terrible wounds to her head. The front door was shut and the gas-light switched off. Sarah's shoes had been placed neatly on the hall table, and were free of bloodstains. A crowbar was lying on the floor, but there was no blood on that, either.

The friend opened the front door to get help and there she saw an old woman, sheltering from the rain. When asked to help she said, 'Oh no, I can't come in,' and ran away into the night. Was the mysterious old woman the killer of Sarah Millsom? Nothing had been stolen and no motive could be identified. The strange case was never solved

LOCATION: CANNON STREET STATION

A night-time burial in the dreaded plague pit

Plague Pits In desperation, the Mayor of London bought a 2½-acre (1ha) patch of land called No Man's Land – later renamed Pardon Churchyard – for the burial of the plague victims. It was soon filled.

Then Sir Walter Manny bought a further 12 acres (5ha) of land next to the churchyard, and large pits were dug. There was no time, or space, for individual Christian burials, and London's dead were hastily shovelled into the pits dotted all over this vast site. Records indicate that some of those buried with the dead were still alive, so great were the numbers of sick.

LOCATION: BARBICAN STATION

Carthusian Street EC1

The Black Death The Black Death, or bubonic plague, had a devastating effect across the whole of Europe in the 14th century. It has been compared to World War I in the huge number of dead and the social changes that followed. The disease was spread by the fleas on rats that lived in the sewers and thatched roofs of buildings. There was no cure and no escape. In the last months of 1348 approximately 40% of the population of London died, a total of 50,000 people.

The Charterhouse (Charterhouse Square) EC1

Dissolution by force In 1371 Sir Walter Manny gave the Carthusian Order of monks his acreage where the plague pits were together with Pardon Churchyard, and they established a monastery.

In the 1500s, the monks would not accept Henry VIII as head of the Church in England. They did not want to lose their faith – or their revenue, for the monastery brought in £650 a year, an enormous sum in those days. Henry arrested their prior, John Houghton, and had him hanged, drawn and quartered. In a savage parody of Luther's nailing his *Ninety-five Theses* to the church door of Wittenburg in 1517, symbolically the start of the Reformation, one of Houghton's arms was chopped off, nailed to the monastery door and left to rot. The monks still held out, but after

16 more had been executed, Henry sent his soldiers to occupy the monastery and the other monks fled.

LOCATION: BARBICAN STATION

Covent Garden WC2

Mohocks We may worry about modern youth, but gangs of drunken young men have always roamed London. In 1175 Roger Hoveden wrote of a 'crew of young and wealthy citizens' attacking the houses of the rich. In 1711 the journalist, Richard Steele, described a club called The Mohocks, who 'attack all that are so unfortunate as to walk the Streets through which they patroll.' These men, after drinking in the taverns of Covent Garden, would form rings around their victims and slash them with their swords. Faces were 'carbonadoed', that is, cut crossways like meat in preparation for grilling. One man had his nose slit open, another his eyes gouged out. The Mohocks enjoyed their 'ripping rings'. The victim was poked with a sword from all directions, and, whirling about in terror, made to dance as he was being cut.

LOCATION: COVENT GARDEN STATION

Gloucester Road SW7

Serial killer John George Haigh was one of London's worst murderers. His first victim was a wealthy young man, Donald McSwan. Haigh owned a basement at 79 Gloucester Road and there he murdered McSwan in 1945. He dissolved the body in vats of sulphuric acid, and poured what little remained of Donald down the drain. A while later Haigh persuaded McSwan's parents to the basement where he murdered them both and again destroyed the bodies in acid. The money he stole from the McSwan estate kept Haigh going for two years, but by late 1947 he needed more. Dr Archibald Henderson and his wife were murdered next and destroyed by acid in early 1948. In 1949 Olivia Durand-Deacon thought Haigh could help manufacture the false finger-nails she had invented. She was soon disposed of, but a friend of hers notified the police and Haigh was finally caught.

It is not easy to dissolve a body in acid. It takes many hours, and the clear liquid turns into a filthy brown sludge. Bits of teeth and bone remain. In Haigh's case, the police investigating his cellars found a partially eaten-away left foot. Haigh was executed in Wandsworth prison on 10 August 1949.

LOCATION: GLOUCESTER ROAD STATION

39 Hilldrop Crescent N7

Dr Crippen is a notorious name among London murderers. He was American, small, shy, not very successful. His wife, Cora, a music-hall singer, quickly grew tired of him. When Crippen met Ethel le Neve, a 20-year-old typist, he found his soulmate and they were happy. Driven by some force, maybe the stifling conventions of the time – the year was 1910 – Crippen did not leave his wife, but rather poisoned her. The doctor used his medical skills to cut up her corpse and hide the bits in the cellar. Her head was never recovered. Crippen was hanged, but he loved Ethel so much that he fought to keep her out of the case.

LOCATION: KENTISH TOWN STATION

When Crippen tried to flee to the USA by sea, a suspicious captain radioed the police, making Crippen the first criminal ever to be caught by the use of radio-telegraphy.

Lambeth High Street SE1

Spring-heeled Jack This nightmare haunted the streets of London in the 1830s, a grotesque figure in a mask and white oilskin suit, with metallic claws and springs in his shoes. He breathed fire at his victims and slashed at them with his claws. There are many accounts, but Jane Alsop of Lambeth gave the clearest one. When she found him in her doorway, he belched flames at her, then grabbed her head and slashed her clothes. Her sister dragged Jane back into the house, but Jack was holding so tight he pulled some of her hair away. Then he knocked on the door three times as the women cowered inside.

A contemporary account of the notorious criminal

It is possible that a man dressed up in a mask, learned to breath fire, sheathed his hands in claws and put springs in his shoes, but who thought up such details and then acted on them? We'll never know; he vanished and was never caught.

LOCATION: LAMBETH NORTH STATION

Lincoln's Inn Fields WC2

A traitor's death In 1586 the 14 conspirators in the Babington Plot, which had aimed to kill Queen Elizabeth I and put Mary, Queen of Scots, on the throne of England, were sentenced to a traitor's death: to be hanged, drawn and quartered. Their leader, Antony Babington, suffered horribly. He was still alive when the hangman cut him down and slit his stomach open, then burned his guts in front of his eyes. It wasn't until he was butchered into four pieces that he was finally dead. The scene was so awful that the Queen decreed that the others must be hanged to the point of death before the rest of the sentence was carried out.

A traitor's d
suffered hor
when the ha
and slit his s
burned his g
It wasn't un
four pieces

LOCATION: HOLBORN STATION

London Bridge EC4

Queenly revenge The first London Bridge was built by the Romans in about AD 50, soon after their invasion of Britain. The uneasy peace was often broken by uprisings, sometimes sparked by heavy-handed Roman action. When Boudicca, widow of the chief of the Iceni, was stripped of her powers, flogged, and saw her daughters raped by Roman soldiers, she took spectacular revenge. Boudicca's armies invaded London where citizens

th – Antony Babington, bly. He was still alive gman cut him down omach open, then ts in front of his eyes. l he was butchered into hat he was finally dead.

were 'massacred, hanged, burned and crucified', according to the Roman historian, Tacitus. Then she torched the city itself, probably starting at a point just north of the bridge. Thousands died in the fire. Boudicca left the city to meet the Romans north of London, but there her armies were destroyed. A statue of Boudicca and her daughters riding in their war chariot stands beside Westminster Bridge, opposite Big Ben.

Fire on London Bridge In 1598 John Stowe recorded that London Bridge seemed 'a continual street rather than a bridge'. Houses, shops and even public lavatories were strung along both sides of it. On 10 July 1212 a fire started in Southwark, south of the bridge, and many people gathered on the bridge itself to gawp. Strong winds carried sparks over the river and the north entrance to the bridge caught fire. At almost the same time the fire in Southwark reached the south entrance. Thousands of people were trapped with flames blocking both ends of the bridge. Rescuers in boats tried to take people off, but in the panic many boats overturned and sank, drowning the just-rescued. The two walls of fire burned buildings and people until they met in the middle. Three thousand drowned and burned bodies were found, but many more were completely incinerated, trapped in that 'continual street' over the Thames.

LOCATION: MONUMENT STATION

Right: The grim reality of prison life

Far right: Punishment was meted out from the Old Bailey

Newgate Prison Newgate Street EC1

Limbo and Hell Newgate, built in 1188 and not demolished until 1902, was notorious as one of the worst prisons in Britain. It was '... a Hell such as Dante might have conceived', in the words of the 18th-century Venetian adventurer Casanova, a connoisseur of jails. The hold for condemned prisoners, called Limbo, was the worst part – a place without light, crawling with lice and rats and with an open sewer running through the middle. Here prisoners lay chained to the floor.

In the early years, Newgate prisoners were reduced to cannibalism, and from that time the legend of the Black Dog of Newgate comes, only appearing when someone was executed and bringing with it a foul smell. This creature seems to have grown out of the real horrors of the place: the floggings, the violence of old prisoners to new arrivals, or the cruelty of the jailers themselves. The area is to this day a place of crime and punishment, for the Old Bailey courthouse stands on the same site.

'...a Hell s
might hav

Deadman's Walk, off Warwick Lane, is a passageway behind Newgate through which prisoners were led on their final journey to their execution.

LOCATION: ST PAUL'S STATION

Ratcliff Highway (now The Highway) E1

In 1811 the murder of two families caused great terror in London. One shopkeeper sold 300 alarm rattles in an hour.

The murder of the Marrs Mr Marr kept a shop at 29 Ratcliff Highway. On the night of 7 September 1811, the maid went out to buy some food. When she came back she found a scene from a slaughterhouse. Marr, his wife and baby, and the apprentice boy were all lying around the house, with their heads brutally smashed in and their throats cut. Nothing of value was missing from the shop. The several weapons used on the Marrs included a sailor's knife, a mallet, a chisel and a crowbar.

The murder of the Williamsons Mr Williamson was landlord of the Kings Arms at 81 New Gravel Lane (now Garnet Street). On the night of 19 September 1811,Williamson, his wife and the maid were all murdered. Like the Marrs, their heads were staved in and their throats cut. The maid's head was just hanging from her shoulders by a strip of skin. Williamson's lodger saw a figure leaning over the bodies as he escaped to raise the alarm.

uch as Dante
e conceived'

The murderer John Williams, a labourer, was accused of the murders. His motive was never clear and today some people think he was not the culprit. Williams was imprisoned in Cold Bath Fields, where he hanged himself – one more crime, as suicide was illegal.

Williams' corpse was propped in a cart and paraded past the scenes of the murders and on to the crossroads of Cannon Street and New Road. Here it was buried in unconsecrated ground, with a stake driven through his heart to ensure that he would never rest.

One hundred years later Williams' body was dug up and the bones were divided up as relics around the area. His skull is in a pub at the crossroads where he was buried.

LOCATION: TOWER HILL STATION

St Giles (St Giles High Street) W1

Hell hole For hundreds of years St Giles was the worst slum in London. A hospital was established here for lepers in 1117, and the poorest and most desperate people clustered round it. St Giles had very few amenities, but one thing it never lacked was ale-houses; in the 16th century the condemned on their way to Tyburn stopped here for a last drink of ale. Here syphilitic prostitutes plied their trade and poverty-stricken men and women drank their lives away with cheap gin.

In the early 19th century, houses in St Giles were called the Rookeries; close-packed tenements set around a maze of alleys and passages that provided criminals with any number of secret bolt holes and escape routes.

Many people lived in the cellars of these houses, sometimes 20 families in one space no better than a hole in the ground, without the basics of light or sanitation. Conditions such as these bred disease. A 19th-century commentator, Thomas Beame, noted among the tragic victims a young man dying of consumption lying naked under a rag, completely alone, no charity or hospital prepared to take him in.

But St Giles harboured a worse disease, a disease which killed in the hundreds of thousands – for it is notorious as the starting point of the Great Plague (see pages 54–55).

LOCATION: TOTTENHAM COURT ROAD STATION

THE GREAT PLAGUE (The Black Death) 1664-5

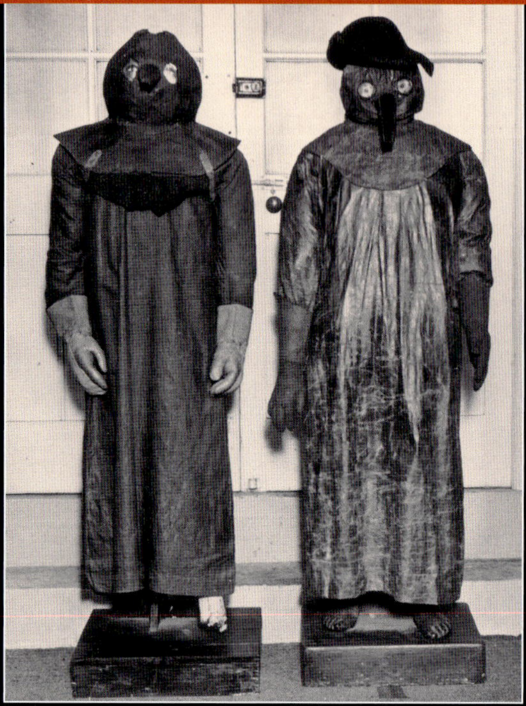

'Serjeant Death hath arrested them'

The Great Plague began in Ashlin's Place, Drury Lane, in the parish of St Giles and spread quickly through the 'Congestion of mishapen and extravagant Houses', as the contemporary diarist John Evelyn described London.

The plague was widespread, and often regarded as God's judgement on the wickedness of the city. 'Fear you not some plague...blown with the breath of the Almighty?' thundered one clergyman in 1657. The real cause, an infection spread by rat fleas, was not traced until the 19th century. Almost half the population of London died in 1348 from the Black Death, the first great epidemic in Europe; and in 1603, the last outbreak before the Great Plague, 30,000 Londoners died. But by the end of 1665 approximately 120,000 Londoners were dead, 25% of the city's population. (The equivalent today would be 1.75 million deaths.)

Doctors dressed in outlandish protective gear were more likely to scare their patients to an early death than effect a remedy.

'Fear you not som
the breath of the A
one clergyman in

Guards, nurses and Searchers of the Dead

Once plague was confirmed in a family everyone was sealed up in their house for 40 days, with a guard set at the door. This usually condemned them all to a slow and horrific death. Plague doctors – nightmarish figures with sharp, beak-like masks filled with protective herbs and long covering robes, resembling giant birds of prey – might visit, but there was little they could do. The parish sent nurses to the families, but these fearsome creatures killed more than they cured. Pronouncing 'distemper of the throat', they strangled their dying patients, or deliberately infected healthy people with runnings from the sores of their sick relatives in order to steal their property. Desperate to escape from this trap many people killed their guards. One family attacked their guard with gunpowder, blowing him up and burning him alive in the street. They escaped, but no-one would come near the infected house to help the guard.

Once death had come, the Searchers of the Dead visited. These were old women who had to verify the cause of death to the parish clerk. Finally the bodies were abandoned to the death-

LONDON

Corpses of plague victims were buried with much haste and little ceremony

plague...blown with mighty?' thundered 657

carts and taken to plague pits. The carters, constantly drunk to keep up their spirits, and with that black humour that tries to defy death, would hold up the bodies of children and shout, 'Faggots! Faggots! Five for sixpence!'

The city of the dead

In that stifling summer the death toll was 4,000 or more each week. Shops and taverns closed, the court and government had left the city long before. Chroniclers wrote about the eerie details of neglect: the empty streets, the River Thames flowing quietly without boats on it, grass growing in the road at Whitehall. Smoke from cleansing fires drifted about but stung no-one's eyes. In the shops that remained open, coins were placed in vinegar, and customers would not take change. The disease attacked so suddenly that people would sit down in the street and die where they sat. At night the cry of 'Bring out your dead!', the ringing of the death-carts' bells and the rumbling of their iron-clad wheels was ceaseless. The short nights of summer darkness could not hide what they were doing.

The end

The harsh winter of 1665-66 cut the death toll dramatically as the rats and their fleas died off, and people started to return to London. But it was not until the Great Fire of September 1666 that the plague vanished. By that time another 100,000 people had died of the disease throughout the rest of the country.

The picturesque Tower of London served as a state prison from the 15th to the 18th centuries

St Giles in the Fields W1

Death of a Lollard St Giles' Church saw the gruesome death, in 1414, of Sir John Oldcastle, a member of the heretical Lollard Rebellion. Special executions were often thought up for traitors and heretics, although the most usual method was to be hanged, drawn and quartered. Oldcastle was partially hanged, then he was strung up by his arms and legs in chains from a large gibbet. A fire was lit below him, so that he slowly roasted, then burned alive as the iron chains glowed red-hot.
LOCATION: TOTTENHAM COURT ROAD STATION

Smithfield EC1

Smithfield was once known as 'Smooth-field', a meadow outside the city walls. In the 12th century it was used for horse-fairs and the slaughter of pigs and oxen, and it is still the site of London's major meat market. But the meadow had a more sinister use as a place of execution.

Braveheart William Wallace of Scotland fought a spirited war against the English and their King, Edward I, and he terrified and angered them. His execution in 1305 was long drawn-out and bloody.

According to an eye-witness, Wallace was 'hung on a noose and afterwards let down living, his privates cut off and his bowels turned out and burned.' His body was then quartered and his head stuck on a pole on London Bridge, the common fate of all traitors. Some men were hanged to their death before the mutilation began, but not Wallace, who remained alive throughout much of his tortures.

Boiled alive Among the varieties of death practised at Smithfield, boiling alive seems to have been reserved for poisoners. In Henry VIII's time one victim was Richard Ross, a cook, so he had plenty of opportunity to poison his 16 victims. How long it took to boil him to death is not recorded, but executioners were placed on each side of the cauldron and used long poles to push Ross down again and again as he cooked.

Far right: The rack proved a most efficient torture

Protestant martyrs Queen Mary's reign was short (1553–58), and unhappy. She was a sick woman, desperate for a child, but spurned by her husband, Philip II of Spain. Mary was a devout Catholic, and an energetic prosecutor and killer of Protestants. Some 300 Protestant martyrs were burned to death on Mary's orders, many of them at Smithfield. The Queen took a great interest in their sufferings and wanted to make sure they lasted as long as possible. The martyrs were not to be strangled first, and Mary decreed that no green wood was to be used because this could produce smoke that might suffocate the victims before the flames reached their bodies. She wanted them to burn alive, and scream in agony.
LOCATION: FARRINGDON STATION

Tower of London EC3

The Tower of London was built by William the Conqueror in 1070 to subdue his conquered Saxon subjects. It has always inspired awe and terror. Only a few years after the Tower was built Thomas Fitz-Stephen wrote that 'the mortar thereof is

tempered with the blood of beasts.' It is also tempered with the blood of men and women imprisoned and tortured here.

Instruments of torture The rack was popularly known as the 'Duke of Exeter's Daughter', and was supposed to have been invented by the Duke in 1446, although it actually goes back to Roman times. The rack worked by stretching the victim's body until bones were pulled out of their sockets and tendons were torn apart. It was used in England until about the 1670s and was always regarded as the most painful torture. There were many famous victims, including Guy Fawkes. King James I, Fawkes' intended victim, said chillingly to the jailers, 'the gentler tortures are to be used first'. The rack was to be used only if these 'gentler' tortures failed, which they did. On the rack Fawkes confessed everything after 30 minutes.

The 'Scavenger's Daughter' could be called the rack's little sister but worked in the opposite way. It compressed the body into a ball, slowly squashing the innards, crushing bones and breaking limbs. Henry Skeffington invented this instrument in Henry VIII's time. It consisted of a set of irons that forced the victim into a crouching position; side bars were then ratcheted tighter and tighter, causing extreme agony.

The 'Little Ease' was first mentioned in 1534 and was probably at the base of the White Tower. It was a cell just 1½ feet (45cm) wide, 4 feet (1.25m) high, and 2 feet (60cm) deep, set behind a door with a metal grille at the top. The victim would be pressed into this space and then left, unable to stand, sit or lie for as much as a week, before the tortures began in earnest. These might consist of the bilboes that crushed ankles, the pilniewinks that crushed the victim's fingers, or the brakes that crushed their teeth.

The Princes in the Tower The 'Little Princes', Edward V, aged 12, and the Duke of York, aged 9, disappeared in 1483. They had been imprisoned in the Garden Tower by their uncle, Richard III. No-one knows what happened, but given Richard's tigerish nature it seems unlikely that he would have allowed them to live as their claim to the throne was stronger than his. In 1674 two small skeletons were discovered, crammed under a staircase in the White Tower, which were later identified as those of the missing princes. Were they suffocated, strangled, stabbed, or maybe drowned in one of the river entrances?

The fate of the Princes in the Tower remains a grisly mystery

The execution of the feisty Countess of Salisbury

Tower of London (CONT)

The Countess of Salisbury The Archbishop of Canterbury had dared to criticise Henry VIII for his actions against the Catholic Church. As the Archbishop was in France, Henry took his revenge on the man's mother, the Countess of Salisbury: she was sent to the Tower and condemned to death in 1541. The Countess, by now well into her seventies, refused to admit any guilt, and on the scaffold bravely shouted insults at the executioner. She would not kneel at the block – instead, she ran around the scaffold screaming her innocence. The executioner, axe in hand, chased her, and finally hacked her to death where she fell.

The Duke of Monmouth The Monmouth Rebellion against James II in 1685 failed miserably, but the Duke of Monmouth was still a glamorous and popular man. He was one of the last victims of the bungling Jack Ketch, official executioner for 23 years. Royal traitors like the Duke were sent out of the world with great drama. The scaffold at the Tower was draped in black and the Duke had to lie out full-length on a low block. In this atmosphere, Jack Ketch failed to deliver. He was notorious for hacking away at his victims' necks. He took five blows of the axe to the Duke and cut him badly but did not kill him. At one point, it is recorded, Monmouth twisted his half-severed head and grinned up hideously at his executioner. Eventually, Ketch knelt down and sawed Monmouth's head off with a knife.

LOCATION: TOWER HILL

Tyburn Connaught Place W2

Popular entertainment

Tyburn was London's theatre of execution from about 1196 to 1783. Today it is a massive roundabout, pounded by traffic, but in its heyday thousands of people came to see men and women hang here. The condemned came on a long journey through London from Newgate (see page 52). Some were finely dressed and threw flowers to the crowd. They stopped at St Giles to drink ale, then at Tyburn they died by slow, struggling strangulation on the gallows. Friends would pull on their feet to hasten death.

The crowd, believing the body to have magic power would fight to touch the corpse, while friends tried to take it away for burial. Whole families came to watch, pies were sold and hawkers sold printed ballads often describing the supposed misdeeds of the criminals. The popular highwaymen were adored, while informers and traitors had filth and insults thrown at them.

Mass production John Derrick, the public executioner around the year 1600, tried to kill as many people as possible in one go and invented an admirable system of hoists still in use today in the dockyards of the world for quite other purposes. London's appetite for execution was insatiable and

150 people a month were mounting the scaffold. Derrick's new gallows on which 23 people could be hoisted, hanged and cut down all at once proved useful on busy days.

The Triple Tree In the 1670s, Richard Jacquet invented a gibbet that went literally one better than the Derrick by accommodating 24 people. It was a triangular affair with three legs as support and three arms at the top, each of which could take eight victims. A popular ballad of the time named it the Triple Tree and claimed that an evil spirit picked it up by the roots in a storm. It was not reckoned worthwhile to take the Triple Tree down between executions, and it stood there until 1759.

Oliver Cromwell, one-time Lord Protector

Rituals of death There was an ancient, pagan ritual of death at public executions. Young women put the hand of a recently hanged man on their breast for its restorative powers, and sometimes the

Cromwell's body was dug up, put on trial and duly found guilty. The rotting corpse was then paraded through the streets of London...

body was dissected and studied for signs of evil. In January 1661, three years after his death, Oliver Cromwell experienced an ancient form of savagery. After the restoration of the monarchy, Cromwell's body was dug up, put on trial and duly found guilty. The rotting corpse was then paraded through the streets of London, where it was hanged until the sun set. The head was cut off, dipped in tar and spiked above Westminster Hall. Cromwell's body was then thrown into a pit under Tyburn. In a ghoulish reversal of fortune, Charles I's body was dug up, the head sewn back on and given a royal funeral.

LOCATION: MARBLE ARCH STATION

Wapping E1

Pirates on the Thames A bleak stretch of the river at Wapping was used for hundreds of years to dispatch pirates into another world. After hanging, the bodies were generally left on the riverbank to be washed away by the tide. The more famous pirates such as Captain Kidd, who was hanged in 1700, were exhibited at Graves Point as a horrible warning to sailors as they put to sea. The bodies were dipped in tar then suspended from gibbets or in special cages and left there until they fell apart.

LOCATION: WAPPING STATION

> **“a filthy sight it was to see his flesh shrunk upon his bones”**
>
> SAMUEL PEPYS

Wardour Street W1

Murder in wartime In 1942 the West End, in an area bounded by Marylebone Road at the north and Piccadilly to the south, was haunted by its own Jack the Ripper. The darkened streets of London at the height of war had the same nightmarish quality as the streets of Whitechapel in the 1880s. Four women were murdered and two more savagely attacked. The murderer killed day after day, and only a silly mistake gave him away.

The worst murder occurred at 153 Wardour Street, where Nita Ward was found on 10 February with her throat slashed and her body mutilated with a tin-opener. On 9 February Evelyn Hamilton had been found strangled, and just two days later Florence Love's daughter found her mother dead – strangled and then slashed with a razor. Doris Jouannet, too, was murdered in the same way.

Two luckier victims survived, despite having spent time with a young airman who became violent. After one attack he ran off leaving his gas mask behind. It had his service number on it and the police traced it to Gordon Frederick Cummins, a 28-year-old RAF cadet. He was executed on 25 June 1942, just five months after the first murder.

LOCATION: OXFORD CIRCUS STATION

JACK THE RIPPER

In 1888 the East End of London was terrorised by five horrific murders, all of prostitutes. The story has become world-famous. No-one was caught, but Jack the Ripper in some ways still haunts the streets of Whitechapel.

The murders

1 Bucks Row (now Durward Street) E1, Mary Ann Nicholls, 31 August. Her throat was slashed and her body slit open from throat to stomach.

2 29 Hanbury Street E1, Annie Chapman, 8 September. Her throat and body were slit. This time the intestines were placed over the right shoulder and the uterus and bladder were missing. Now the great fear began.

3 Berner Street (now Henrique Street) E1, Elizabeth Stride, 30 September, the night of the double murder. Elizabeth's throat was slit but there were no other mutilations. Perhaps the murderer was disturbed.

4 Mitre Square EC3, about a quarter of a mile away, Catherine Eddowes was found at 1.45am, attacked in the same way as Annie Chapman. In a development, her face had been mutilated.

5 Dorset Street (now demolished, the corner of Whites Road and Crispin Street) E1, Mary Kelly, 9 November. The last murder was the worst. Mary's legs were skinned and her throat severed, her nose and breasts cut off and placed by the bed, her heart and kidneys ripped out, and there was such an attack on her face that flesh spattered the walls.

Mary Ann, Annie, Elizabeth, Catherine and Mary

These five women lived in terrible poverty and might only earn pennies from their customers, but they all had a life story and died a horrible death. Mary Kelly, so violated that photographs of her body seem hardly human, was a lively, pretty woman from Ireland. She married at sixteen, but when her collier husband died, Mary had to make her own way. Once she went with a rich protector to Paris. She probably had the time of her life.

Who was Jack?

After Mary Kelly, the murders stopped suddenly, It is believed, however, that serial killers do not stop unless they are caught or they die. So who was Jack the Ripper, and why did he stop?

The list of suspects is bizarre, and includes the Queen's grandson, men in snowshoes, Russian agents and angry abortionists. Montague J Druitt is a more likely candidate. Educated and intelligent, Druitt may have studied medicine before switching to the law. There was insanity in his family and he had no alibis for the murders. In 1888 he became sick, lost his job and, fearing permanent insanity, committed suicide on 3 December.

The ghost

On 31 December around midnight, a shadowy figure is sometimes seen to leap from Westminster Bridge into the Thames. Legend says it is the ghost of Jack the Ripper; it echoes the fatal leap taken by Montague Druitt.

Despite public interest, Jack the Ripper was never caught

SOUTH-EAST ENGLAND

When it comes to bloodshed, murder and massacre, south-east England scores particularly high on two important counts: invasion and smuggling. The proximity of France and the Low Countries meant that this was always the first part of the country to be invaded. Whenever taxes were high, violent smuggling gangs threatened the populace. There were other problems, shared with the rest of the country. Inland, people eking out a subsistence living from the land challenged high taxes and the introduction of machinery that threatened their livelihoods. Religious persecution and witchcraft also touched this region many times, notably between the 16th and 18th centuries.

Detail of the exterior of Canterbury Cathedral, scene of a notorious murder

Invasion

The shortest crossing of the English Channel proved irresistible to many would-be conquerors from mainland Europe, threatening in particular the people of Kent. The Romans invaded southern Britain in AD 43, and from their strongholds in the south and east they moved to dominate most of England. When the Roman Empire crumbled, boatloads of Angles, Saxons and Jutes came across the sea. Between the 9th and 11th centuries, the Vikings attacked Britain and engaged in plundering raids and bloody battles such as that at Maldon in Essex in 991.

The last successful invason of Britain was by the Normans, who landed near Hastings in 1066. Although the country was never invaded again, this region has remained vulnerable to attack, from the Spanish Armada in 1558 to Napoleon Bonaparte in the early 19th century. Defences were tightened again during World War I, and the possible invasion of Hitler's forces was a very real threat in the 1940s. German V1 and V2 rockets during World War II brought death and destruction to Kent and Sussex as well as London.

Uprisings, wars and riots

South-east England has witnessed its share of riots and disputes, most notably the Peasants' Revolt of 1381, a violent reaction to excessive taxation, which was led by a Kentish man, Wat Tyler. The Civil War saw a large concentration of activity in the region. To the west in Oxfordshire and Berkshire there was support for the King, while the east stood for Parliament and Cromwell. News travelled slowly, and despite the fact that some 100,000 men died throughout the country in this war, there were isolated enclaves in the south-east where the people hardly knew the conflict existed.

In the 19th century, labourers in the agricultural south tried to defend their livelihoods by breaking new mechanised farm equipment. As in the industrialised north, some men died trying to save themselves and their families from the indiginities of the poorhouse.

Belief, persecution and witchcraft

The 16th and 17th centuries were marked by religious persecution across Britain. The south-east saw the greatest concentration of the burning of Protestant martyrs under Queen Mary, with some 230 out of the total 300 killed coming from this region. Vivid accounts of the burnings are recorded in *Foxe's Book of Martyrs* (1563), with deaths occurring from Kent and Sussex to Buckinghamshire and Oxfordshire.

Alongside this persecution came the investigations into so-called witches. Witch trials had been prominent in Europe since the 15th century, and the fears spread to Britain. East Anglia saw the highest proportion of trials and subsequent deaths in the 16th and 17th centuries. In the mid-17th century this was very largely due to the work of one man, Matthew Hopkins, the self-styled 'witchfinder-general'. Hopkins had a thirst to seek out the devil, which to him was manifested in the form of witches and their familiars. Although decreasing in number, witchcraft trials continued into the 18th century.

Society and death

Until the 20th century death was perceived as very much a part of life. Dead bodies were regularly seen in the streets, in the home and on the battlefield. For those who lived lives of endless toil, the fascination and blood lust for criminals and the nature of their death was an escape from the drudgery. Watching the flames lick around the religious martyrs, observing the drowning of witches or a body rotting on a gibbet, acted not only as a warning and deterrent but also as an entertainment. Hang fairs at Horsham, witch trials at Chelmsford, dissections at Cambridge, all had a bloodthirsty following. Cruel sports such as bull baiting, popular in Wokingham, and fist fights in Farnborough attracted huge crowds of all ages.

Sensitivity and morality began to creep in at the beginning of the 19th century, and during the Victorian period you find the last public hangings, such as in Oxfordshire in 1851, and the last fist fight at Wadhurst in 1863. Bull baiting was finally banned in 1835.

Alton HAMPSHIRE

Sweet Fanny Adams The horror surrounding the brutal murder of eight-year old Fanny Adams from Alton not only sent shock waves through the community and the country at large but it also ensured that the girl's name lived on in the English language.

Fanny was murdered by Frederick Baker on 24 August 1867 while playing in Flood Meadow, a short distance from her home. Thomas Gates made the horrific discovery of the child's head resting on two hop poles at the foot of a hedge. Close by was a leg and thigh, complete with stocking and boot. More pieces of the body were found, including the torso, which had been hideously mutilated. Baker was tried, convicted and executed at Winchester in December 1867.

The little girl's name was immortalised by sailors in the Royal Navy, who nicknamed newly introduced tins of inferior meat Sweet Fanny Adams, as an explanation of the body parts never found. In time the name was shortened to Sweet FA, meaning nothing, or worthless.

LOCATION: 10 MILES SOUTH-WEST OF FARNHAM ON A31

Amersham BUCKINGHAMSHIRE

Martyred for a cause A series of trials of Lollards – followers of the teachings of John Wycliffe (see opposite) – took place at Amersham in the 16th century. These Protestants did not approve of worshipping images of the saints or praying to them.

A particularly zealous churchman, Bishop Longland, set about holding inquisitions and meting out punishments to the Lollards. These ranged from wearing badges of faggots on their sleeves to indicate moral wrongdoing, to branding on the face with hot irons, and – the ultimate – burning to death at the stake. The names of those burned in Amersham are engraved on the Martyrs Memorial, erected in 1931.

LOCATION: 9 MILES NORTH-EAST OF HIGH WYCOMBE ON A404

Arreton ISLE OF WIGHT

Legend of the skull The responsibility of looking after his baby grandson, James Dove, fell upon Michael Morey after his daughter died giving birth. Morey was a woodcutter, leading a hard and isolated life. James suddenly disappeared in 1736, and since Morey could not offer any explanation, he was taken into custody. Three months later the boy's remains were found, dismembered and placed in two leather bags, and concealed with an old billhook and bloodstained gloves.

Morey was executed despite the circumstantial nature of the evidence. His body was hung in chains from the gibbet located on a Bronze Age barrow near Arreton, which is now known as Michael Morey Hump. Excavations revealed several skeletons and skulls, one supposed to be that of Michael Morey. Although this was later revealed to be of prehistoric origin, the legend around it lives on.

LOCATION: 7 MILES SOUTH-EAST OF NEWPORT ON A3056

Aylesbury BUCKINGHAMSHIRE

Battle of Aylesbury Aylesbury was the scene of a bloody battle of the Civil War fought between the Royalists under Prince Rupert and the Parliamentarians led by Sir William Balfore, in 1642.

Furious fighting using a combination of muskets, swords and poleaxes meant a short-lived battle, and soon hundreds of Royalists lay dead. In 1818 a large number of human bones were discovered near the battle site. They were buried in a tomb at the churchyard at Hardwick with a tablet including the grim epitaph, 'united in one common slaughter.'

LOCATION: 16 MILES WEST OF HEMEL HEMPSTEAD

BURNED AT THE STAKE

Throughout the 16th century there were waves of persecution against Protestants. In the early days these were directed at the Lollards, Protestants following the heretical teachings of reformer John Wycliffe (1329–1384).

South-east England saw the largest number of martyrs burned at the stake during the brief reign of Queen Mary (1553–58). 'Bloody Mary' had received a harsh upbringing at the hand of her father, Henry VIII, for remaining true to Roman Catholicism. It was followed by the difficult short reign of her brother Edward VI. On inheriting the throne she determined to restore her religion in England, but met with fierce resistance.

While most of the country was still Catholic, there were Protestant strongholds in London and the south-east. Nearly 300 martyrs were cruelly burned during her reign, with 78 dying in London, 62 in Kent, 23 in Sussex and some 70 in East Anglia. A gory account of the martyrs' deaths can be found in John Foxe's *Book of Martyrs*, published in Strasbourg in 1563. More dramatic than accurate it promoted anti-Catholic hysteria.

The burnings were carried out in front of huge crowds who had come for a good day out, often bringing their children along. The actual suffering varied from case to case. England was regarded as less cruel than other European countries – in France and the Netherlands the tongues of heretics were often cut out or bored through. Some victims bribed officials to get a bag of gunpowder to put round their waist or neck to cause an explosion and quicken death. Much depended on the state of the fuel – whether it was damp or green. Wind direction also played a part, either encouraging the flames or blowing them away from the victim, thus prolonging death. For many it was God's will and they bore their suffering with great fortitude.

The burning of Protestant martyrs provided a memorable warning to would-be followers.

Banbury OXFORDSHIRE

An execution too far John Kalabergo was an immigrant who fled persecution in Italy for a new life in England. He soon set up a successful business, and his reluctant nephew William was sent to help him. Bitter at having to leave Italy, and seeing his chance for an inheritance, William shot his uncle in the back of the head when they were out delivering in 1851. The boy's trial and subsequent execution caught the public attention. He was described as 'deathly pale and ghastly'. A huge crowd gathered to watch the execution, when his body convulsed with such violence that his legs were drawn up and down, a truly terrible sight. As a result, the authorities banned public hangings in Oxfordshire from this date.

LOCATION: 25 MILES NORTH OF OXFORD OFF M40

Barnet HERTFORDSHIRE

Battle of Barnet, 1471 This was one of the bloodiest battles fought between the houses of Lancaster and York during the 15th-century Wars of the Roses. The Yorkists were led by Edward IV, and the Lancastarians by Warwick, 'the Kingmaker'.

The bloody battle took place in heavy fog and was fought at such close quarters that Warwick's soldiers attacked each other by mistake. Warwick was killed when he was cut down trying to remount his horse, and on this occasion the Yorkists triumphed.

LOCATION: 12 MILES NORTH-WEST OF LONDON ON A1000

Basingstoke HAMPSHIRE

Buried alive Imagine, if you dare, being buried 6 feet (2m) underground. You would struggle in every possible way to attract attention, and try desperately to gain the smallest amount of air. This ghastly fate struck Mrs Blunden in 1674. She had complained of a fearful headache and was told to drink poppy-water, a mild form of opium. She drank too much of this soporific medicine and fell into a deep sleep. Pronounced dead by a physician, she was promptly buried at the Liten, close to the Holy Cross. When boys from a nearby school heard tapping underground the grave was opened up. But it was too late: Mrs Blunden was dead, her body badly bruised by her desperate attempts to escape.

Basingstoke riots When the Salvation Army first came to the Hampshire town in 1880, they innocently provoked demonstrations because of their opposition to alcohol, for many residents earned their living in Basingstoke's breweries. As the Army paraded through the streets, spreading their message, ill-feeling simmered. In December of that year the violence errupted, involving a

drunken mob of over 1,000 people. The rioters were clubbed, hurled into railings and ducked in the Basingstoke Canal. Finally, the Riot Act was read from the town hall and the horse artillery was ordered to clear the streets.

LOCATION: 14 MILES SOUTH-EAST OF CAMBERLEY ON M3

Battle EAST SUSSEX

Battle of Hastings The most famous battle in British history was fought in 1066 at Senlac Hill, just outside the town of Battle. King Harold's men fought with swords, axes, spears and slings, but the Norman invader William also had the use of archers and cavalry. Harold caught William by surprise while his army was plundering the neighbourhood and scavenging for food, but the French knights cut the less disciplined men of Harold's army to pieces, moving the dead and wounded to the front of the shield-wall to provide an obstacle to the English. The final assault produced a change of tactics as William's archers shot their arrows in the air. Harold was shot through the eye by a falling arrow, and died. Dismayed, the English retreated, pursued by the Normans in the fading light. Few English soldiers escaped the resulting slaughter, and William the Bastard became King William I of England.

LOCATION: 10 MILES NORTH-WEST OF HASTINGS ON A2100

Bedford BEDFORDSHIRE

The evil Sheriff The cruel and unhappy reign of King John was punctuated with uprisings by the troublesome barons. In 1217 the King granted Faulkes de Breauté the title of Sheriff of Bedfordshire and the use of Bedford Castle. Faulkes embarked on a life of murder, cruelty and eviction, even depriving the people of water. By the time Henry III came to the throne, the reports from Bedford were so bad that a deputation was sent to investigate. Eighty men of the castle were hanged. Faulkes himself escaped back to France, where he died of disease soon after. His legacy was the demolition of Bedford Castle.

Thomas Dun, murderer and highwayman

One of England's most notorious villains was Thomas Dun, who operated around the Bedford area in the 11th century. He began his thieving career as a child, and become a master of disguise, feared throughout the land for his violence and evil. He is said to have butchered men, women and children. Finally a mob caught up with him and, without trial, he was sentenced to death. Reports say he fought his executioners, and the wilder tales tell how his hands were chopped off, his arms at the elbows, feet at the ankles, legs from the trunk and his head was severed and burned to ashes.

LOCATION: 15 MILES NORTH-EAST OF MILTON KEYNES ON A421

Scenes of the Battle of Hastings vividly depicted in the stitches of the Bayeux Tapestry

Bognor Regis WEST SUSSEX

Pressed to death Thomas Wells will be remembered less as the supposed murderer of Elizabeth Symmonds at Bognor in 1735 than for his refusal to plead and subsequent torture: he was the last recorded person to be 'pressed' to death. Anyone refusing to answer questions could be subjected to pressing to induce a confession. The torture took place at Horsham jail, where a 100lb (45kg) weight was placed on him. On the second day a further 100lb (45kg) was added, and on the third a monstrous 150lb (68kg). Wells still refused to plead, so the weight was increased by another 50lb (23kg) – at which point he died, without ever speaking.

LOCATION: 7 MILES SOUTH-EAST OF CHICHESTER ON A259

Borley ESSEX

The most haunted house in England

Borley Rectory, built in 1863, was destroyed by fire in 1939. Labelled the most haunted house in England, the Rectory featured in many newspaper articles of the day. How much is fact and how much elaboration is debatable, but there is no doubt many strange happenings and sightings have been associated with Borley and its church. Legend says the rectory was built on the site of a medieval monastery. A nun from the nearby convent at Bures tried to elope with a monk from the monastery but they were apprehended. The monk was hung but the unfortunate nun was walled up in the monastery to die a horrendous death. Their ghosts haunted the house – the nun's ghost was seen so often that the dining-room window was blocked up. In later years, poltergeist activity and an odd atmosphere made the rectory notorious. Excavations after the rectory had burnt down revealed a skull believed to be that of the nun.

LOCATION: 2 MILES WEST OF SUDBURY OFF A134

Braughing HERTFORDSHIRE

A lucky jolt In 1595 a wealthy farmer named Matthew Wall, from the parish of Braughing, was declared dead. As his coffin was being sedately carried to the churchyard the bearers unfortunately dropped it in Fleece Lane. Not so unfortunate an event, for the occupant was revived by the jolt and knocked on the coffin lid, to everyone's surprise. Wall went on to live for many years, and Old Man's Day is still celebrated every October by village children in his memory.

LOCATION: 7 MILES WEST OF BISHOP'S STORTFORD OFF A120

Brighton EAST SUSSEX

Trunk murders On 17 June 1934, the decaying torso of a middle-aged but pregnant woman was discovered in Brighton railway station's left luggage

Brighton Station, where bodies were mysteriously left in 1934

office. On 18 June another trunk containing two legs and two severed feet, believed to be of a victim aged around 25 years, turned up at King's Cross station in London. Little progress was made in finding the murderer until prostitute Violet Kaye was declared missing. On interviewing her associate, Tony Mancini, police found a trunk containing Miss Kaye's body.

Mancini was tried under the name of Jack Noytre, but was acquitted of all the trunk murders as he had been at work when the Brighton and King's Cross trunks had been deposited, and claimed that he had found Violet Kaye dead and

panicked, putting her body into a trunk. The murders were never solved.
LOCATION: 59 MILES SOUTH OF LONDON ON A23

Burwell CAMBRIDGESHIRE
Puppet show fire One day in 1727 over 140 villagers assembled in a barn at Burwell, awaiting the imminent arrival of Mr Shepheard and his puppets. Their excitement soon turned to terror as an 'awful catastrophe and melancholy event' began to unfold. The whole tragic sequence was witnessed by 16-year-old Thomas Howe watching from a beam just under the great thatch roof. At about 9 o'clock Richard Whitaker came in to feed the horses and, to avoid paying to watch the show, took his lantern and candle into the stable and climbed up into the straw stored above. Somehow the straw caught fire. Only small at first, the fire spread along the roof like lightning. Panic ensued in the rush to escape, but a table blocked the door and the roof came down, crushing and burning those below. Over 80 people died in the tragedy.
LOCATION: 14 MILES NORTH-EAST OF CAMBRIDGE ON B1102

Thomas Howe remarked, 'In the morning that was a hideous scene – skulls, bones and carnage. The mangled relics were gathered up, shovelled into carts and buried in two large pits dug in the churchyard.'

Bury St Edmunds SUFFOLK
St Edmund the Martyr King Edmund's army attacked a Danish army in AD 870 after they had continually invaded his kingdom. Overwhelmed by the Danes' ferocity, he disbanded his men and fled, hiding under a bridge over the River Waveney. There he was discovered and captured by the Danes, who beat him and tied him to a tree; his flesh was torn with whips and he was shot with arrows. Finally his head was struck off. His remains were moved to Bury St Edmunds, where a great abbey was built in 1020 in the name of St Edmondsbury.
LOCATION: 32 MILES EAST OF CAMBRIDGE ON A14

Archbishop Thomas à Becket was struck down in his own cathedral

Calverton BUCKINGHAMSHIRE

A butcher's tale A gibbet used to stand in Gib Lane, and it is said to be haunted by the ghost of Lady Grace Bennett who was murdered in the 17th century. Her assassin was Adam Barnes, a butcher from Stony Stratford, who broke into her home in search of money. Barnes was convicted and hanged, his body suspended in irons from the gibbet until it decomposed as a warning to all.

LOCATION: 2 MILES WEST OF MILTON KEYNES OFF A5

Cambridge CAMBRIDGESHIRE

Body experiments Thomas Weems confessed in Cambridge jail to the murder of his wife Mary Anne. He alleged that she had falsely claimed pregnancy to trick him into marriage, and subsequently made his life a misery. He was duly hanged on 6 August 1818, left for one hour, then cut down and taken to the Chemical Lecture Room in the Botanic Garden. Crowds gathered, straining to get a view of the corpse. The experiments, however, were conducted in front of an invited audience, who paid well to see the spectacle. They firstly connected wires to his neck and chest, and by operating a battery caused Weems' body to shudder. Making deeper incisions, the scientists made him shudder more. The next day the body was put on display and crowds flocked to see it. A final dissection took place behind closed doors.

LOCATION: 60 MILES NORTH OF LONDON ON M11

Canterbury KENT

Murder of Thomas à Becket One of the most infamous crimes in history, the murder of Archbishop Thomas à Becket in his own cathedral at Canterbury, shocked contemporaries even in an age used to violent acts. Henry II and Becket had been close friends, and the King had appointed a reluctant Becket to be archbishop in 1162. Tensions grew between Crown and Church, and Becket fled to France for eight years.

On his return in 1170, to great acclaim, legend tells how the King remarked, 'who will rid me of this turbulent priest?' An army was dispatched to Canterbury to carry out the deed, sack the cathedral and kill all the monks. The monks scattered, and four of the king's loyal knights carried out the assassination as Becket stood in the transept of the cathedral. He was repeatedly bludgeoned, and the final blow shattered his skull; a messy bundle of rags and torn flesh was all that was left of the Archbishop of Canterbury.

LOCATION: 26 MILES EAST OF MAIDSTONE ON A2

Cardington BEDFORDSHIRE

Airship crash The ill-fated airship, *R101*, took off from here in October 1930, heading for Eygpt in poor weather conditions. Having circled Bedford, the airship had to fight against a rising wind and one engine shut down above London. The storm took a hold as they flew over France and the crew lost control of the airship. It narrowly missed hitting Beauvais Cathedral and crashed into hills near by. Only 6 of the 54 passengers survived; some died instantly, some of hideous burns later.

The victims lay in state in Whitehall and were driven on 24 artillery carriages to Euston Station. Crowds lined the route to the church in Cardington, where they were laid to rest in a single grave. A memorial tomb was erected in 1931.

LOCATION: 3 MILES SOUTH-EAST OF BEDFORD FF A421

The tangled remains of airship R101, which had been designed and built in the great hangars of Cardington

Caxton CAMBRIDGESHIRE

Caxton Gibbet At a crossroads between Cambridge and St Neots, Caxton Gibbet is a lonely place and the focus of many tales. One story maintains a murderer was hanged alive in an iron gibbet, to remain until he starved to death. A baker who handed him a piece of bread as a kind gesture was also hanged from the same gibbet. It is thought more likely that the gibbet was erected for a Royston highwayman named Garwood, executed in 1753 for robbing mail coaches.

LOCATION: 9 MILES WEST OF CAMBRIDGE ON A428

Chale Bay ISLE OF WIGHT

Sinking of the *Clarendon* A terrible storm raged around the south-west coast of the Isle of Wight on 11 October 1836, as a West Indiaman, the *Clarendon*, was trying to clear Chale Bay. Gradually driven closer and closer inshore, she finally grounded at the bottom of Blackgang Chine. Despite the valiant efforts of the villagers only 3 of the 27 passengers and crew survived. All they could do was bring the bodies ashore, and many of the victims are buried in St Andrews churchyard. It is said that in certain weather conditions the cries of the lost souls can be heard screaming in the wind.

LOCATION: 6 MILES WEST OF VENTNOR ON A3055

Chelmsford ESSEX

Witch trials Essex has the dubious distinction of having hanged more witches than any other county. The notorious Chelmsford witch trials spanned the mid-16th to mid-17th centuries. A trial of 1566 concerned Agnes Waterhouse, her daughter Joan and Elizabeth Francis, all from nearby Hatfield Peverel. Agnes was 63 years old and kept a cat and a toad. All three women were accused of having possession of a cat named Satan that apparently changed shape and caused the death of several people and domestic animals. It is said she rewarded the cat by allowing it to suck blood from her face. Agnes finally 'confessed' to save her daughter's life. Probably the first woman to be executed for witchcraft in England, she was hanged on a cross-beam beside the Chelmsford–Braintree road. Elizabeth Francis survived, only to be hanged in 1579 as the result of a later witch trial.

LOCATION: 35 MILES NORTH-EAST OF LONDON ON A12

Chichester WEST SUSSEX

Persecution of priests The reign of 'Bloody Mary' had been a time of terrible persecution for Protestants. When her half-sister Elizabeth I came to the throne in 1558, it was the Catholics who suffered. In particular, Catholic priests were singled out as they were considered to be in league with Elizabeth's Catholic enemies.

Two men, Ralph Crockett and Edward James, were accused of such sympathies and met their deaths in 1588 after the successful defeat of the Armada invasion fleet sent by Catholic Spain. Their trial took place in Chichester and they were then drawn on a hurdle to Broyle Heath, to the west of the city, where they absolved each other before being brutally hanged, drawn and quartered as traitors.

LOCATION: 16 MILES EAST OF PORTSMOUTH ON A27

Coggeshall ESSEX

The Coggeshall Gang Victorian England had its fair share of hooligans, and between 1844 and 1848 a series of violent crimes took place in and around the attractive Essex village of Coggeshall.

Locals feared for their safety as the gang of 14 men terrorised the community. Based at the Black Horse Inn in Stonegate Street, the gang had the ear of the landlord, who also received the stolen property. Wearing masks and bearing pistols and cudgels, the men operated at night stealing and burning down property. They even tortured people to find the whereabouts of valuables, holding their victims over fires or tying ropes around their necks and hoisting them up. Finally caught, they were tried, convicted and sentenced to transportation for life.

LOCATION: 10 MILES WEST OF COLCHESTER ON A120

MATTHEW HOPKINS: THE WITCHFINDER-GENERAL

The mid-17th century was a dark time – England was at war, a bitter Civil War which set neighbour against neighbour. People of the eastern counties were predominantly Protestant, and haters of Catholicism and its elaborate religious ritual. Suspicion and fear were growing and began to centre on witches. Witchcraft had been around for centuries, and although previously witches had been more avidly persecuted in mainland Europe, England was now seeking them out.

Matthew Hopkins, an unsuccessful lawyer who was born in a Suffolk village in the early 1620s, moved to Manningtree in Essex in the 1640s. It was at the Thorn Inn in the adjacent parish of Mistley that he examined his first suspects. Hopkins was convinced that all witches had made a satanic pact with the devil, and that their evil work was done through their 'imps' or 'familiars'. These took the form of everyday creatures, and in particular cats, toads and dogs, which were said to suckle blood from their owners. Hopkins was commissioned by Parliament to seek out these so-called witches and he was particularly active in his home counties of Essex and Suffolk. The witch-hunt began in the Chelmsford–Colchester area, and he and his assistants interrogated many suspects in the intimidating vaults of Colchester Castle.

Left: Anti-witch hysteria was fed by images of lascivious dancing and devil worship

Far left: Matthew Hopkins, a figure of fear who died in 1647

Various methods of trial were implemented; Hopkins' specialities were watching, searching and swimming. The suspect, usually an elderly woman, was stripped and put in a loose dress. She was then forced to sit on a stool for days, often bound, without food or sleep. She was watched by witnesses to see if she was secretly feeding a familiar, and regularly walked round and round to keep her awake. Many became confused and confessed after this treatment. In a second trial the victims would be searched for witch's marks – a nipple with which to feed the imps. The inquisitors often took warts or moles to be these marks. The third trial was swimming: the suspects were stripped and their thumbs tied to their toes. Then they were bound and thrown into a pond or deep stream. If they sank they were innocent and often drowned; if they floated, they were declared guilty. The women were sometimes pushed under at this point and then dragged to the surface so they could face their fate. Death would follow by drowning, hanging or burning.

Some 400 people in the region were executed as a result of Hopkins' witch trials; 68 in Bury St Edmunds alone and a staggering 19 in Chelmsford in one day. By 1646 some people were beginning to question Hopkins' motives, and he retired to Manningtree a wealthy man.

Colchester ESSEX

Siege of Colchester As the Civil War errupted in England, Colchester declared for Parliament as early as 1642. Most of the townspeople supported the fight against the monarchy. In 1648 a few remaining Royalists, including Sir Charles Lucas and Sir George Lisle, raised a new army in Kent. Threatened by Parliamentary forces they sought sanctuary in Colchester. After an initial skirmish they were allowed in under a peace agreement. However Sir Thomas Fairfax arrived at the head of the Parliamentary army, and attempted to storm the town. When this failed he decided to besiege it.

The siege of this ironically pro-Parliament town was to last for 76 devastating days. The people slowly starved during one of the coldest and wettest summers known and were reduced to eating dogs, rats and even candles. When the town at last surrendered, Lucas and Lisle were imprisoned in the castle and finally executed outside by firing squad. The spot where they fell is marked by an obelisk.

LOCATION: 22 MILES NORTH-EAST OF CHELMSFORD ON A12

Colnbrook BERKSHIRE

Ostrich Inn murders There has been a pub on this spot for centuries. Its notoriety stems from the 12th century, when it was run by a man named Jarman. The Ostrich was a staging post, often used by the wealthy on their way to Windsor. Jarman devised a dastardly scheme to steal from the visitors. After providing a good meal and copious amounts of ale, he would lead his victim to his best room. Once the guest was deeply asleep Jarman would pull a secret lever and the occupant of the bed would slide into a vat of boiling ale below. Drowned or boiled to death, it was undoubtedly a horrendous end for the victims. The villain would then take their belongings and dump the body in the river. When finally apprehended Jarman laid claim to 60 murders, and was duly hanged.

LOCATION: 4 MILE EAST OF SLOUGH OFF A4

The stark landmark of Combe Gibbet

Combe BERKSHIRE

Combe Gibbet A strange and eerie place, the setting for the gibbet on Combe Down is the highest point on the Berkshire–Hampshire border, and recalls a chilling and barbarous tale of the 17th century. George Brougham had taken a lover and wanted rid of his wife, Martha, so he decided to kill her.

On their way to market one day he saw a wasps' nest at the roadside. Putting on gloves, he went to investigate. Martha's curiosity was aroused and she, too, peered at the nest. Her husband moved silently behind her and pushed her head into the nest and held it there. The furious insects stung angrily, and Martha died in agony, her body covered and bloated with stings.

Brougham's downfall came when he told his lover of his dreadful deed and was overheard. He was arrested and ordered to be hanged in chains near the place of his wife's death – and so the gibbet was erected on this grim spot.

LOCATION: 8 MILES SOUTH-WEST OF NEWBURY OFF A343

Dartford KENT

Murder of Wat Tyler There is a certain mystery surrounding the death of local man Wat Tyler, the leader of the Kentish men during the Peasants' Revolt of 1381. Tyler is said to have led the peasants to the City of London to complain about the new poll tax. He was stabbed to death there, supposedly by the Lord Mayor. Other accounts suggest that as he brazenly approached the king he was intercepted and wounded by the mayor. His head was displayed on London Bridge.

LOCATION: 15 MILES EAST OF LONDON ON A2

Dunnose Head ISLE OF WIGHT

Sinking of the *Eurydice* HMS *Eurydice* was a fine two-decked, fully rigged sailing frigate that was converted into a Royal Navy training ship in 1877. The ship was ordered to Bermuda with a full load of passengers, and set sail in March 1878. Local accounts tell of terrible weather that day but the *Eurydice*, sheltered by the cliffs of Dunnose Head, did not realise the danger until it was too late. The ship's portholes had been left open to give ventilation to the passengers and, in the stormy conditions, she took on water and sank. Three hundred perished in the freezing waters.

LOCATION: 3 MILES SOUTH OF SHANKLIN ON A3055

Egham SURREY

Last fatal duel Englefield Green, on the edge of Egham, was the scene in 1852 of the last fatal duel fought on English soil. Two Frenchmen, Cournet and Bartholmy, came here to settle a dispute. At the first attempt Bartholmy's pistol misfired and Cournet missed. The duellists took aim once more, and this time Cournet fell to the ground – this was the man who had a return train ticket in his pocket, he was so confident of winning. He was taken to the nearby Barley Mow inn where he died, and his body now rests in Egham churchyard. Bartholmy's triumph was short-lived, however he was tried for murder and hanged.

LOCATION: 3 MILES WEST OF STAINES ON A30

Four 'seconds' attended the duel, to ensure that it was conducted in an honourable way.

Elstree HERTFORDSHIRE

Thurtell-Hunt murder case of 1823 One of the most famous and sensationalised events of the age, this case provoked a fascination reflected in the newspapers of the day. Thurtell and Hunt were accused of murdering William Weare, an unscrupulous gambler, whom they pulled from his horse-drawn gig and killed in Gill Lane. A third man, Probert, turned King's Evidence and escaped punishment. Thurtell was executed at Hertford before a crowd of 15,000, who watched as the hangman had to pull on his feet 12 times to kill him. The gallows and drop were later exhibited in the 'Chamber of Horrors' in London. Hunt was transported for life.

LOCATION: 12 MILES NORTH-EAST OF LONDON ON M1

Etton CAMBRIDGESHIRE

Civil War horror Woodcroft House, at Etton, hides a tale of a grisly end which dates back to the Civil War. Dr Hudson, a Royalist, was attempting to escape his Roundhead pursuers by dangling from the battlements, preparing to jump into the moat. Before he had time to jump, a solider cut cleanly through his wrists so that he fell into the moat. A second soldier fished the poor man out, knocked him unconscious and cut out his tongue. Dr Husdson died of his brutal wounds. The soldier kept the tongue as a good luck charm for a number of years.

LOCATION: 3 MILES NORTH OF PETERBOROUGH OFF A15

Farnborough HAMPSHIRE

Bare-knuckle boxing Billed as the greatest fist fight of all time, in 1866 Tom Sayers, England's champion, faced the much larger American, John Heenhan at Farnborough. This was one of the last such fights before the introduction of the Queensbury rules in 1867, and it was raw stuff: bare fists and round after round until one man was either knocked out or failed to get back to the centre in 30 seconds. Trains from London brought crowds of all classes of society, hungry for a bloody fight. And the blood certainly flowed that day. Sayers arm was broken and Heenhan was almost blinded. By round 42 both men were in a terrible state and the police, against the crowd's wishes, intervened to stop it. The fight lived on in ballads.

Two plane crashes In August 1913 the Texan-born Sam Cody – the first man to fly an aircraft in Britain – met his death while flying from Farnborough airfield in his latest seaplane, which had been specially equipped with a wheel and skid undercarriage. Cody took off with one passenger, and all seemed well until the plane turned near Cove Common and suddenly failed. The great wings crumpled, the plane nose-dived and the men fell to their deaths. Cody was greatly mourned with 100,000 people lining the route of his funeral.

After the Farnborough tragedy, questions were raised over design faults and whether the aircraft should ever have been allowed to take off.

An eerie coincidence occurred at the Farnborough Air Show in 1952, as the first prototype of the de Havilland DH 110 was giving a display over the main runway. The pilot, making a turn close to Cody's route of 39 years before, was heading for the densest part of the crowd in a low dive when suddenly the wings began to buckle. In a split second they were ripped from the fuselage, and the tail engines broke away and hurtled into the crowd. Thirty died in the tragedy and many more were seriously injured.

LOCATION: 3 MILES SOUTH OF CAMBERLEY ON A331

FIST FIGHTING

Fighting with fists was part of athletics in ancient Greece and of gladiatorial entertainment in Rome, but did not appear as an organised sport in England until the early 18th century. Prize fighters competed for a purse of money while others gambled on the result. Before Broughton's Rules for prize fighting were introduced in 1838 anything went, with hair pulling, eye gouging, head butting, choking and neck throttling all commonplace and cheered on by the crowds. There were prolonged and violent contests with bare fists and little regulation. It was not until the London Prize Rules of 1839 that kicking, biting and blows below the waist were declared to be fouls. On 8 December 1863 the last bare-fisted prize fight in England took place at Wadhurst in East Sussex between Tom King and John Heenhan. There was a public outcry over the brutality of the fight and calls for reform. As a result, public bare-fisted prize fighting was made illegal.

Bare-knuckle or fist fighting was outlawed as a public spectacle in 1863.

Flimwell EAST SUSSEX

Three hundred beheaded Flimwell lies on the Kent–Sussex border, on the road from London to Hastings. In 1264, Henry III and his army rested here on their way to fight the rebel barons at the Battle of Lewes. During an argument some of the locals, loyal to the barons, killed the King's cook. In bloody retribution, the army gathered together 300 local people in a field near the village and cut off their heads.

LOCATION: 13 MILES SOUTH-EAST OF TUNBRIDGE WELLS ON A21

> **During an argument som loyal to the barons, kille cook. In bloody retributi gathered together 300 lo near the village and cut**

Great Yarmouth NORFOLK

Bridge disaster When William Cooke's Circus visited Great Yarmouth in 1845, they decided to advertise the show with Nelson, the clown, sailing down the River Bure in a washtub drawn by four geese. Thousands of people lined the riverbanks o watch, with 300 to 400 at a prime vantage point on the Yarmouth Suspension Bridge. At about 5.30pm the clown passed under the bridge and the crowd surged to the other side to get a better view. Two rods appeared to give way and an alarm was given, but as the chains of the bridge broke on one side, several hundred people, mostly women and children, were thrown into the river. Some were rescued by boats and revived by bystanders, but 130 people were drowned in the tragedy.

LOCATION: 20 MILES EAST OF NORWICH ON A47

Guildford SURREY

Massacre at Guildford On the death of King Canute there was a crisis over the royal succession. Alfred Atheling, son of Ethelred 'the Unready', sailed to England from Normandy to claim the throne. In 1036 he was met by Earl Godwin, the powerful Earl of Essex. Godwin laid on a feast for Alfred and his followers, and after a good meal they retired for the night. Many never woke again, hacked down by Godwin's men as they slept. Others were rounded up and murdered or sold as slaves. Alfred was deliberately blinded and sent to Ely, where he died of his wounds. It may be that some of the 200 mutilated skeletons that were excavated in the town's Mount Cemetery were those of Alfred's men.

LOCATION: 30 MILES SOUTH-WEST OF LONDON ON A3

Hawkhurst KENT

Hawkhurst Gang William Galley, the Custom house keeper and David Charter, a shoemaker, were in possession of damning evidence against the Hawkhurst Gang, notorious smugglers, for their part in an attack on Poole's customs house. In 1748 the two men were on their way to give evidence against the gang when they stopped at an inn – the 'simple rustics' they found inside were the smugglers in disguise. Plied with drink, the two witnesses were then overpowered. Tied back-to-back on a horse, with their legs bound under the girth, they were whipped until Galley expired. His body was left on the Downs. Charter was thrown to his death down a 30-foot (9m) well, with several large stones dumped unceremoniously after him. After the trial in Chichester four of the gang were hanged, and a fifth died in jail before he reached the gallows. The bodies were carried to Broyle Heath where they were hung in chains.

LOCATION: 16 MILES SOUTH-EAST OF TUNBRIDGE WELLS ON A268

f the locals,
he King's
, the army
ls in a field
f their heads.

SMUGGLING – THE MYTH

From the coast of Norfolk to the West Country the dubious trade of smuggling has been a ready source of money for centuries. The south coast of England is most associated with the crime, especially Kent and Sussex during the18th century.

The name 'smuggler' may conjure up a jolly felon taking a little extra brandy on the side with the connivance of all, but this would be far from the truth. Smuggling was big business in the 18th and 19th centuries, and along with the crime came the murder, torture and brutality implemented by organised gangs. Before the 18th century smuggling had been small scale, but excise duty was vastly increased to pay for a constant state of war. Not only the luxuries of tea, brandy and chocolate but staples such as soap and salt were taxed, too. In fact, taxes rose so high that most of the rural community became involved in smuggling in some way or other.

Organised gangs ruled the roost; along the south coast it was the Hawkhurst and the Groombridge gangs. They worked the runs along the marshes, and could operate as many as 500 pack horses at one time to transport their contraband to various rendezvous points between here and London. They looked after their own, and any dragoon or customs officer who got in their way was ruthlessly treated. After a series of brutal killings the leaders of the Hawkhurst gang were executed. The gangs gradually lost their grip on the community and, with the reduction of taxes, smuggling went into a less brutal phase. By the 1840s a free trade policy was introduced, ending high import duties, and the crime of smuggling gradually waned. Today, drugs and illegal immigrants are making it big business again.

The Deviil's Punchbowl is a natural hollow in the hills near Hindhead

Henley-on-Thames OXFORDSHIRE

A genteel poisoning Wealthy widower Francis Blandy was keen to see his daughter, Mary, marry before she got too old. Unfortunately, Mary's choice was to be his downfall. Blandy tried to warn his daughter off Captain Cranston, a Scottish officer, suspecting that the man already had a wife in Scotland. Mary, however, was obsessed with Cranston. Cranston, too, was obsessed – with Mr Blandy's fortune. When the older man threw him out of the house, he promised Mary some special powder to help 'sweeten' her father. It arrived, with the pretence that it was to clean pebbles to make into earrings. Trustingly, she administered it to her father. In great agony Mr Blandy died, and Mary was full of remorse. The case of 1750 drew much attention as Mary was considered too much a gentlewoman to be guilty. She was, however, sentenced to death. Her final request before execution was that she should not be hanged too high, to retain her modesty from the crowds below.

LOCATION: 9 MILES WEST OF MAIDENHEAD ON A4130

Herne Bay KENT

Brides in the bath By the time George Joseph Smith arrived in Herne Bay he had already spent a lifetime of crime ranging from larceny to bigamy, committed under a host of aliases. Bessie Mundy married Smith as 'Henry Williams' in 1910 and the couple moved to the High Street in Herne Bay. Smith took Bessie to the doctor, claiming that she was suffering from fits. On 13 July 1912, Bessie was found dead in the bath, just five days after making out a will in favour of her husband. The police were suspicious of the death, but there was no sign of a struggle, and the doctor diagnosed an epileptic fit, because of her history.

Smith nicknamed the unfortunate Bessie the first of his 'brides in the bath,' and went on to murder two more women in this manner. He was finally rumbled when a victim's father started to piece together newspaper reports and told the police of his suspicions. The case became a major sensation; Smith was hanged at Maidstone in 1915.

LOCATION: 10 MILES NORTH OF CANTERBURY ON A291

Hindhead SURREY

Sailor hacked to death In 1786 an unknown sailor, walking from London to Portsmouth, fell in with three men, one a former shipmate. As they approached the outskirts of Hindhead the men knocked the sailor to the ground and then each cut his throat. First taking their victim's money, they then dumped him in the Devil's Punch Bowl, unaware that they had been observed. The next day they were caught and made to return to the scene of the crime. The locals, pitying the unknown victim, paid for his funeral and erected a headstone in nearby Thursley church. All three murderers were hanged and their bodies suspended in the gibbet on the hill above Hindhead.

Wigwam murder In 1942 two soldiers made the gruesome discovery of a woman's body on Hankley Common at Thursley, near Hindhead. The body was badly decomposed, rats had penetrated her skull and several fingers had been eaten off. It was apparent that the woman had been beaten to death with a blunt instrument and sustained stab wounds of an unusual hooked pattern. Investigations finally led to a half-Canadian, half-Cree Indian soldier who had shared a wigwam on the common with the unfortunate Joan Wolfe. She had been anxious to marry him when she discovered she was pregnant. Not until a knife shaped like a parrot's beak was found in his possession could the police finally charge him with the murder of his lover. August Sangret was found guilty and hanged in April 1943.
LOCATION: 12 MILES SOUTH OF GUILDFORD ON A3

Horsham WEST SUSSEX

Hang Fairs Horsham was the location of the county assizes, and there was once a prison on Gaol Green. Until 1844, gruesome Hang Fairs here attracted huge crowds from all over the county. To encourage maximum attendance, they were always held on Saturdays. As part of the spectacle, the final words and confessions of convicted criminals were taken down (or concocted) by ballad makers and pamphleteers and sold on at considerable profit.
LOCATION: 6 MILES WEST OF CRAWLEY ON A264

Kingley Vale WEST SUSSEX

Viking ghosts The Vikings and the men of Chichester fought it out here in the mid-9th century. You will find a fine grove of dense yew trees, which were said to have been planted to commemorate the battle. The burial mounds (barrows) at the top of the vale known as the King's Graves or the Devil's Humps are reputed to be the graves of the Viking leaders. Legends tell of menacing Viking ghosts seen at this place.
LOCATION: 4 MILES NORTH OF CHICHESTER OFF A286

King's Lynn NORFOLK

Boiled alive The Tuesday Market Place in King's Lynn was a place of punishment over the years. In 1531 Margaret Day was found guilty of poisoning her mistress and family, for which the punishment was the ghastly one of boiling alive. Screaming, Day was suspended over a boiling vat of water and lowered and raised until death occurred. At the moment of death it was said her chest burst open and her heart flew out and hit the wall of a nearby house.

Some 85 years later Mary Smith was accused of witchcraft and sentenced by the Reverend Alexander Roberts to be burned at the stake. As she had prophesised, her heart also flew out of her chest and struck the wall of her accuser's house. Today a diamond-shaped brick with a carved heart can be seen high on a house at the north-east end of the market place.

LOCATION: 27 MILES NORTH-EAST OF THETFORD ON A10

Littleport CAMBRIDGESHIRE

Enclosure Act riots In 1816 the men of Littleport rebelled against the Enclosure Act that was causing starvation and poverty in rural areas. They gathered at the Globe Inn to demand concessions for prices and dole equal to those that had already been granted in Suffolk. Some drifted away from the meeting and ransacked houses. Armed with pitchforks, guns, butchers' cleavers, clubs and iron bars, they broke into the house of magistrate John Vachell. The milita came and read the Riot Act, but fighting broke out nevertheless and shots were fired. The rioters were overpowered and fled, and one was shot through the head as he ran.

Eighty-six rioters were imprisoned in Ely jail, where 23 men and one woman were later convicted for capital offences. In the event all but five received mercy. The unlucky five were put in a cart adorned with black cloth and hanged before a large crowd.

LOCATION: 5 MILES NORTH OF ELY ON A10

Lowestoft SUFFOLK

Lowestoft witch trials Two elderly widows from Lowestoft, Amy Denny and Rose Cullender, were tried and convicted of witchcraft in 1664. Rose was stripped and searched by six women who reportedly found the Devil's Mark from which she was alleged to have suckled demons. Both women were sentenced to be hanged.

LOCATION: 26 MILES SOUTH-EAST OF NORWICH ON A146

Maldon ESSEX

A bloody battle The Battle of Maldon is evocatively recorded in a fragment of a famous poem written in Old English at the end of the 10th century. It tells how the Vikings landed near Maldon in AD 991 and demanded tribute from the rich spoils of the Royal Mint here. The ensuing battle was ferocious, with blood spilled on the stones and running away into the oozing mud of the banks of the River Blackwater.

'The onslaught of battle was terrible, warriors fell on either side, young men laid dead... cruelly cut to pieces.'

LOCATION: 10 MILES EAST OF CHELMSFORD ON A414

Merstham SURREY

Murder in the tunnel In June 1881, the sound of gunshots in the Merstham tunnel alarmed passengers on the London-to-Brighton train. A man in bloodstained clothing was spotted alighting from the train near Brighton. When apprehended, the man, Percy Lefroy, told police that he had been knocked unconscious as the train went into the tunnel and the other people travelling in his compartment had disappeared. Later the body of Isaac Gold, a retired coin dealer, was found near the entrance to the Balcombe tunnel. He had been stabbed and shot. On searching Lefroy, the police found coins in his pocket and he was convicted of the murder. He finally confessed to the killing, shortly before being hanged in Lewes prison.

A second murder In September 1905 the body of a woman, still warm, was discovered about 400 yards (400m) into Merstham tunnel. A silk scarf had been pushed into her mouth, and it appeared that she had been thrown from the train. She was identified as Mary Money by her brother Robert, who had last seen her setting off for Victoria Station but didn't know whom she was meeting. A guard saw a couple arguing on the 9.33pm train out of London, but by Redhill they had left the train.

No one was ever apprehended for the murder, but there is a postscript to this mystery. Seven years later in a house in Eastbourne, Robert Money shot two women and his three children. He then poured petrol on the bodies and set light to them, after which he shot himself. One of the women survived the carnage. It transpired that Money had many aliases and possibly suffered from mental instability. Did he perhaps play a part in his sister's death?

LOCATION: 8 MILES SOUTH OF CROYDON ON A23

Far left: the Tuesday Market Place, King's Lynn

The Rufus Stone marks a historical uncertainty – was this unpopular king murdered?

Micheldever HAMPSHIRE

Martyr of the Swing Riots The Swing Riots were a response to the new agricultural machinery might put many farm labourors out of work. The men rioted to demand food and work, and also destroyed machinery wherever they could. One such labourer was 19-year old Henry Cook of Micheldever, who ended up on the scaffold in 1830 after taking part in a mob protest. Armed with a sledgehammer, he was arrested for the apparently trivial offence of striking the hat brim and coat collar of a landowner. Cook was hanged for assault and intent to murder.

LOCATION: 10 MILES SOUTH OF BASINGSTOKE OFF M3

Minstead HAMPSHIRE

Accident or regicide? William Rufus, the second son of William I, came to the throne in 1087, usurping his brother Robert who was in Normandy at the time. His reign was bloody, with battles against Normandy and Scotland and warlike expeditions into Wales. Monkish chroniclers considered his government arbitrary and ruthless, and his personal conduct outraged many. While out hunting in the New Forest in 1100, the king's huntsman Walter Tyrell shot at a stag. The arrow was deflected and pierced the lungs of William Rufus, and Tyrell fled. Was this accident in fact a murder on the order of his younger brother, who then succeeded him as Henry I? North of Minstead, the Rufus Stone, erected in the 18th century, marks the spot where William fell. Legend has it that, as it was carried back to London, his body left a trail of blood all the way.

LOCATION: 6 MILES WEST OF SOUTHAMPTON OFF A31

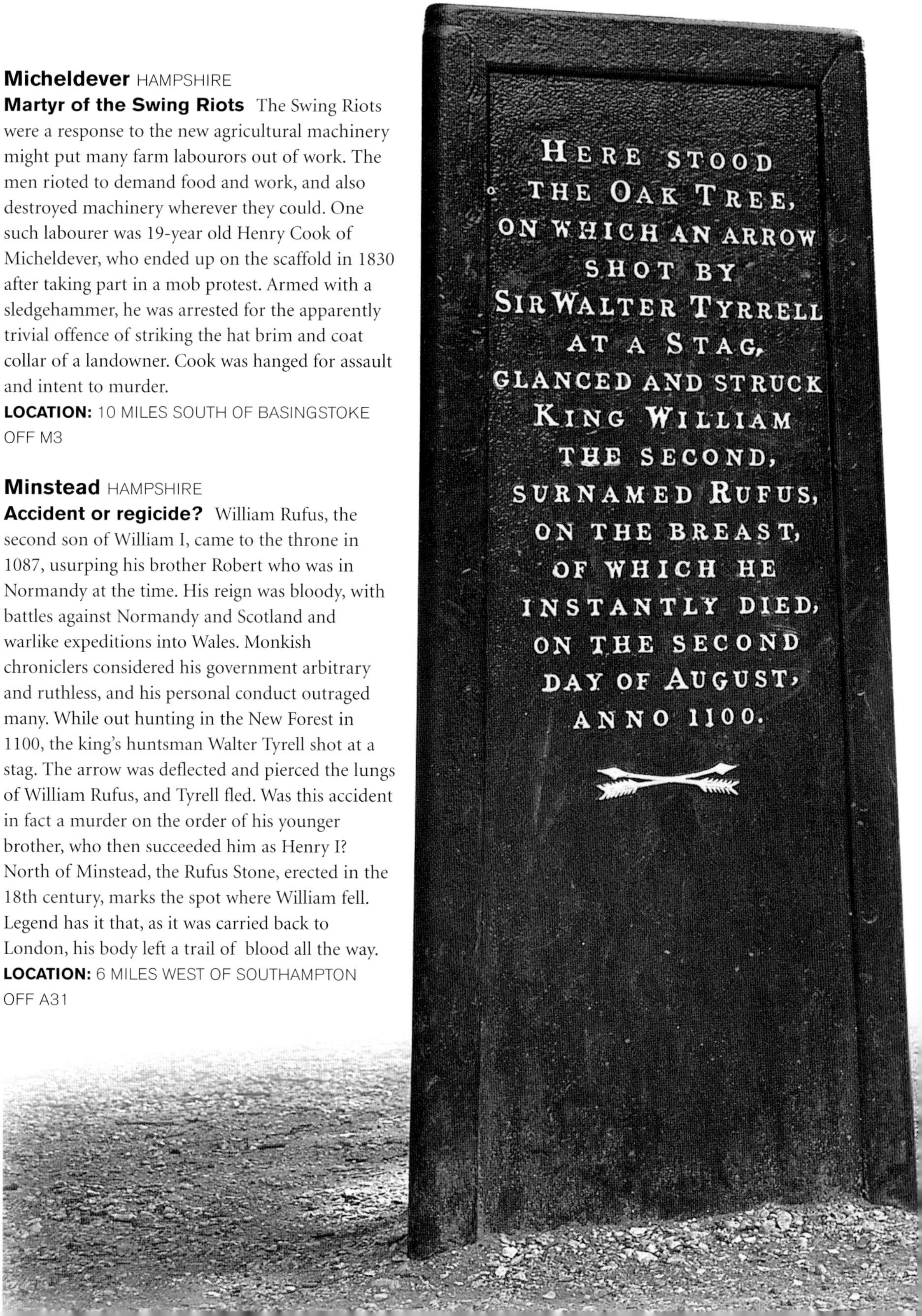

Norwich NORFOLK

Hanging goes wrong Not all hangings go according to plan. One that was bungled took place in Norwich on 16 August 1819. John Pycraft, a small, crippled man, was found guilty of poisoning his infant child and sentenced to hang at Norwich Castle. The hangman made a mistake with the distance of drop needed and Pycraft was left choking helplessly at the end of the rope. Coolly the hangman fixed weights to the man's legs and he finally died an agonising eight minutes later.

A dismembered wife William Sheward confessed to the murder of his wife Martha 18 years after the event when he staggered into a police station in a drunken state.

It had been in the summer of 1851 when Sheward, a tailor by trade, had stabbed his wife to death with a pair of scissors. He dismembered the body and scattered the parts throughout the city of Norwich – a foot here, a bone there, a piece of skin, a portion of thigh. He boiled the head to prevent the smell of putrefaction. He then threw it in bits about the streets. But it wasn't until April 1869 that Sheward was finally hanged. No-one knows why he confessed.

LOCATION: 115 MILES NORTH-EAST OF LONDON ON A11

Oakley BEDFORDSHIRE

Shocking witch hunt Even as late as the 18th century witches, were still being persecuted in England. In Oakley, near Bedford, an elderly woman was pronounced a witch and consented to undergo a 'swimming test' in order to be freed. The theory was that if she floated she was a witch, and if she sank she was innocent. She was tied up in a wet sheet, her thumbs and toes bound together and with a rope around her waist, before being dragged into the River Ouse. Her body floated but her head stayed under the water. The trial was repeated three times with the same result. The cry went up to hang her, but first she was cruelly beaten. A kindly bystander intervened at this point with an alternative trial. He suggested she be weighed against a bible. As it weighed only 12lbs (5.5kg) she outweighed it, was declared innocent, and escaped with her life.

LOCATION: 4 MILES NORTH OF BEDFORD OFF A6

Oxford OXFORDSHIRE

Burning of martyrs In April 1554, the prominent Protestant bishops Latimer, Ridley and Cranmer were condemned as heretics for refusing to convert to Catholicism. As part of their punishment, they were separated from each other, and were deprived of all books and writing materials. Ridley and Latimer were burned together at the stake in October 1554, in the centre of Oxford, where a memorial now marks the spot. The fire burned fiercely around Latimer and soon engulfed him, but on Ridley's side it burned more slowly, causing great agony. Around his neck he carried a bag full of gunpowder, and he forced his head into the flames to ignite this. It exploded and he was finally at peace.

In prison Cranmer recanted and signed a proclamation of Roman Catholic belief. But he soon rejected it and he, too, was burned for his faith. As the flames rose round him, he thrust his right hand into the flames, declaring that as it had signed the recantation, it should burn first.

Courtroom cursed Rowland Jenks was examined by the Queen's Council on suspicion of heresy and committed for trial at Oxford in July 1577. The trial lasted two days and Jenks was sentenced to have his ears cut off. As he left he cursed the court, and soon after a terrible smell arose from the building, choking the occupants. Most of the magistrates on the bench and all the jury died. A pestilence raged across the city and surrounding villages and some 510 people died. The plague went as fast as it had come, giving rise to the legend of the Black Assize. It was almost certainly jail fever; Jenks walked free and lived to be an old man.

Oxford (CONT)

Back from the dead Brought to trial for smothering her illegitimate child, Anne Greene was found guilty and hanged in Castle Yard in Oxford in 1649. Her body was taken down and, as was usual, kicked and stamped upon to check she was dead. She was taken to the Anatomy School for dissection. However, as he raised his scapel Dr Petty felt the body to be unusually warm. He set about reviving her, and astonishingly, in a few days she recovered. When questioned she remembered nothing of the ordeal. Anne got her reprieve, married, had a family and lived into old age. Dr Petty's reputation was assured.

LOCATION: 56 MILES NORTH-WEST OF LONDON ON A40

Padworth BERKSHIRE

Hanged in chains For murdering old William Billimore on Padworth Common in 1787, two young men were doomed to the gibbet. Abraham Tull, 19, and William Hawkings, 17, beat the old man to death for money to spend at Reading fair. They were caught a few days later in Maidenhead, trying to sell their victim's watch. A gibbet was erected near the scene of the crime; the boys were hanged,and their bodies clapped in chains and left to rot. A crowd of 10,000 people attended at the spot still known as Gibbet Piece.

LOCATION: 5 MILES SOUTH-WEST OF READING OFF A4

Peasenhall SUFFOLK

Murder of Rose Harsent This mystery of 1902 has never been solved. Rose Harsent's father went to visit his daughter who was in service in Providence House in Peasenhall. There he made the ghastly discovery of his daughter's body, with a livid gash across her throat and a stab wound to the chest. There was a smell of charred flesh, and her nightdress had been singed. The most likely culprit for the murder was William Gardiner, with whom Rose had a relationship, but despite two trials, the juries could not deliver a verdict. Rose had received a letter telling her to put a light in the window to indicate an assignation could take place. Who wrote the note and who did the murder was never discovered.

LOCATION: 25 MILES NORTH OF IPSWICH ON A1120

Penn BUCKINGHAMSHIRE

Wartime child killer The bodies of eight-year-old Doreen Hearne and six-year-old Kathleen Trendle were found in Rough Wood, near Penn, on 22 November 1941, after the children had been missing for three days. The post mortem revealed that the girls had been partially strangled and then stabbed in the neck. The crime shocked the neighbourhood. Tyre marks of a lorry were found close to the bodies, together with a patch of oil, a khaki handkerchief with the laundry mark 'RA 1019', a hair ribbon, sock and gas mask container. A boy, age 12, had seen the girls talking to the driver of an army truck and gave the police a good description. It was traced to the 86th Field Regiment, Royal Artillery at Yoxford in Suffolk, and to 26-year-old Harold Hill as the murderer. Hill pleaded insanity, but was executed at Oxford.

LOCATION: 2 MILES EAST OF HIGH WYCOMBE ON B474

Pevensey EAST SUSSEX

Murder at the Mint The Old Mint House stands in Pevensey High Street, and is haunted by the ghost of a young woman. In 1586 it was rented by a successful London merchant, Thomas Dight, to house his young mistress, Eleanor Fitzjohn.

Far left: The peaceful High Street of Pevensey today

Left: A sensational contemporary account of the Red Barn Murder

With Dight often absent, Eleanor turned her affections to a handsome young fisherman. Returning early one day Dight discovered the pair in bed together and flew into a jealous rage. He cut out the girl's tongue and bound her, forcing her to watch him hang her lover in chains from the ceiling. Dight then lit a fire under him, and she was forced to watch him die from the effects of heat and smoke. Eleanor was left tied up in an upstairs room where she died of starvation. Dight confessed to these awful deeds on his deathbed.
LOCATION: 4 MILES EAST OF EASTBOURNE ON A27

Polstead SUFFOLK

The Red Barn Murder This is one of the most famous murders in English history, partly because of the sensational publicity it attracted, and partly because it became the subject of a thrilling melodrama. In 1827 William Corder seduced Maria Marten and she disappeared. Corder claimed he knew nothing of her whereabouts and then disappeared to London. Maria's mother had vivid dreams that her daughter was buried in a red barn. So convincing were the dreams that her husband went to the place she believed Maria to be and began to dig. Maria's body was discovered, and Corder was tracked down to London, where he was arrested, tried and hanged for the murder. In a further gruesome twist, Corder's skin was carefully preserved by the attending doctor, so that it could be used to bind the trial documents. Corder's scalp is on display in Moyses Hall in Bury St Edmunds. The red barn was later destroyed by fire, although the site is marked.
LOCATION: 12 MILES NORTH OF COLCHESTER OFF A12

Quidenham NORFOLK

Death of Queen Boudicca The famous warrior queen supposedly met her end at Quidenham in Norfolk, where a mound is the alleged burial place. Finally defeated after terrible battles in AD 60–61, she had burned and pillaged her way through a swathe of Roman occupied lands from London to East Anglia. Brutal and savage throughout the conflict, her Celtic warriors beheaded their captives and offered these trophies to the goddess of victory.

The Romans, with their superior weapons, finally overcame Boudicca's army and defeat was imminent. To avoid capture, Boudicca fled northwards to Norfolk, and it is said she and her two daughters ended their lives by taking poison.

LOCATION: 11 MILES NORTH-EAST OF THETFORD OFF A11

Rayleigh ESSEX

The bath chair bombing Archibald Brown was seriously injured in a motor cycle accident when he was 24 and become very bitter and cruel as a result. For 23 years he ruled his wife and son with a rod of iron.

On the afternoon of 24 July 1943, residents of London Road heard a loud explosion but thought nothing of it as they were used to the sound of war bombing. What had exploded was Archibald's invalid chair, leaving a devastating tangle of metal and human remains in the road. His left leg was 15ft (5m) up a tree and his right 48ft (15m) away in a front garden.

Archibald's son Eric was on leave and had placed a mine taken from his barracks below the seat of the chair. Eric suffered from severe mood swings, and believed the only way his mother could lead a normal life was to release his father from his sufferings. Diagnosed as schizophrenic, Eric spent 32 years in prison.

LOCATION: 6 MILES EAST OF SOUTHEND ON A127

WARRIOR QUEEN OF THE CELTS

Boudicca, often known by her Latin name of Boadicea, lived in the first century AD and was wife of Prasutagus, the King of the Iceni, a tribe inhabiting an area now known as Norfolk and Suffolk. The Iceni were tolerated by the Romans, for Prasutagus had made a pragmatic pact to submit to Roman rule in return for his tribe being allowed to continue with their own customs.

On the death of Prasutagus in AD 60, Boudicca declared herself queen. However, the Roman governor, Suetonius, wished to make the Iceni a subject population. He seized Boudicca, had her flogged and forced her to witness the rape of her two daughters by Roman soldiers.

The Iceni regarded Boudicca as their natural leader; the role of women in the ruling class was equal to that of men, and women held high positions and even owned land. While Suetonius was involved in quashing a rebellion in the north-east the proud queen plannned her revenge. The chronicles of two Roman writers, Tacitus and Dio Cassius, written some years after the events and with a Roman bias, give lurid accounts of the brutality and savagery of the Iceni rebellion led by Boudicca. She was described as huge of frame and with a harsh voice. She had a great mass of long red hair, and apparently struck fear and awe in everyone who saw her. She and her daughters rode in a chariot at the head of her people; legend has it that she fixed knives to her chariot wheels to slash opponents trying to reach her.

With the support of the neighbouring tribe, the Trinovantes, she left a trail of destruction as her army burned and pillaged Roman lands from Colchester to London and St Albans. Backed by an army of 100,000 men she laid waste to the cities. Her army was awesome with their tattoos and painted faces. As they went into battle they screamed, blew trumpets and terrified the Romans. They gloried in the piles of dead bodies and held great banquets and sacrifices all in the name of victory. Some 70,000 died in the battles, and disease and famine affected both sides. Boudicca, however, found it difficult to maintain order among the Celts; they looted and burned with a manic frenzy. Roman women who were captured were particularly cruelly tortured and murdered. Their breasts were cut off and stuffed into their mouths, and their bodies skewered on large stakes.

The Romans' fighting superiority finally won the day. Few escaped, but Boudicca and her daughters fled and committed suicide. This 'honourable' death was recognised by the Romans, who declared her the first British heroine.

A statue of Boudicca stands beside the Thames in London

Reading BERKSHIRE

Baby farm murder In the 1890s Amelia Dyer ran a 'baby farm', where servant girls could leave their illegitimate babies while they were at work. The hideous murders were discovered in London, when the bodies of over 40 babies were retrieved from the River Thames. All had been strangled. Shortly afterwards, six more bodies were found in the river at Caversham, near Reading, all with red tape around their necks. One parcel containing a body had the address of a woman in Reading –

The hideous murders were discovered in London, when the bodies of over 40 babies were retrieved from the River Thames. All had been strangled.

Amelia Dyer. On searching her house the police found letters from mothers and a quantity of baby clothing. Arrested, Dyer tried twice to kill herself – once with scissors and once with a boot lace. Despite claiming insanity, this most hated of women was hanged in 1896.

LOCATION: 40 MILES WEST OF LONDON ON M4

Richmond SURREY

Boiling up a body Kate Webster stole money in her early teens to sail to Liverpool from her native Ireland. Moving to London, she continued her life of crime. In 1879 she took a job in Richmond as a maid to the wealthy Julia Thomas, but after only a month she was sacked. In revenge, Kate struck her employer with an axe and pushed her down the stairs. She then dismembered the body, hacking it to pieces and boiling parts in a pot. Kate then put the reduced body fat into jars and sold it as dripping; the bones she burned on the fire. Putting the remaining body parts in a bag and a box, she threw them into the river. Calling herself Mrs Thomas, she sold as many of the lady's belongings as possible but this finally raised suspicions and she was arrested and subsequently hanged.

LOCATION: 9 MILES SOUTH-WEST OF LONDON ON A316

Far right: Contemporary records of the unusual 'burial' of Henry Trigg

Rye EAST SUSSEX

Butchers and lambs Butcher John Breeds had a grievance against the Mayor of Rye, James Lamb, and in March 1742 he set about killing him. By mistake he stabbed Lamb's brother-in-law, Alan Grebell, who had borrowed the mayor's cloak to wear to a party. Breeds had boasted in the pub that 'butchers should kill lambs,' and with his name stamped on the knife that was the murder weapon, it was an open and shut case. He was hanged on the marshes, and put in a iron gibbet which remained there for many years. Part of the skull survived and can still be seen in an upstairs room of Rye Town Hall.

LOCATION: 12 MILES NORTH-WEST OF HASTINGS ON A259

St Albans HERTFORDSHIRE

First English martyr The first recorded English martyr, Alban, was a 3rd-century soldier living in Verulamium (now St Albans), who worshipped Roman gods. One day he gave shelter to a Christian priest, who greatly impressed him. When orders came for the priest to be arrested, Alban donned the priest's clothes and was taken prisoner himself while the real priest made his escape. The Roman governor demanded that Alban should make a sacrifice to the gods. When he refused and told them he was a Christian, he was whipped, taken to a hill above the town and beheaded.

LOCATION: 20 MILES NORTH-WEST OF LONDON OFF M10

Staplehurst KENT

Charles Dickens in train crash On 9 June 1865, just outside Staplehurst, the Folkestone-to-London express train, travelling at 50 mph, was derailed on a viaduct where maintenance work was being undertaken. Much of the train tumbled off the bridge, and many passengers were killed or badly injured. Charles Dickens, the famous writer, was travelling in the first of the derailed coaches, returning from a holiday in Paris with his young mistress, Ellen Ternan, and her mother. Their coach was left hanging on part of the broken bridge. Dickens was able to climb out of the window and rescue the two women before he returned to help the dying and the wounded. Later, he suffered severe shock, and never quite recovered from the trauma. When he died five years later it was on the anniversary of the date of the crash.

LOCATION: 8 MILES SOUTH OF MAIDSTONE ON A229

Stevenage HERTFORDSHIRE

Avoiding the body-snatchers Henry Trigg was a successful grocer who died in 1724. Before his death he had insisted that he should not be buried in the churchyard as he feared the body-snatchers would take him. Body-snatching from graves was prevalent at that time, with the corpses being sold for dissection by medical students. Trigg requested that his coffin be placed in the rafters of a barn on his premises, and this was duly done. His niece Ann left forty shillings in her will of 1769 to have Henry's bones laid to rest in the churchyard and no one is sure if this happened. It is said that soldiers during World War I stole the bones to sell as souvenirs. The coffin is still kept in the premises, now owned by the National Westminster Bank.

LOCATION: 7 MILES NORTH OF WELWYN GARDEN CITY ON A1

THE

ECCENTRIC W

OF THE LATE

HENRY TRIG

OF STEVENAGE.

To be had at the OLD CASTLE, STEVENAGE, where the remains of Henry Trigg are s the West End of the Hovel, and may be viewed by any Traveller who may think it w

The same is recorded in History and may be depended

IN THE NAME OF GOD, AMEN.

I, HENRY TRIGG, of STEVENAGE, in the County of Hertford, Grocer, being very infirm and weak in body, but of perfect sound mind and memory, praised be God for it, calling into mind the mortality of my body, do now make and ordain this my last WILL and TESTAMENT, in writing, hereafter following: that is to say:—Principally I recommend my soul into the merciful hands of Almighty God that first gave me it, assuredly believing and only expecting free pardon and forgiveness of all my sins, and eternal life in and through the only merits, death, and passion of Jesus Christ my Saviour; and as to my body I commit it to the West end of my Hovel, to be decently laid there upon a floor erected by my Executor, upon the purlin, for the same purpose: nothing doubting but at the general Resurrection I shall receive the same again by the mighty power of God; and as for and concerning such worldly substance as it hath pleased God to bless me with in this world, I do devise and dispose of the same in manner and form here following.

Imprimis. I give and devise unto my loving brother Thomas Trigg, of Letchworth, in the County of Hertford, Clerk, and to his Heirs and Assigns for ever, all those my Freehold Lands, lying dispersedly in the several common fields

I have already bequeathed
Trigg, unto my brother Ge
heirs for ever; and if my
should refuse to lay my b
then what I have bequeat
my Lands and Tenements,
unto my nephew William
for ever, upon his seei
decently laid up there as a

Item. I give and beque
William Trigg, the sum o
age of Thirty Years; to hi
of *Twenty Pounds;* to his
of *Twenty Pounds;* and la
the sum of *Twenty Poun*
Thirty Years: to John
Butcher, the sum of *O*
Solomon Spencer, of Stev
Guinea, Three Years next
my cousin Henry Kimpt
Year next after my deceas
Two Years after my decea
Five Shillings; and to Jos
ings and Sixpence, Two Ye
to my tenant Robert Wr
Shillings, Two Years next
to Ralph Lowd and John
each, Two Years next afte

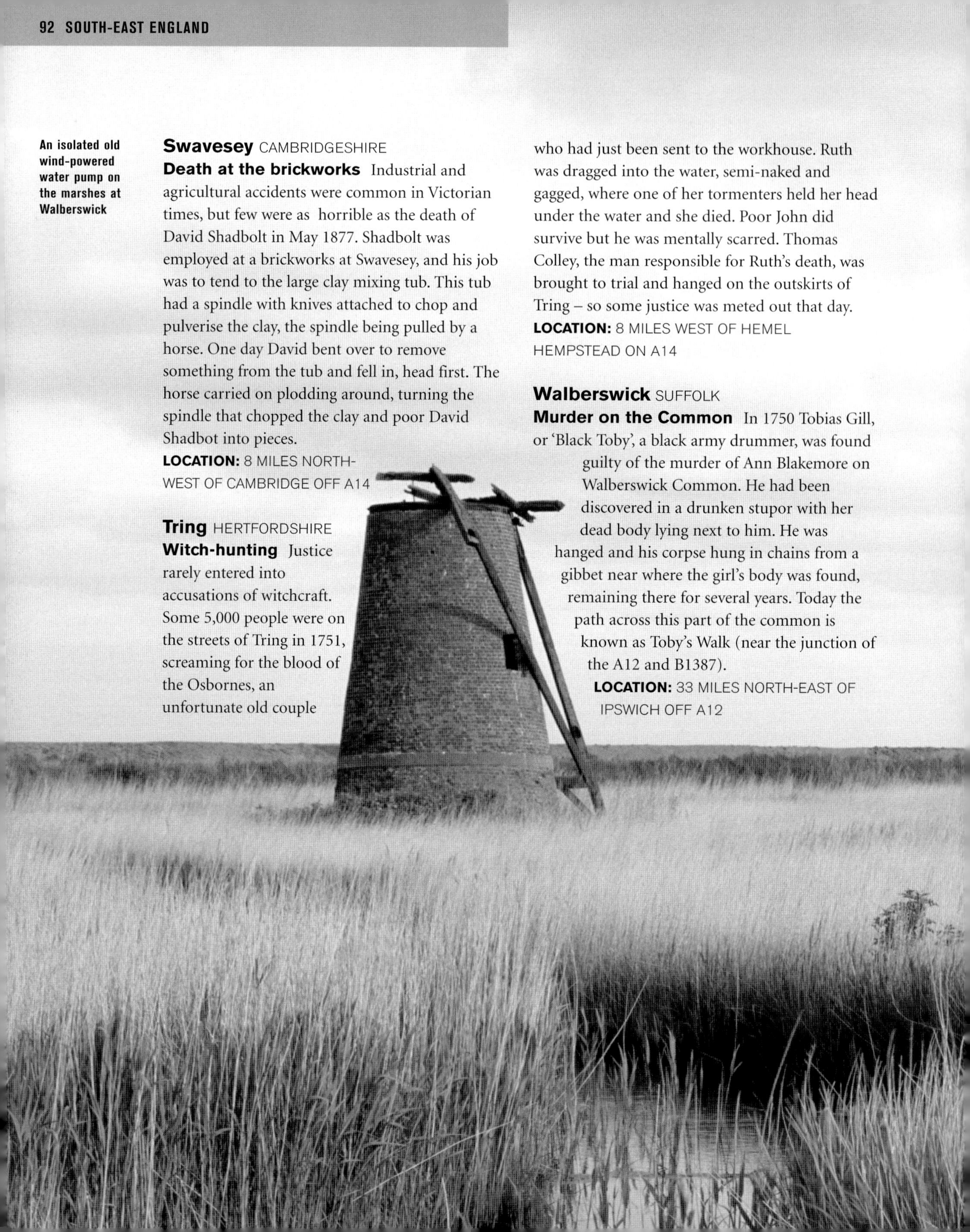

An isolated old wind-powered water pump on the marshes at Walberswick

Swavesey CAMBRIDGESHIRE

Death at the brickworks Industrial and agricultural accidents were common in Victorian times, but few were as horrible as the death of David Shadbolt in May 1877. Shadbolt was employed at a brickworks at Swavesey, and his job was to tend to the large clay mixing tub. This tub had a spindle with knives attached to chop and pulverise the clay, the spindle being pulled by a horse. One day David bent over to remove something from the tub and fell in, head first. The horse carried on plodding around, turning the spindle that chopped the clay and poor David Shadbot into pieces.

LOCATION: 8 MILES NORTH-WEST OF CAMBRIDGE OFF A14

Tring HERTFORDSHIRE

Witch-hunting Justice rarely entered into accusations of witchcraft. Some 5,000 people were on the streets of Tring in 1751, screaming for the blood of the Osbornes, an unfortunate old couple who had just been sent to the workhouse. Ruth was dragged into the water, semi-naked and gagged, where one of her tormenters held her head under the water and she died. Poor John did survive but he was mentally scarred. Thomas Colley, the man responsible for Ruth's death, was brought to trial and hanged on the outskirts of Tring – so some justice was meted out that day.

LOCATION: 8 MILES WEST OF HEMEL HEMPSTEAD ON A14

Walberswick SUFFOLK

Murder on the Common In 1750 Tobias Gill, or 'Black Toby', a black army drummer, was found guilty of the murder of Ann Blakemore on Walberswick Common. He had been discovered in a drunken stupor with her dead body lying next to him. He was hanged and his corpse hung in chains from a gibbet near where the girl's body was found, remaining there for several years. Today the path across this part of the common is known as Toby's Walk (near the junction of the A12 and B1387).

LOCATION: 33 MILES NORTH-EAST OF IPSWICH OFF A12

Wannock EAST SUSSEX

Airship disaster There was an airship base on the hill above Wannock during World War I, and the iron moorings set in concrete still survive. Tragedy struck one foggy night in December 1917, when one airship landed on the Aldis lamp of another and exploded, killing the pilot and badly burning two crew members. The moored airship caught fire and its bombs exploded, severing the arm of Lieutenant Victor Watson, who was trying rescue the crew.

LOCATION: 2 MILES NORTH-WEST OF EASTBOURNE ON A22

Winchester HAMPSHIRE

Civil War ghost Dame Alice Lisle, owner of Moyles Court in Ellingham, had been a staunch supporter of the Parliamentarian cause. In 1685 she hid two of the rebel Duke of Monmouth's soldiers at her house. Betrayed, arrested and tried for high treason, she was sent before Judge Jeffreys at the Bloody Assizes in Winchester and sentenced to be burned alive. The clergy appealed that she was an elderly, deaf woman and the sentence was reduced to beheading. She spent her last night in the Eclipse Inn in Winchester, and could see the scaffold from her bedroom window. The ghost of a tall, motionless figure now haunts the pub.

LOCATION: 20 MILES SOUTH OF BASINGSTOKE OFF M3

Wokingham BERKSHIRE

Bull baiting One of the most popular sports in the 18th and 19th centuries was bull baiting, and Wokingham was a major venue for this bloodthirsty sport. The annual meeting on 21 December was particularly popular. The bull was brought into the arena tethered on a 15ft (5m) chain and the first dog was let loose. The dog had to attempt to 'pin' the bull by the nose (the bull's only vulnerable point) and if the dog failed it would be gored. Dogs would be released until one managed to set its teeth into the bull's nose. Then a dozen men would separate bull and dog and the bull was killed. The sport began to be seen as barbaric, and bull baiting shows often led to brawls and drunkenness. In 1835 it became illegal.

LOCATION: 10 MILES SOUTH OF MAIDENHEAD OFF M4

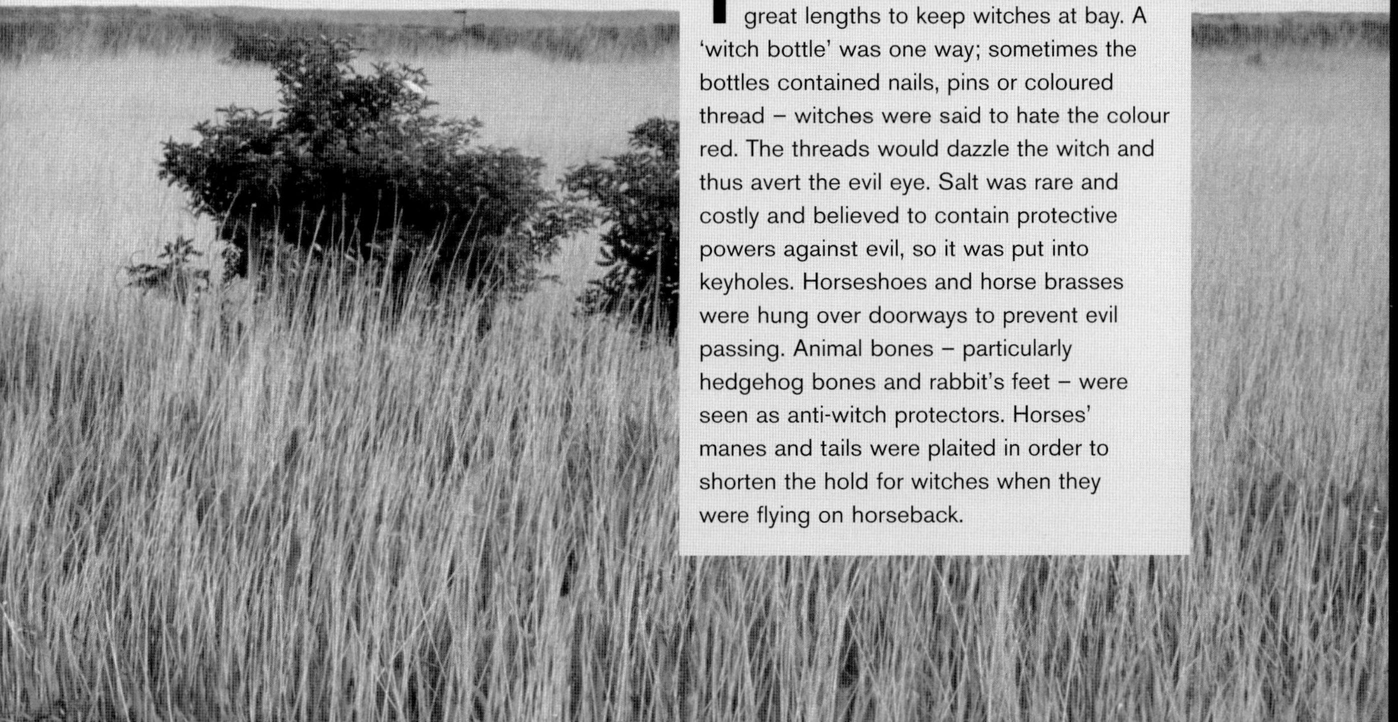

TO WARD OFF WITCHES

Throughout history, people have gone to great lengths to keep witches at bay. A 'witch bottle' was one way; sometimes the bottles contained nails, pins or coloured thread – witches were said to hate the colour red. The threads would dazzle the witch and thus avert the evil eye. Salt was rare and costly and believed to contain protective powers against evil, so it was put into keyholes. Horseshoes and horse brasses were hung over doorways to prevent evil passing. Animal bones – particularly hedgehog bones and rabbit's feet – were seen as anti-witch protectors. Horses' manes and tails were plaited in order to shorten the hold for witches when they were flying on horseback.

CENTRAL ENGLAND

The counties at the heart of England have played a central part in the nation's history over the course of two millennia. Medieval power struggles took place on and around their fields and mighty castles. In the 18th century a wealth of mineral deposits and the region's wide rivers, offering abundant water power, made it the natural birthplace of the Industrial Revolution. As a result, parts of the Midlands were swallowed up in urban sprawl and choked by the smoke of factories and furnaces. At the same time, wide expanses of the region remained wild and rural, from the rolling Cotswold hills to the peaks of Derbyshire, and from the woods of Nottinghamshire to the Lincolnshire coast. The variety of murder and mayhem in its past is as wide as the variety of landscape: dark deeds in the forest; the clash of steel on the battlefield; the poverty, disease and desperation of city slums – Central England has witnessed every twist and footnote of human history.

The Romans established themselves in force in the English heartlands, driving out or relocating local tribes and building cities such as Chester, Worcester and Lincoln as centres of administration. After the Romans' departure the country was left to the machinations of competing kingdoms, one of which, Mercia, dominated the scene in the 7th and 8th centuries. Set between the east coast Anglo-Saxons and the Britons of the west, Mercia took in present-day Staffordshire, Leicestershire, Nottinghamshire and parts of Derbyshire and Warwickshire. Its mighty king, Offa, was responsible for erecting the 167-mile-long dyke which still more or less follows the English/Welsh border. The country around this area, the Marches (borderlands), became a lawless and troubled territory, where bandits and outlaws lurked and hardly a week went by without a bloody spat between Welsh and English.

The magnificent battlements of Warwick Castle

The cockpit of England

After the Norman invasion, the barons who ruled the Marches became formidable political heavyweights, who could make or break a monarch depending on their allegiances. This was the beginning of the Midlands' role as 'cockpit of England', a time when armies fought and dynasties were created and dashed on its fields. King John had to contend not just with the loss of his crown jewels in the Wash and the defiance of outlaws such as Robin Hood, but also with rebellions that posed a serious challenge to the Crown and which were met with the harshest reprisals.

In the 1260s another power struggle took place between the forces of Henry III and the barons' champion, Simon de Montfort, at Evesham. During the Wars of the Roses, Lancastrians and Yorkists conducted their vicious tug-of-war over the crown in Northamptonshire, Warwickshire, Shropshire and Herefordshire. It was a skirmish near Worcester that started the Civil War of the 17th century, and a savage battle at Naseby that decided its outcome.

Back to business

After the bloodshed came a new struggle: the struggle to produce goods and make profits. The Darby family set up their pioneering ironworks in a wooded gorge in the Severn Valley between Coalbrookdale and Coalport, and made it a centre of industrial production. Canals and railways were soon snaking their way across the region, carrying raw goods and finished products to factory and market.

By the 19th century new forms of manufacturing, transport and communications had changed society beyond recognition, and poor people left the countryside to find work in the rapidly developing towns and cities. Birmingham, 'city of a hundred trades', grew to be the nation's largest urban centre outside London, and areas such as the Black Country, the Potteries and the coalfields of Nottinghamshire were notorious for their inhumane conditions and polluted air.

The modern age

Modern war has left its mark on the Midlands – most notably in Coventry, whose medieval core was wiped out during World War II, and whose modern cathedral stands next to the poignant remains of its predecessor. In recent years, though, the region's urban centres have found new life; the reputation earned during the height of industrial activity has been overtaken by a new appreciation of the area's rich heritage, factories and workshops included, and its cultural life.

Beyond the towns and cities, Central England is still a place of staggering variety and beauty, attracting tourists in their thousands to the picture-pretty Cotswold villages, to fortresses and manor houses and, of course, to Stratford-upon-Avon and 'Shakespeare country'. But the real vibrancy of the central counties comes from their part as a backdrop to the most dramatic, and frequently most bloody chapters of British history.

Ashby-de-la-Zouch

LEICESTERSHIRE

Lost his head The late 15th century was a dangerous time to be a high-flyer, as the proud owner of Ashby-de-la-Zouch castle found out to his cost. William, Lord Hastings seemed unstoppable during Edward IV's reign, and in 1474 he could afford to flash his money around, building the huge castle and its magnificent 80ft (24m) Hastings Tower.

After the King's death he supported the young heir, Edward V, who was, unfortunately, spirited away with his brother to the Tower of London to be killed (see page 57), probably on the orders of Richard of Gloucester, their 'Protector'. Hastings clung on to power, switching loyalties to the new king, Richard III, but the good times couldn't last. On 13 June he was summoned to a Privy Council meeting, and before he could say 'any other business' was seized by the guards, dragged outside and had his head hacked off on a block of wood.

Clamped by the fin
interrupting the flo
could be hauled ou
taken to the finge
like a crocodile's j
to clamp over the f
culprit was ready t

Clamped by the finger Centuries later, there were still harsh penalties for anyone suspected of defying authority, whether it be King or Church. In St Helen's Church there's evidence of the grim punishment meted out just for the odd idle comment during the vicar's sermon. Even as late as the 19th century, anyone interrupting the flow could be hauled out of the pew and taken to the finger pillory, designed like a crocodile's jaw with ridges to clamp over the finger until the culprit was ready to hear the Word.

LOCATION: 16 MILES NORTH-WEST OF LEICESTER ON A50

Barton-upon-Humber LINCOLNSHIRE

Poor Grace Poor Grace Tripp, born in Barton in 1691, lived a short and dismal life. Having made it into the service of a Lord Torrington, she made the mistake of befriending a bad lot called Peters, who promised to marry her as long as she helped him rob her master's house first.

Swept along with the romance of it all, Grace let Peters into the house one night when nobody was at home except the housekeeper. All went smoothly at first, as Grace and her lover packed up boxes of silver, but before they could slip away the housekeeper arrived to investigate the noise. As she entered the darkened room she was suddenly grabbed from behind; while Grace held up a candle to light the scene, Peters produced a knife and sliced through the housekeeper's throat. As the woman lay bleeding, he coolly searched her pockets and took 30 guineas. Peters and Grace

r – Anyone
of the sermon
of the pew and
illory, designed
with ridges
ger until the
ear the Word.

THE PERILS OF PREGNANCY

Pregnancy and childbirth could be a risky business before the development of modern medicine. Infant mortality was shockingly high, and mothers who survived the process of giving birth were often killed by later infections. Obstructed labour caused excruciating pain and often death; one solution in the 18th century was to sacrifice the baby by crushing its skull and delivering the rest piecemeal. Ectopic pregnancies, where the egg lodges in the Fallopian tube first blocking then rupturing the tube as it develops, so causing a haemorrhage, was almost always fatal. Some of the treatments used included electric shocks, injecting narcotics into the embryo, and much deliberate bleeding. In 1883 Robert Lawson Tait successfully opened a patient's abdomen and removed the Fallopian tube, saving her life and confirming his title 'father of modern abdominal surgery'.

fled with their booty, leaving the street door open, but were soon picked up, and for her part in the crime Grace was hanged by the neck on 27 March 1710. She was just 19 years old.

LOCATION: 8 MILES NORTH-EAST OF SCUNTHORPE ON B1218

Birmingham WEST MIDLANDS

City of a thousand trades Long before it flourished as the industrial 'city of a thousand trades', Birmingham was a town full of smithies, which were kept busy during the Civil War producing over 15,000 swords for use on the killing fields. Markets were conducted on the Bull Ring, where butchers tethered their bulls and baited them with vicious dogs, in the belief that an angry bull produced tastier meat.

But it was during the Industrial Revolution that Birmingham saw its greatest boom, and by the 1860s the poorest workers were living in crowded and disgusting conditions. Politician Joseph Chamberlain complained that they had to rely on contaminated wells, and were, as he put it, 'compelled to drink water which is as bad as sewage before clarification'. Over 14,000 dungpits lay open to the air, and intestinal disease spread unchecked. Living packed into hovels, the badly nourished people succumbed easily to waves of smallpox, a highly contagious disease causing high fever and a foul rash of pustules.

Birmingham's sorry state made it a target for reformers and a centre of medical research and practice. In 1879 pioneering surgeon Robert Lawson Tait, who worked in the city, carried out Europe's first successful removal of a diseased gall bladder; he also managed to remove a gangrenous appendix lying in an abscess cavity, the first success of its kind, and revolutionised the treatment of women with ectopic pregnancies (see above).

LOCATION: OFF M5/M6/M42

Black Country STAFFORDSHIRE

Hooked In 1843 a visitor to the Black Country, the south Staffordshire coalfield, described an infernal scene of close packed two-storey houses surrounded by blazing furnaces and burning coal-heaps, rubbish and slag, forges and chimneys spewing filth. The land around Wolverhampton, Willenhall and Bilston was gouged by mines; engine houses leaned and cracked, and whole rows of houses occasionally disappeared into the earth as old mining tunnels collapsed beneath them. No wonder that the area was a hot-spot for riots and strikes. In 1842 detachments of troops were sent in to bludgeon Chartist demonstrators calling for political reforms.

Disease and violent crime were rife in these miserable circumstances: crimes such as the murder of Reuben Curtis, found early one Sunday in the mid-19th century, suspended upside-down from a hook over a narrow engine pit full of hot water. Curtis had been beaten up by his estranged wife's lover, one George Clarke. He was still alive when rescued, but only just, and after a few gasps died, apparently from the effects of the hot water's vapours.

'Cutting and wounding' Alcohol was, then as now, often a cause of conflict. Benjamin Hayes turned up one night in the 1840s at Samuel Jukes the beer-seller's house, in search of a pint. Jukes had shut up shop and locked him out. Undeterred, Hayes found his way into the kitchen and with a trowel, the tool of his trade, stabbed his host in the face four times before running off. Remarkably, despite his injuries Jukes managed to chase and catch his attacker, who was sent to jail for 'cutting and wounding'.

LOCATION: REGION NORTH-WEST OF BIRMINGHAM OFF M5/M6

Blore Heath SHROPSHIRE

Lancastrian defeat In 1459 Henry VI's realm was on the point of collapse, with no law courts sitting, no parliament summoned, and a king who was powerless and bankrupt. The country was ripe for war, and the powerful Yorkist faction duly went head-to-head with the royal Lancastrian house.

On 23 September the King's man, Lord Audley, was sent to intercept an army of 3,000 led by Lord Salisbury at Blore Heath, near Market Drayton. Salisbury was heavily outnumbered but played a canny game, pretending to retreat and drawing on a charge by Audley's cavalry, which was promptly cut to pieces. Without the cavalry to help them, Audley's infantry were exposed and vulnerable. Seeing the enemies' arrows, pikes and swords making mincemeat of their colleagues, 500 Lancastrians defected to the other side. Salisbury's men showed no mercy, even when the Lancastrians turned tail and fled. They chased them for 2 miles,

They chased them for 2 miles, slashing and slaughtering as they went, until around 2,000 mutilated Lancastrian corpses littered the Shropshire fields.

slashing and slaughtering as they went, until around 2,000 mutilated Lancastrian corpses littered the Shropshire fields. Fewer than 200 Yorkist lives had been lost.

LOCATION: 2½ MILES EAST OF MARKET DRAYTON OFF A53

Bulwick NORTHAMPTONSHIRE

Becket's murderer This stone village was the home of Fitzurse, knight of the realm, who earned notoriety as one of the four knights who took Henry II at his word when he demanded to be rid of the 'turbulent priest,' Thomas à Becket, Archbishop of Canterbury, and sliced Becket's skull in two even as he claimed sanctuary in the cathedral's transept (see page 70).

LOCATION: 6 MILES NORTH-WEST OF OUNDLE ON A43

Bunbury CHESHIRE

Revenge set in stone The Image House in Bunbury, adorned with stone heads covering the outer walls, was built with more than decoration in mind. Each head represented one of the figures of authority – the sheriff, his officers, the judge and so on – who were involved in the apprehension and sentencing of a poacher during the 18th century. This wasn't simply an insult: this was revenge. The cottage was designed along the principles of witchcraft, which made gruesome use of representation. Just as witches claimed to cause illness by sticking pins into clay or wax images, and long, lingering death by leaving them to decay underground or melt, so the builders of the Image House were claiming power over the fate of all those portrayed on the walls. Its actual effects are unknown, but to the victims, the sight of their stone 'heads' must have been chilling.

LOCATION: 3 MILES SOUTH OF TARPORLEY OFF A49

Burton Lazars LEICESTERSHIRE

Leper hospital The 13th-century leper hospital that once stood here was one of many houses of refuge for the victims of this terrible, disfiguring, infectious disease. Now known as Hansen's Disease, the condition was for centuries confused with a term used in the Bible for spiritual uncleanliness. So as well as suffering inflamed nodules under the skin and the deformity and loss of parts of their bodies, the wretched lepers were shunned as unholy, and unworthy of life. In order not to contaminate others physically or spiritually, many were forcibly removed from their families and sent to colonies, or 'living tombs'. At least in the medieval hospitals such as that at Burton Lazars they could be sure of care and shelter.

LOCATION: 1 MILE SOUTH-EAST OF MELTON MOWBRAY ON A606

To warn people of their approach, lepers were made to ring a bell or carry a wooden rattle and call out 'Unclean!, unclean!'

Burton upon Trent STAFFORDSHIRE

The Boy of Burton Accusations of witchcraft were flung around with abandon during the 16th century. One famous case, exposed even at the time as a pack of lies, involved the 'Boy of Burton', Thomas Darling. On 27 February 1596, the teenager was wandering through Winsell Woods when he came across Alice Gooderidge, a 60-year-old local woman. As he passed, Thomas broke wind, and Alice responded with a neat rhyming couplet:

> *'Gyp with mischief and fart with a bell;*
> *I will go to heaven and thou shalt go to hell!'*

'Gyp with mischief an
I will go to heaven an

Returning home, the humiliated boy fell into fits and claimed to be hallucinating, seeing, among other wonders, a man emerging from a chamber pot. He blamed Alice's 'spell', and the miserable process of interrogation and trial of the supposed witch began. Alice's body was shaved and searched for the Devil's Mark; she was ordered to recite the Lord's Prayer, and failed; she was made to wear a pair of new shoes and seated near a fire until her feet were scalding.

Eventually the miserable Alice confessed that she was in the Devil's pay, and was thrown into prison. By the time Darling admitted his deception it was too late: Alice had died in her damp and filthy cell. Darling got his come-uppance seven years later when he had his ears cropped for libelling the Vice-Chancellor of Oxford University.

LOCATION: 11 MILES SOUTH-WEST OF DERBY OFF A38

Chester CHESHIRE

Gory gladiators Chester has seen more than its fair share of murder and mayhem. The Romans built their fortress Deva here in the 1st century AD, strategically placed to fend off attacks from Wales and the North. It included a huge amphitheatre where the legionaries could take a break from fighting with a little recreational bloodshed. A slate relief found on the site suggests that the speciality was gladiatorial shows featuring *retiarii* – the 'net-and-trident' fighters who wore virtually no defensive armour and were therefore guaranteed to suffer serious wounds on the body and face.

Chester beseiged In 1069 Chester was flattened by William the Conqueror, and after a few hundred years of relative calm, the city was back in the thick of it during the Civil War. In September 1645 the Royalist garrison at Chester came under siege. Charles I sent Sir Marmaduke Langdale to relieve it, but Langdale himself came under attack from a Parliamentarian army led by General Sydenham Poyntz. Cavalry and musketeers engaged in a ferocious battle at nearby Rowton Heath, firing into each other's faces and slashing wildly with their swords, while the King himself watched the carnage from a tower in the city. When his cavalry had been destroyed and the battlefield was a mound of dead horses and soldiers, Charles fled to Wales. Meanwhile his garrison was left to struggle on, still starving and still under siege, for another five ghastly months.

LOCATION: 34 MILES SOUTH-WEST OF MANCHESTER OFF M53

Coleshill WARWICKSHIRE

A tidy punishment solution In an age when corporal punishment was common, Coleshill introduced economy and efficiency to the whole process. To avoid wasting time and money on various individual methods of inflicting discomfort and pain, they had a contraption made that could conveniently combine a pillory, a whipping post and stocks in one go.

Miscreants would sit with their legs pinned into the lower loops, or, to receive the lash, have their hands shut into the smaller, upper loops. If condemned to a spell in the pillory, they would stand on a shelf and place their necks into the larger loop. The Coleshill contraption could even take several culprits at once, thus providing a whole festival of suffering instead of a solo turn.

LOCATON: 9 MILES EAST OF BIRMINGHAM ON B4117

Coventry WEST MIDLANDS

Destruction of the city Coventry's rebuilt centre and old cathedral ruins bear testament to the 20th century's technological advances in massacre and destruction. On the night of 14 November 1940, the city, targeted because of its armaments production, was the victim of a devastating air raid. During ten hours of unremitting bombardment, 500 German planes dropped 500 tons of explosives and nearly 900 incendiary bombs on the city – the biggest single bombing raid of its time.

LOCATION: 17 MILES EAST OF BIRMINGHAM OFF M6

fart with a bell; thou shalt go to hell!'

Dane Hills LEICESTERSHIRE

Black Annis As late as the 1870s, parents were scaring their children with the horror stories surrounding a local cave, and keeping alive the folk memories of what may have been a Celtic sacrificial site dedicated to Anu, the mother goddess.

Over the centuries Anu had been transformed into Black Annis, a fierce creature with long, sharp teeth and nails, who was said to lie in wait for children. Anyone foolish enough to venture near the cave was likely to be scratched to death by Annis, who would proceed to suck their blood and hang their skins out to dry.

LOCATION: OUTSKIRTS OF LEICESTER OFF A47

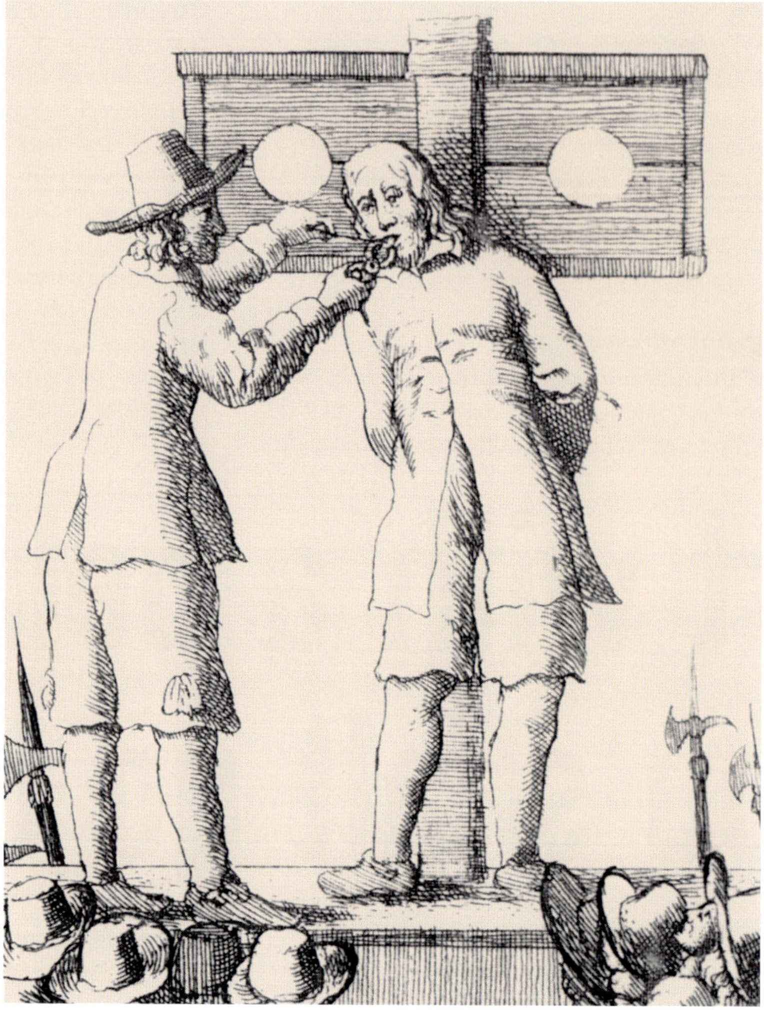

Having your teeth extracted at the pillory was no soft punishment

Derby DERBYSHIRE

Martyred for her faith

Derby town boasts the county's only female martyr, Joan Waste, who was born blind during the reign of Henry VIII. A devout Protestant, Joan was in the habit of visiting Derby jail to hear the prisoners read aloud from her Bible. During Catholic Queen Mary's reign, Joan refused to renounce her faith. She was incarcerated in the same prison, then burned at the stake before a horrified crowd on 1 August 1556.

Ordeal of the pillory

Two centuries later the crowds were still gathering eagerly in Derby to witness the misery of others. In 1732 they enjoyed a few hours' hands-on abuse, hurling apples, eggs, turnips and dung at Eleanor Beare, landlady of the White Horse inn. One of Mrs Beare's regulars, Hewitt the butcher, had starved and mistreated his wife before finally finishing her off with the help of Beare and her maid, Hannah Ollerenshaw, who was also Hewitt's lover. The unfortunate Mrs Hewitt was invited to a tea of arsenic-laced pancakes, prepared by Beare and Ollerenshaw, and was dead within three hours.

Hewitt and his mistress were executed; Beare escaped with her ordeal in the pillory. It was no light punishment. The ill-effects of her vicious pelting included severe illness and swelling; Beare was said to have aged by 30 years. During the three years of imprisonment that followed, however, she recovered her health, and her eventual release was celebrated with a musical procession by the fickle public.

Luddite traitors In 1817 the crowd sided with the victims when it gathered for the execution of three Luddites – Brandreth, Turner and Ludlam – convicted for their role in the 'Pentrich Uprising'. As traitors they suffered an elaborate ritual punishment which culminated in death by hanging, followed by a particularly messy beheading (see opposite).

LOCATION: 15 MILES WEST OF NOTTINGHAM OFF A45

THE FATE OF TRAITORS

In 1606 Sir Edward Coke gave detailed judgement against the Gunpowder Plotters, spelling out the long and involved punishment reserved for traitors. Every element bore a symbolic significance, which Coke was careful to explain, and which continued to be applied into the 19th century.

First a traitor was dragged to his execution across bare ground, being unfit to tread the earth. He was dragged backwards, to show that his crime made him unnatural, and must lie as near as possible to the ground, undeserving of the common air. Having been hanged by the neck between heaven and earth – unworthy of both – the traitor would be cut down alive, so that he could see his 'privy parts' cut off and burned, and appreciate the message that he was unfit either to be begotten or to beget. His bowels and guts were then removed and burnt to signify the evil 'inward conception' of his treachery; and just to ram the message home, the head that had thought up the wicked plot was finally chopped off. As a grand finale, what was left of the traitor was quartered and hung out as a prey for birds.

Coke's judgement was rarely carried out to the letter, although it was ritually acknowledged. Convicted traitors would be dragged on hurdles, rather than on bare ground; most were hanged until dead before being mutilated, and aristocrats had their own five-star service, being decapitated straight away, as a special royal favour.

By the 18th and early 19th centuries, despite continuing to pronounce Coke's sentence in full on male traitors, judges routinely left the deed to the executioner's discretion, who usually plumped for strangulation and decapitation, and left out the added extras.

Women found guilty of treason were burned at the stake, for their modesty's sake: it was considered improper to expose a lady's private parts, even for the purposes of butchery.

The 6,000 people who assembled in Derby in 1817 were treated to a modified version of the penalty for treason. The three labourers convicted for their part in a riot had already been dragged around the prison quad on sledges harnessed to horses. They were hanged until dead – though it took a good 30 minutes to finish them off, and according to local newspaper reports Ludlam suffered several convulsions in that time. It was just as well, though, that the three were beyond suffering by the time the next stage was underway. The masked coalminer who hacked off their heads made a particularly clumsy job of it, and his assistant had to saw through the sinews with his knife. As Brandreth, the first victim's head was held up with three cries of 'Behold the head of a traitor', the spectators gasped and shrieked, and ran in all directions. The soldiers posted at each end of the street drew their swords ready for a fight, but by the time the executioner had finished his job the crowd had dispersed, having had its fill of inhumanity for one day.

Edgcote NORTHAMPTONSHIRE

Family affair 'At Edgcot in this county upon Danes More a bloody battell was fought,' noted chronicler John Speed, summing up a conflict that saw thousands of hideous deaths in the cause of political ambition. This episode in the long Wars of the Roses began with the Lancastrian Earl of Warwick's rebellion against Edward IV in the north of England. As Warwick's forces advanced from Northampton, the King's army set off from Banbury, and the two sides clashed on Danesmore plain on 26 July 1469. On the King's side alone, 5,000 men were cut down. To compound the disaster, the Queen's father, Earl Rivers; her brother, John Woodville; and the army's commander, the Earl of Pembroke; and Warwick's brother, Richard, were all captured after the battle, carried off to Northampton and beheaded.

LOCATION: 5 MILES NORTH-EAST OF BANBURY

Dramatic events unfolded at the bloody Battle of Evesham

Edgehill WARWICKSHIRE

First battle of the Civil War On Sunday 24 October, 1642, Charles I led his forces to the top of Edgehill and looked down over Keynton, where he could see the Parliamentarian army falling in, ready for the first battle of what would become known as the Civil War. The action began well for the Royalists: a group of musketeers hidden in a hedge ready to take pot shots at the ranks was beaten off; the King's cavalry then thundered down on the rebel infantry, hacking at them with their swords for a good 3 miles as they fled in panic. Unfortunately they were so preoccupied with chasing and killing the enemy that they left the rest of their army to the mercy of the Parliamentary horsemen, and by the time they returned to the field chaos reigned.

As darkness fell the commanders retired, afraid that too many of their own men's heads would be lopped off by mistake. 'For the slain on both sides', remarked one survivor, 'the number is uncertain'. But it was certainly high. For every Royalist killed, the Parliamentarians had lost five, and the following day, exhausted and depleted, they retreated to Warwick, pursued by Prince Rupert and his insatiable troops.

LOCATION: 7 MILES NORTH-WEST OF BANBURY OFF A422

Evesham WORCESTERSHIRE

Revenge of the rebel baron Simon de Montfort, Earl of Leicester (1208–65) has been variously described as a man of the people, the father of parliaments and an arrogant fanatic. He was certainly a force to be reckoned with, and gave Henry III a difficult time when he gathered the barons of England to demand a greater say in government. The two sides had already fought several times, and both the King and his eldest son, Edward, had been at times captured by the barons. Edward made the defeat of de Montfort and the rebel barons his personal mission: according to a contemporary chronicler, he 'thirsted for their blood'.

While de Montfort and his men were resting at Evesham on 4 August they heard that Edward was heading their way. 'A wonderful conflict' took place on a hill outside the town, and the rebels were virtually wiped out. Edward's special wrath was reserved for de Montfort himself, whose head, hands, feet and genitals were cut off in a display of vengeance that was shocking even in that brutal age.

De Montfort's mutilated remains were buried in Evesham abbey, where they soon made it a centre of pilgrimage, despite attempts to suppress the cult. It was said that in the 13 years after his terrible death, the baron leader's relics were responsible for over 200 miracles.
LOCATION: 13 MILES SOUTH-EAST OF WORCESTER OFF A44

Eyam DERBYSHIRE
Plague quarantine When George Viccars started unpacking his luggage at Eyam on 7 September 1665 he set in train a calamitous sequence of events. Viccars was a tailor, who had brought a supply of clothes from London. He must have been glad to leave the capital, which had been hit by a catastrophic wave of bubonic plague. But as Viccars unfolded the garments he was bitten by plague-infected fleas, which had stowed away in their folds. He was the first person in the locale to die, and soon other villagers were suffering the chills, delirium and pus-filled buboes that characterised the disease. There was a real danger that the epidemic might spread through the district, and it was rector William Mompesson who had the idea of putting the whole village into quarantine. No-one was allowed in or out of the community; food and supplies were left on a stone on the outskirts, and payment left on collection. Life for the imprisoned residents must have been unspeakable: in this small village of under 600 people, over 300 had died in agony by the end of 1666. On the heights above Eyam, a stone enclosure containing a group of gravestones recalls the tragedy of one family; Mrs Hancock was the sole survivor, and had to haul the bodies of her husband and six children up to this plot, one by one. Mompesson lost his wife but lived to continue leading his flock, whose selflessness had saved countless others from the ravages of the plague.
LOCATION: 5 MILES NORTH OF BAKEWELL OFF A623

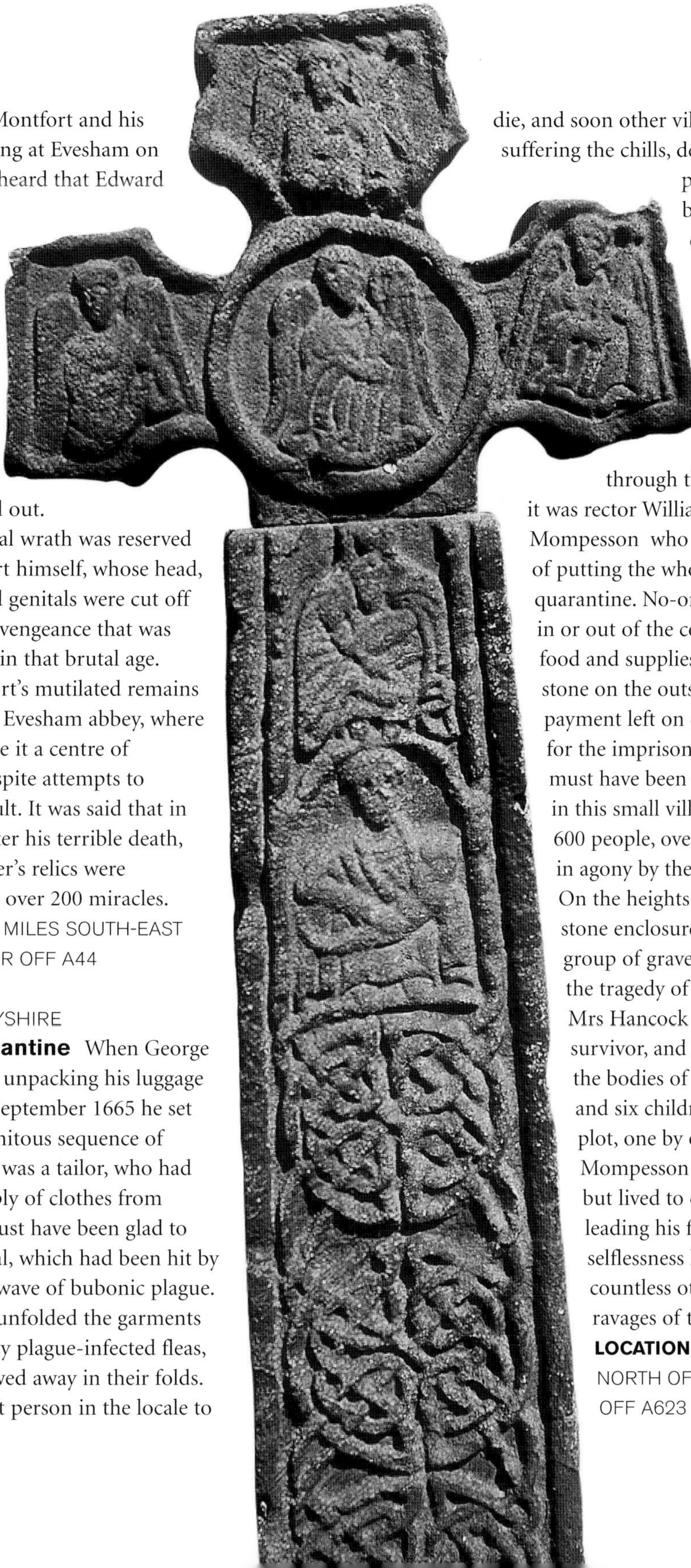

Memorial cross at the lost village of Eyam

Mary Stuart was a constant thorn in the side of Elizabeth I, and met her end at Fotheringhay Castle (now a ruin)

Fotheringhay NORTHAMPTONSHIRE

A royal beheading Mary, Queen of Scots, had been a problem for Elizabeth I since taking refuge in England in 1568. Kept under strict surveillance and moved from place to place, Catholic Mary still provided a focus for opposition to Elizabeth's Protestant regime. In 1587 she was found guilty of conspiring against the Queen and, on 8 February, brought to the Great Hall of Fotheringhay Castle to be executed. Dressed in a blood-red gown, Mary knelt and placed her head on the block. Mr Bull, the nervous executioner, failed to make a clean job of it, and took two swipes to cut through her neck. As he grabbed her red hair to hold up the head, it came away in his hand: under her wig, Mary was completely grey. As her trunk lay bleeding on the ground her little dog emerged from under her skirts, where it had hidden during its mistress's ordeal.
LOCATION: 4 MILES NORTH-EAST OF OUNDLE OFF A605

Ironbridge SHROPSHIRE

Birth of the Industrial Age This beauty spot in the wooded Severn Valley was a hell-hole of furnaces and factories in the 18th century, when the Darby family undertook their pioneering work in iron-smelting, forging and casting. Thousands of men and boys toiled in sweltering furnaces, producing rails, engine parts, fireplaces and bridges; a pall of stinking fumes and pollution hung over the entire area. The gorge is now a collection of industrial museums, including Blists Hill, a re-created 19th-century working town, complete with slaughterhouse and a surgery equipped with blood-curdling implements.
LOCATION: 3 MILES SOUTH OF DAWLEY OFF A4169

Kenilworth WARWICKSHIRE

Kenilworth Castle has a long and violent history. In the 13th century its occupants, supporters of Simon de Montfort (see page 104), endured a nine-month siege before starvation and disease forced their surrender. In 1326 Edward II was imprisoned here en route to his final and hideous fate at Berkeley Castle (see page 14). John Dudley, Duke of Northumberland, took up residence in the 16th century and could hope for a quieter life, being king in all but name during the reign of young Edward VI. Dudley showed his true nature while suppressing the Peasants' Revolt, when he had an urchin shot for making a rude gesture, and presided over the slaughter of 3,500 peasants. But his luck ran out after he dared to place his own daughter-in-law, Lady Jane Grey, on the throne. He was thrown into the Tower and put to death.

A suspicious death Dudley's handsome and dashing son Robert, Earl of Leicester, was a favourite with Elizabeth I, and spent a fortune on Kenilworth Castle so that he could entertain the Queen there in style. Some said she would have married Dudley had he not already had a wife, Amy Robsart. When Amy was found dead, with a

broken neck, suspicion fell on Dudley, but he had the perfect alibi – he was with Elizabeth at Windsor at the time.

LOCATION: 5 MILES SOUTH-WEST OF COVENTRY OFF A46

Leicester LEICESTERSHIRE

Cooking the evidence At the age of 21, James Cook inherited his late master's bookbinding business and started to trade in a workshop off Wellington Street. In May 1832 he received a letter from Mr Paas, a London manufacturer of bookbinding instruments, who was coming to Leicester to collect money due to him. On 30 May Paas set off on his debt-collecting rounds. After visiting Cook he met another customer, and mentioned that he'd been told to call back later for the money. Mr Paas was never seen alive again.

That evening, Cook popped into the Flying Horse for a beer and a game of skittles. Apart from carrying a purse stuffed full of money, he behaved normally, and soon went back to work. Between 10.30 that night and 4.30 the following morning he was seen moving around in his workshop. The following night, neighbours were alarmed by the sight of flames behind the workshop's drawn blinds. One managed to break down the door and found a large hank of flesh burning over the fire. Cook was summoned, and claimed that he was cooking horseflesh to feed a dog. But this was human flesh. Hanging from a cord in the chimney were two thighs and a leg, hacked apart by a knife and a saw. Elsewhere, the neighbours discovered the leg of a pair of trousers covered in blood, along with some of Mr Paas's belongings. In the ashes of the grate were burnt fragments of human bone.

Cook was convicted of murder and hanged. His head was shaved and tarred, and his body hung in a gibbet in Saffron Lane, on the outskirts of town.

LOCATION: OFF M1

Ironbridge is a tranquil place now, the industrial bustle replaced by tourists

Leominster HEREFORDSHIRE

The last ducking In 1809 the passing of an ancient tradition was marked when Jenny Pipe was strapped to the ducking-stool and plunged in to the river at Kenwater Bridge. The stool and its tumbrell are now preserved as museum pieces in Leominster town hall. Mrs Pipe doesn't seem to have suffered too badly from the effects of her soaking: as soon as she emerged from the water she began soundly cursing the magistrate who passed the sentence.

LOCATION: 12 MILES NORTH OF HEREFORD ON A49

Lichfield STAFFORDSHIRE

A bad lot Lichfield was the birthplace of Jack Withers, 'a sacrilegious villain' who fell into bad company after leaving his apprenticeship at the family butcher's shop. Apprehended for thieving, Jack was drafted into the army in Flanders, where he was caught with his fingers in the cathedral's donation box. Withers claimed to have been directed by a statue of the Virgin Mary, and was subsequently carried in triumph, shoulder-high, to cries of 'miracle!' Back in England, Withers took up highway robbery, and put his butchering skills to use after taking 8 shillings from a postman. First he cut the poor man's throat and ripped out his bowels, then he filled the body with stones and threw it into a pond. Withers was caught committing another robbery, and executed on 16 April 1703.

LOCATION: 15 MILES NORTH OF BIRMINGHAM OFF A51

Lincoln LINCOLNSHIRE

A slow burning Eleanor Elsom was found guilty of murdering her husband in 1722 and sentenced to be burned at the stake, a punishment considered by some at the time to be more humane than hanging. A description that survives of Elsom's fate puts paid to that theory. She was brought barefoot from the prison, saturated with tar, placed on a tar barrel, 3 feet (1m) high, and secured to the stake with three iron bands. Elsom herself put a noose around her neck; it was then pulled tight several times, while the barrel was removed and the fire lit. This rope-pulling was the basis of the belief that burning was an easy option, the idea being that the victim would be strangled before the flames took hold, but theory and practice were sometimes at odds.

LOCATION: OFF A46

Lindow Moss CHESHIRE

Murder confessed – in error In 1983 a murder investigation brought Cheshire police to the home of Peter Reyn-Bardt, suspected of murdering his wife, Malika, 23 years earlier. Despite having boasted in the past of killing her and dismembering and burying her body, Reyn-Bardt now denied all knowledge of her fate. But on 13 May that year workers on the peat extraction site that bordered his back yard unearthed a female skull. The forensic pathologist pronounced it to be 30 to 50 years old, and Reyn-Bardt confessed all. But before he came to trial there was a strange twist to the tale. The skull was sent for further study to Oxford University, where it was found it to be at least 1,660 years old, remarkably preserved in the organic chemicals of the bog.

'Lindow Man' A second body subsequently retrieved from Lindow Moss in the 1980s dates back to about the 2nd century BC. 'Lindow Man' was discovered in pieces: his arms had already deteriorated, probably soon after death, and four years elapsed between finding his head, torso and right foot and the recovery of his legs and the skin of his buttocks. Some believe him to have been the victim of a ritual sacrifice, perhaps by the triple method employed by Celts. His throat was split end to end, possibly by a garrot; his head shows evidence of bludgeoning by an axe, and there were stab wounds on the neck and torso. Grains of mistletoe found in his stomach suggest a hallucinatory meal prepared by druids.

LOCATION: OUTSKIRTS OF WILMSLOW OFF A34

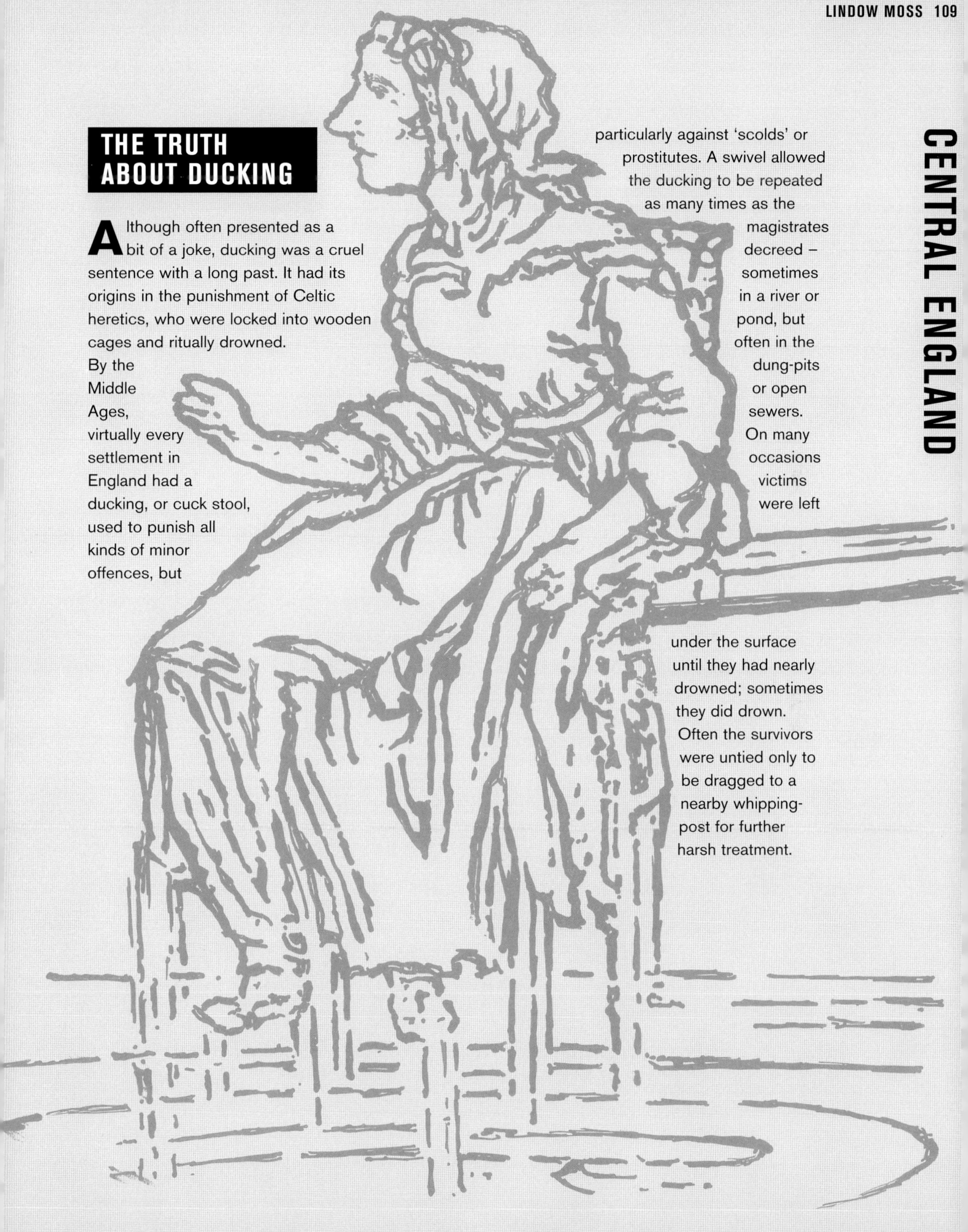

THE TRUTH ABOUT DUCKING

Although often presented as a bit of a joke, ducking was a cruel sentence with a long past. It had its origins in the punishment of Celtic heretics, who were locked into wooden cages and ritually drowned. By the Middle Ages, virtually every settlement in England had a ducking, or cuck stool, used to punish all kinds of minor offences, but particularly against 'scolds' or prostitutes. A swivel allowed the ducking to be repeated as many times as the magistrates decreed – sometimes in a river or pond, but often in the dung-pits or open sewers. On many occasions victims were left under the surface until they had nearly drowned; sometimes they did drown. Often the survivors were untied only to be dragged to a nearby whipping-post for further harsh treatment.

Background: The gaunt ruin of Ludlow Castle

Litton DERBYSHIRE

Murder under the gibbet The hanging of executed murderers in gibbets was in part a form of deterrent. That was certainly the idea behind the gibbeting of Anthony Wingard in the early 19th century. Wingard had murdered Hannah Oliver, a widow who kept the turnpike gate at Wardlow Miers. The judge who sentenced him to hang specifically ordered that, instead of being dissected after death, Wingard should be hung to rot in a metal cage, as an example to others. It didn't work. Days later, Hannah Pecking, a 16-year-old from Litton, fed her friend Jane Grant a poisoned cake while the two were fetching cattle from a field, virtually under the feet of the swaying corpse. Her motive was said to be jealousy; her inevitable end was on the gallows.

LOCATION: 8 MILES SOUTH-WEST OF SHEFFIELD OFF B6049

Louth LINCOLNSHIRE

Royal revenge Having quarrelled with Rome over his divorce from Catherine of Aragon, Henry VIII proceeded to make himself head of the Anglican Church and dissolve the monasteries, pocketing their wealth and rewarding his friends with their land and buildings. In 1536 these policies sparked an uprising, known as the Pilgrimage of Grace, which began at Louth and quickly spread north (see page 169). Within a year it had been suppressed, but Henry harboured angry resentment against Lincolnshire in general, which he called 'one of the most brutal and beestlie [counties] of the whole realm,' and Louth in particular. The local ringleader was hanged, drawn and quartered, and Henry furthered his revenge by executing 12 abbots.

LOCATION: 14 MILES SOUTH OF GRIMSBY OFF A16

Ludlow SHROPSHIRE

Power struggles Today Ludlow is a beautiful and peaceful border town, but for nearly 500 years this was the centre of ferocious power struggles between the English, the mighty Marcher (borderland) Lords and the Welsh. In 1096 Hugh de Montgomery, Lord of Ludlow, marched a huge army into north Wales and set about massacring the inhabitants of Anglesey. Meanwhile, King Harold's son, Magnus, was trying to land on the island, hoping to reclaim his father's realm. Having been refused anchorage by Hugh, Magnus fired an arrow straight into the Lord of Ludlow's face, killing him stone dead. Hugh's brother, Robert, followed in the family tradition, making his mark as 'a most inexorable butcher, exceedingly cruel, covetous and libidinous', until he was finally arrested by Henry I and thrown into a prison cell to rot.

A later ruler of Ludlow, Roger de Mortimer, Earl of March, included among his adventures a rebellion against Edward II, a dramatic escape from the Tower of London and a spell as Queen Isabella's lover. He was also accused of involvement in the hideous murder of the king in 1327 (see page 14), but was eventually brought to book and hanged 'two days and two nights, a public and gladsome spectacle'.

Ludlow Castle became a well-used royal residence, and it was here that the doomed young princes were brought after the death of Edward IV, to await their last journey to the Tower, where they would be murdered (see page 57).

LOCATION: 24 MILES SOUTH OF SHREWSBURY OFF A49

THE BARBAROUS BRIDLE

Women who scolded, nagged or gossiped, who flouted sexual and social convention or who were aged, alone and therefore liable to charges of witchcraft – all were treated as dangerous criminals up until the 18th century and even later.

The 'branks', or scold's bridle, was a means of redress which could be used for any length of time and made with any extra features that took the fancy. At Doddington Park, Lincolnshire, the bridle took the form of a helmet with a long, pointed snout, based on the armour used by soldiers in the time of Richard II. Chester city had no fewer than four branks, each one with a metal rasp fitted to the gag, which would lacerate the victim's tongue as she was led around town on a leash. The branks at Frankwell, near Ludlow, included a revolving wheel at the end of the gag to inflict even greater pain with every movement; other particularly disgusting examples had iron spikes attached to the ball to tear at the tongue. Some victims died of blood-poisoning after suffering these torments. The last use of the branks at Nottingham, known as 'the iron gag', was, unusually, on a man. Blind murderer James Brodie (see page 115) made such a loud fuss while awaiting his execution in prison that the warder made him wear the bridle, to prevent him from speaking.

Macclesfield CHESHIRE

One of the earliest descriptions of an English scolds' bridle, or 'branks', is found in Macclesfield's town records for 1623. This almost cosy-sounding 'bridle for cursed queens' (prostitutes or women of loose morals) was actually a horrifying contraption designed not just to silence the victim, but to torture her at the same time (see left).

LOCATION: 10 MILES SOUTH OF STOCKPORT ON A52

Market Rasen LINCOLNSHIRE

Post-boy murder A horrible discovery was made at Faldingworth Gate, near Market Rasen, one morning in 1733. Covered with a seat-cloth in a post-chaise was 18-year-old William Wright, his head almost severed from his body. It took a month to hunt down his killers, two brothers called Isaac and Thomas Hallam, and for the whole ghastly story to unfold.

Wright, a post-boy, had been overpowered by the Hallam brothers, who forced him to blow his post-horn as a 'death-peal' before cutting his throat and that of his horse. As the brothers were brought into Lincoln to be jailed, all the city's post-boys gathered to greet them with horn-blasts, reducing one of the brothers to tears of remorse.

Nevertheless, the Hallams tried to escape from prison, sawing off their irons with a notched pen-knife and trying to dig through the prison wall. The attempt was foiled and the two were hanged, in 'violent agonies and perturbation of mind', on the spot where William Wright had died.

LOCATION: 14 MILES NORTH-EAST OF LINCOLN OFF A46

Mortimer's Cross HEREFORDSHIRE

Gory victory In 1461 the Wars of the Roses were raging, and the 19-year-old Earl of March, the future Edward IV, was already a battle-weary veteran. Hearing that his father had been killed at Wakefield, Edward marched to Mortimer's Cross to meet the Lancastrian army, led by the Earl of

Wiltshire and Jasper Tudor, Earl of Pembroke. Legend has it that due to a freak atmospheric condition, three suns could be seen on that day, 2 February, which Edward took to be a good omen. Sure enough, his army won the day and pursued the desperate Lancastrians 16 miles south to Hereford. Hundreds of soldiers were hacked down and the prisoners included Pembroke's father, Owen Tudor, who was executed in Hereford.

LOCATION: 5 MILES NORTH-WEST OF LEOMINSTER OFF A4110

Myddle SHROPSHIRE

A 17th-century memoire At the age of 66, a yeoman called Richard Gough started writing down his memories and the stories he had heard about his Shropshire parish. It was 1700, and Gough's colourful anecdotes, family histories and quirky details were destined to be a valuable source of information about ordinary life in Stuart England. Myddle is near the Welsh-English border, and fierce enmity existed between the two nations. Gough reports frequent raids of cattle and goods across the border river; once the thieves had crossed Platt Bridge to Wales no one dared follow them further, but if caught on English territory they were sure to be put to death.

Death of a debt-collector Among the many cases of murder and mayhem noted by Gough are the quarrel between Sir Edward Kinaston and his tenant Clarke, who got into arrears with his rent. A bailiff and servant sent to collect the debts were set upon by Clarke's son, who struck the servant with a turf spade and 'cloave out his brains'. He fled the country, returning years later only to be killed by his neighbour, who flung a stone at his head during an argument.

Betrayed by a dog Another sorry tale involves Hugh Elks, who led a motley crew to his neighbour's house to steal his money. Wearing visors on their faces, the robbers broke in and found a servant making cheese. As Elks stooped to tie her up she spotted his face under his visor and ill-advisedly blurted out: 'Good uncle Elks, do me no harm'. In a panic, Elks cut her throat and fled with his companions, leaving his dog behind. Neighbours later found the dead girl and the dog, 'almost bursted with eating the cheese', and followed the animal to the house of its master, who was subsequently hanged in Shrewsbury.

Pursued by ravens The Elks family traits re-emerged in one Thomas Elks, who drowned his own nephew in a pail of water in the hope of inheriting the family estate. He was found hiding in a haystack when locals spotted two ravens pecking at the hay. Elks confessed to the murder, adding that the ravens had pursued him relentlessly ever since.

LOCATION: 10 MILES NORTH OF SHREWSBURY ON A528

Naseby NORTHAMPTONSHIRE

A battle lost The Battle of Naseby was one of the most decisive of the Civil War. On 14 June 1645 Oliver Cromwell and Thomas Fairfax led 15,000 soldiers of the New Model Army against Prince Rupert's 12,000 Royalists. The fighting was ferocious, and the Parliamentarian infantry were badly mauled before the tide turned. (In the 19th century a mass grave was uncovered containing the skeletons of the decimated regiment.)

Eventually Cromwell's own crack troop, the Ironsides, delivered a devastating counter-attack, and the Royalists were defeated. An observer described the view from nearby Wadborough Hill, noting that the battlefield was 'so bestrewed with carcases of horse and men as was most sad to behold'. After this the King lost all real hope of winning the war.

LOCATION: 6 MILES SOUTH-WEST OF MARKET HARBOROUGH ON B4036

Northampton NORTHAMPTONSHIRE

An army betrayed One of many battles between Yorkists and Lancastrians took place in a meadow just south of Northampton on 10 July 1460. The Earl of Warwick faced the Duke of Buckingham's Lancastrian forces, entrenched behind earthworks filled with artillery. The troops sat tight in their strong position until Lord Grey of Rhuthun switched allegiance and let in the army of the future Edward IV, which slaughtered several of the enemy's leaders before the day was done.

Whipping up a storm A glimpse of town life some 200 years later shows how tough it could be for anyone who failed to scramble far enough up the heap. Eleanor Childe was a vagrant, which was enough to get her whipped in Northampton market between noon and 2pm on a Saturday, and then driven out of town. It was one more example of the savage treatment meted out to the most powerless members of society (see opposite). But not everyone approved: the Northampton county sessions minutes for 1673 quote an official as complaining that 'people are whipped for speaking true, whipped for lying and sometimes just for holding his peace!'

LOCATION: OFF M1 JUNCTION 16

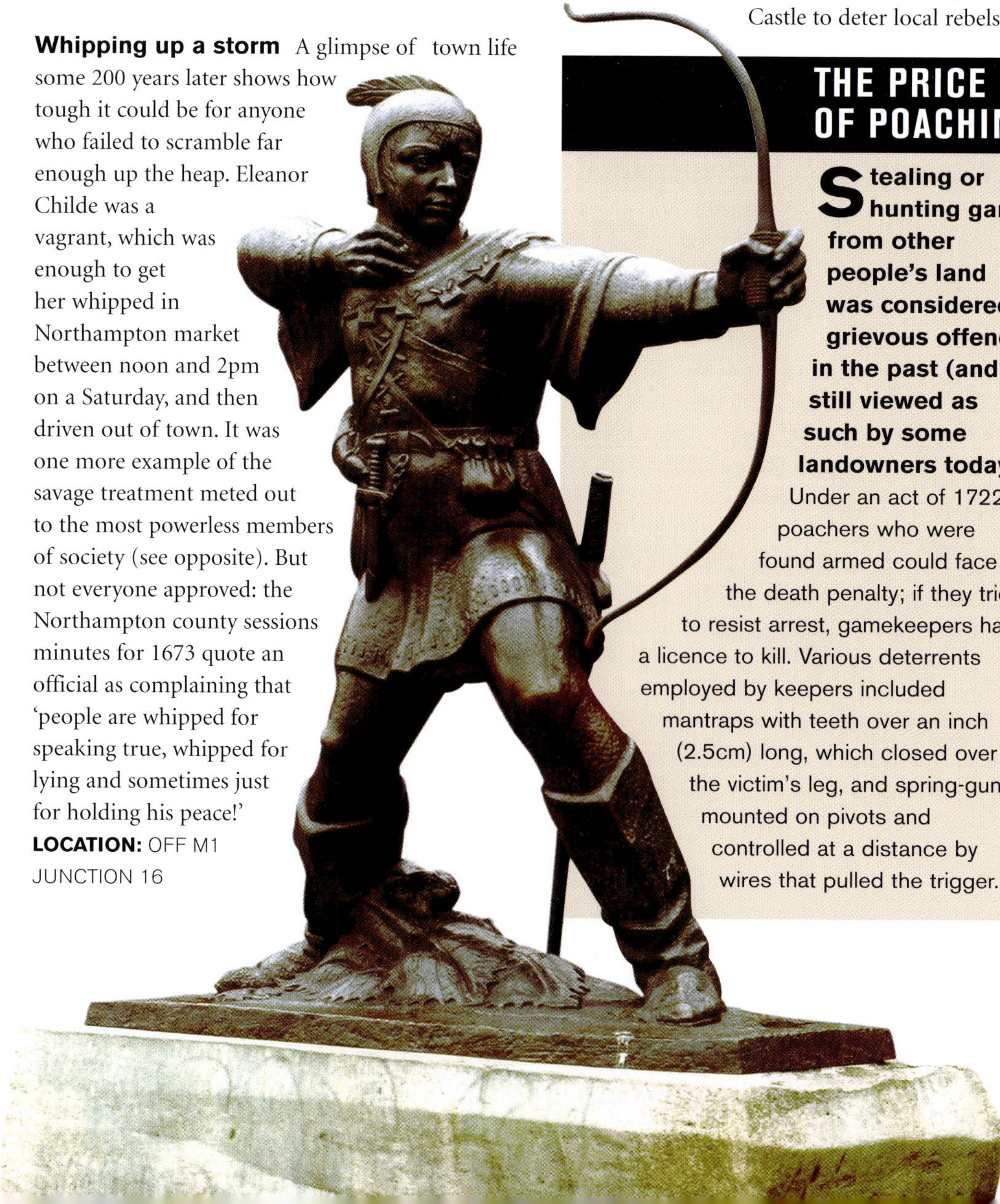

The semi-legendary figure of Robin Hood apparently thrived some time between the mid-13th and mid-14th centuries.

Nottingham NOTTINGHAMSHIRE

Robin Hood Stories of Nottingham's famous outlaw and his sworn enemies the Sheriff and King John, usually have a cheerful, swashbuckling air. The reality was, of course, a lot less jolly. Many outlaws were dangerous characters who terrorised the community. As for Robin's merry men, even hunting game in the royal forest was a very risky business (see below). As for King John, he revealed his true nature by having 28 Welsh boy hostages hanged in 1212 from the walls of Nottingham Castle to deter local rebels.

THE PRICE OF POACHING

Stealing or hunting game from other people's land was considered a grievous offence in the past (and is still viewed as such by some landowners today). Under an act of 1722, poachers who were found armed could face the death penalty; if they tried to resist arrest, gamekeepers had a licence to kill. Various deterrents employed by keepers included mantraps with teeth over an inch (2.5cm) long, which closed over the victim's leg, and spring-guns, mounted on pivots and controlled at a distance by wires that pulled the trigger.

WHIPPING UP TROUBLE

Henry VIII's Act Against Vagrants (1530) decreed that those convicted of vagrancy should be tied naked to the end of a cart and whipped until bloody.

Elizabeth I later spared onlookers' blushes by allowing vagrants to stay dressed from the waist down. A whipping was a gruelling ordeal. It was administered with the 'cat o' nine tails' – a short handle to which were attached nine thongs of dried leather, originally with spiked metal balls at their tips, later simply knotted at the end. Each thong had to be 33 inches (84cm) long to ensure maximum bloodshed. Apart from vagrancy, other transgressions that could lead to a flogging included theft, drunkenness, sexual 'immorality' and open-air preaching. The whipping post was a common feature of towns and villages until the public whipping of women was abolished in 1817.

Justice through the ages Nottingham's Galleries of Justice use chilling exhibits to illustrate 300 years of harsh judicial measures. One of the city's favoured instruments of 'correction' in the 17th century was the branding iron, which was permanently fixed in front of the dock. Magistrates frequently demanded that the branding take place immediately after sentencing, so that they could see smoke rising from the singed skin and be reassured that the iron was red hot.

A blind murderer The use of the scolds' bridle to silence James Brodie has already been mentioned (see page 112). At the time Brodie, a blind man of 23, was in prison awaiting execution for the murder of his young guide, Robert Selby Hancock, in 1800. On 24 March that year a forester had come across Brodie lying on his belly by a river. Brodie claimed that his guide had died during the night, and that he had since been wandering about, unable to find his way. The boy was found 3 miles away, covered with ferns. His skull was fractured, the head bloodied and torn at the ear and the shoulders and arms beaten, according to witnesses, 'to a jelly'. Brodie claimed that Hancock had received his injuries falling from a tree, but a jury decided that he had beaten the boy with his stick, and he was executed.

Caught in the crush Public executions provoked a mixture of reactions from watching crowds. Political prisoners often had the sympathy of the spectators – as did the three Luddite rioters hanged in Nottingham in 1832, to indignant cries of 'Murder! Blood!' Even so, hangings were major attractions. When the mass of people that had watched an execution in the city in 1844 tried to disperse, a dozen women and children were killed in the crush.

LOCATION: EAST OF M1, JUNCTION 25

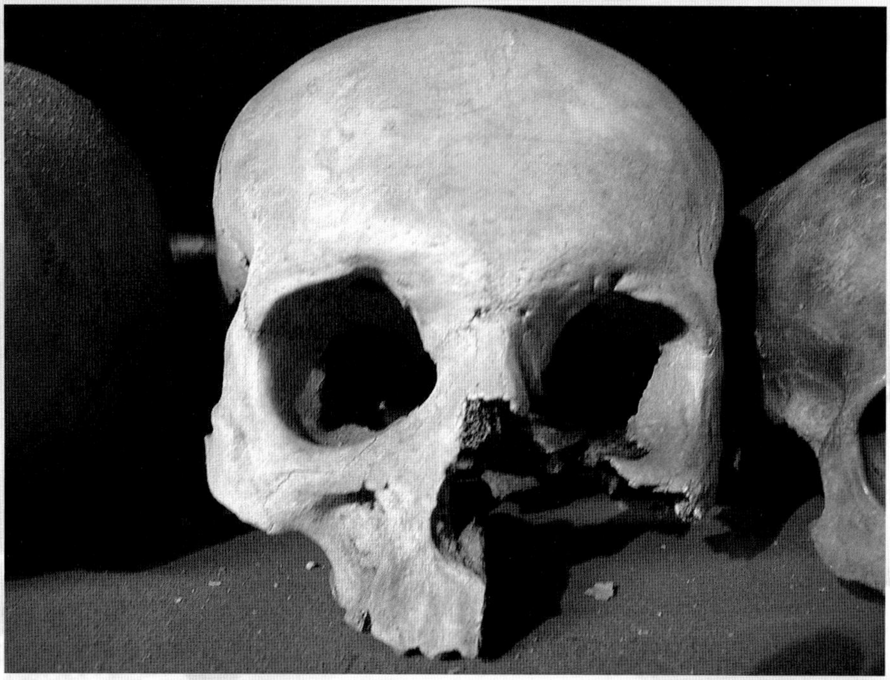

Skull from the bone pit at Rothwell

War poet The town's most famous son is poet Wilfred Owen (1893–1918), who wrote angrily about the sufferings of soldiers on the front in World War I. His bitter poem, 'Dulce et Decorum Est', describes the effects of gas on a fellow soldier, 'the blood gargling from the froth-corrupted lungs'. Owen was killed in action on 4 November 1918 a week before the Armistice.

LOCATION: 16 MILES NORTH-WEST OF SHREWSBURY OFF A5

Ross-on-Wye

HEREFORDSHIRE

Tactics Ross's strategic position on the river that marks part of the English-Welsh border made it a target for raids and bloody battles; the earthen bank and ditch built by King Offa in AD 784 was a front line. Nearby Goodrich Castle, built in around 1300, provides a stark illustration of those turbulent times. Attackers were funnelled into a narrow, 60ft (18m) passage, while the castle's garrison picked them off with arrows from the barbican tower on the gatehouse.

Mass grave A cross in Ross's churchyard is a reminder of the dangers that lay in wait for locals even in times of peace. Over 300 corpses were piled into a mass grave here in 1637, when the town was reeling from a bout of the plague and unable to keep up with the demand for conventional burials.

LOCATION: 9 MILES NORTH-EAST OF MONMOUTH OFF A40

Oswestry SHROPSHIRE

Oswald's Tree Violence marked the beginnings of this border town, according to legend, and it continued to play a part in its history for hundreds of years. The name 'Oswestry' is said to be a corruption of 'Oswald's Tree', named after a Christian king who was killed by Penda, King of Mercia, in AD 642. One version of the story tells of Oswald's body being hung from a tree after a battle; another describes an angel flying away with part of his dismembered body before letting it drop, and a holy spring emerging on the spot where it landed.

The 'Weeping Cross' The Normans built a castle here to fend off Welsh attacks, and fighting persisted over possession of the town for centuries until it was officially incorporated into England in 1535. Twenty years later the population had been reduced by a third, not through fighting but through the ravages of plague. The Croeswylan ('Weeping Cross') Stone in town commemorates the victims.

Rothwell NORTHAMPTONSHIRE

Pit of bones In 1700 a sexton was busy preparing a grave near the church of this pretty market town when he made a macabre discovery. As he was digging, more and more human bones came to the surface – in all 1,500 medieval skulls and thigh-bones were recovered. They are now housed in the crypt of Holy Trinity Church, and can be examined at leisure.

LOCATION: 4 MILES NORTH-WEST OF KETTERING ON A6

Rugby WARWICKSHIRE

War crime The Civil War did not only consist of set-piece battles and sieges. Innumerable atrocities and crimes were committed against ordinary people in the brutalised atmosphere of war, as soldiers roamed the country taking food and shelter and delivering their own brand of justice. One victim of their random sadism was Agnes Griffin, caught by Cromwell's troops near Rugby and allegedly crucified on a tree, cut on the body and forced to eat her own flesh and drink her own blood in a sick mockery of the communion. Agnes survived her ordeal, and to make amends, the local justices awarded her four shillings, and a certificate allowing her to beg for alms.

caught by Cromwell's troops near Rugby and allegedly crucified on a tree, cut on the body and forced to eat her own flesh and drink her own blood in a sick mockery of the communion...

Murder of Sir Theodosius Boughton

Just over a century later, more subtle methods were employed in the notorious murder of the youthful Sir Theodosius Boughton. On a Wednesday morning in February 1781, Mr Powell, the apothecary of Rugby, was called to the family estate at Lawton Hall by Boughton's brother-in-law, Captain John Donellan. Powell found Boughton dead in his room; according to Captain Donellan he had suffered a sudden fit of convulsions. Sir Theodosius was 20 years old and due to inherit an annual allowance, which now passed to his sister, Donellan's wife.

It emerged that Donellan had advised his brother-in-law to put his daily medicine in his ante-room so as not to forget his dose. On the morning of his death Sir Theodosius's mother, Lady Boughton, took him his physic, reporting that it smelled 'very nauseous', like bitter almonds. Two minutes after taking a slurp her son was writhing in pain, his stomach 'rattling and guggling'; before half-an-hour was out he was lying open-eyed, his teeth clenched and foam trickling from his mouth. While the apothecary was fetched, Captain Donellan rinsed the medicine bottle and ordered that the dead man's room be cleaned out. An autopsy revealed that Theodosius had swallowed a poison made of laurel leaves, and Donellan was duly charged with his murder. Even on the gallows he professed his innocence.

LOCATION: 11 MILES EAST OF COVENTRY ON A428

Shrewsbury SHROPSHIRE

Rebel Hotspur Tens of thousands of men faced each other across a field near Shrewsbury on 21 July 1403. The Lancastrian king, Henry IV, led an army estimated as between 14,000 and 60,000 strong; facing him were the forces of the rebel Percy family and their star warrior, Harry 'Hotspur' Percy. For a few hours the two sides negotiatied, but talks broke down, commands were barked out and the sky filled with the screech of arrows. Both armies were equipped with the lethal new longbow, which could fire 12 arrows a minute, and the dead soon started piling up.

When word spread that Hotspur had been fatally hit in the face, the rebels lost heart, and their wholesale slaughter began. It was described by observers as the worst ever witnessed in Christian times. About 20,000 men died on the field, some 1,500 of them shovelled into a mass grave on the spot. Hotspur was buried at Whitchurch, Shropshire, but Henry IV wasn't satisfied. To prove that the great soldier was dead, the King had him disinterred and impaled on a spear in Shrewsbury; later the corpse was quartered and distributed around the country for display.

Death of a foster mother By the 16th century the good folk of Shrewsbury were less accustomed to such orgies of bloodshed, and individual murders were enough to cause a sensation. One such was the killing of Elizabeth Bickerstaffe in 1551. Her foster son, Thomas, announced her missing and organised a search with no result. Seven weeks later, his landlord's dog was seen scratching at the bare ground under Thomas's bed; further investigation unearthed the victim's chopped up remains. Thomas Bickerstaffe was convicted of her murder and hanged in chains.

Hiding the gallows Public executions were still common in the mid-19th century. One chronicler described observers flocking to the Shrewsbury gallows in 1841 'as they would to a bull-baiting or a cockfight'. But the whole business made an unfavourable impression on one schoolboy, Gathorne Hardy, 1st Earl of Cranbrook, who rushed to see a hanging after being let out early from Shrewsbury School. As Home Secretary in 1868 Hardy was still haunted by the spectacle, and introduced a Bill to hide the scaffold from public view.

LOCATION: 39 MILES NORTH-WEST OF BIRMINGHAM OFF A5

Hiding the gall were still comm One chronicle to the Shrews would to a bull

Stafford STAFFORDSHIRE

A family man The tragic case of George Allen and his family shocked the nation in 1807. Allen was an epileptic who occasionally suffered disturbing visions. On the evening of 12 January, though, he seemed well, sitting up in bed and smoking a pipe. Next door were three of his children, aged between three and ten; his wife brought the youngest, a baby, to bed to be breastfed. All at once Allen started accusing his wife of having another man in the house, and leapt out of bed in a fury. Seeing him head for the children's room, Mrs Allen tried to restrain her husband, but he stabbed her in the breast and tried to cut her throat. Only a handkerchief around her neck saved her life. Still protecting the infant in her arms, she managed to stumble downstairs, but before she could escape from the house, the body of her six-year-old daughter was thrown after her.

Neighbours summoned by the woman's screams found Allen with a razor in his hand, having cut the throats and mutilated the bodies of his two sons. Allen gave no resistance to arrest, and freely admitted that he had planned to kill all four children and his wife, and then kill himself. He was executed in Stafford on 30 March.

LOCATION: 14 MILES SOUTH OF STOKE-ON-TRENT ON A34

Stamford LINCOLNSHIRE

Villainy unparalleled A shoemaker's apprentice from Stamford, Timothy Buckley, graduated to become 'as unparalleled a villain as ever lived in this kingdom' by the time of his execution in 1701. Buckley ran away from his master, fell into the company of thieves, and tried his hand at highway robbery. He was no great success at first and was arrested and sent to do military service in Flanders. But Buckley soon deserted and, on his return, took his revenge against the arresting constable by raping the man's wife.

The pay-back was to be a familiar feature of Buckley's career. A stock-jobber who had him prosecuted and branded in the hand was promptly robbed of 48 guineas. For this Buckley was sentenced to death, but obtained a pardon and retaliated by setting his adversary's house on fire.

Tim Buckley ran out of luck at the age of 29, when he held up a coach near Nottingham. The footmen and passengers were armed and ready, and a ferocious gun battle ensued. Buckley discharged eight pistols, killing two men, but by then he had 11 wounds in his arms, thighs and legs, and was fast losing blood. He was executed in Nottingham and his body suspended in chains at the scene of his last crime.

LOCATION: 12 MILES NORTH-WEST OF PETERBOROUGH OFF A1

vs – Public executions
n in the mid-19th century.
lescribed observers flocking
ry gallows in 1841 'as they
aiting or a cockfight'.

Stanton Lacy SHROPSHIRE

The wages of sin In days gone by an illegitimate child could bring disgrace and social exclusion to its parents, and if the father was a churchman it could spell absolute disaster. The Reverend Robert Foulkes was minister of Stanton-Lacy in the 17th century, admired by his flock and known to be a devoted husband and father. Everything went wrong when Foulkes became the guardian and tutor of a wealthy young orphan girl. Foulkes and the girl embarked on a passionate affair, and the girl became pregnant. After failing to procure an abortion, Foulkes took her to London, where the baby was born and immediately murdered. The young mother could not keep the guilty secret, however, and confessed to some of the women attending her. Foulkes was executed on 31 January 1679.

LOCATION: 3 MILES NORTH OF LUDLOW OFF B43465

Bottle-shaped kilns in the Potteries

Stoke-on-Trent STAFFORDSHIRE

The Potteries Pottery has been made in this area since the Bronze Age, but it was in the 17th century that the advantages of the local mineral deposits and water power were fully realised. By the 19th century, production in 'the Potteries' was at its height, and the smoke and toxic waste spewing from its 'pot banks' had earned it a reputation as the most unhealthy environment in Britain. Among the diseases that afflicted workers in the potteries was silicosis, or 'potters' rot', caused by the inhalation of crystalline silica dust from the minerals used in the factories. When this white or invisible dust is breathed in, particles get trapped in the lungs, and nodules grow around them. As they increase in size, breathing becomes more difficult. Silicosis still causes hundreds of deaths every year; before awareness grew of the long-term effects of exposure to crystalline silica, no precautions were taken, and countless lives were lost.

LOCATION: OFF M6

Stratford-upon-Avon WARWICKSHIRE

17th-century medicine Shakespeare's eldest daughter, Susanna, married John Hall, a physician, and the couple lived for many years in Hall's Croft, a

Left: Hall's Croft, where early medicine was catalogued

timber-framed house which has now been turned into a museum. Between 1611 and 1635 Hall kept notes on his patients' symptoms and the treatments offered, and these were published in 1657, 22 years after his death, under the title *Select Observations on English Bodies.* They provide a fascinating insight into 17th-century medical practice, much of which seemed to involve the inspection of urine, stools and vomit. One room in the house contains a hair-raising exhibition of Elizabethan and Jacobean surgical instruments, including evil-looking forceps, scoops and drills.
LOCATION: 8 MILES SOUTH-WEST OF WARWICK ON A439

Sutton Cheney LEICESTERSHIRE

Bloody Bosworth Field After the death of Edward IV in 1483 his brother, Richard, took up the reins of government and the title of 'protector' of the late King's two young sons. But after the suspicious death of the princes (see page 57) and his coronation as Richard III, rivals and enemies began to close in. Henry Tudor, the Lancastrian claimant to the throne, returned from exile in 1485 and confronted the royal army just south of Market Bosworth, near Sutton Cheney, on 22 August 1485. Richard's troops, ranged at the top of Ambion Hill, began proceedings by firing massive four-pounder guns into the Tudor ranks below. This was followed by a shower of arrows from the longbowmen, and a headlong cavalry charge of 8,000 horsemen down the slope. Tudor's archers and men-at-arms packed themselves together in a tight wedge, and the cavalry galloped into a hail of arrows and the swiping and slashing of pikemen and axemen, and had to withdraw. The hand-to-hand fighting continued, and men were slashed and stabbed on all sides by spears, daggers and swords.

In desperation, Henry and a few knights rode away from the action to try and engage the services of Sir William Stanley, who had so far been waiting non-commitally on the sidelines with his 4,000 men. Stanley had been hesitant to help Henry, knowing that his son was held hostage by Richard. In fact orders had already been given to have his son executed, but in the chaos of battle they were never carried out.

As Henry broke away from the main action, Richard and his bodyguard came hurtling down Ambion Hill towards them. The King drove his lance clean through Sir William Brandon, Henry's standard bearer, and then, drawing his sword, started to hack a path through to Henry himself. At this point Stanley made up his mind and led his soldiers to the Tudors' rescue. Richard was unhorsed but returned to the fray, fighting until his armour was red with blood. Finally the King was cut down, and his coronet was placed on the head of Henry Tudor, first in a mighty dynasty. Richard's naked body, covered with blood and filth, was put on public display for two days in Newark.
LOCATION: 2 MILES SOUTH OF MARKET BOSWORTH OFF A447

The King drove his lance clean through Sir William Brandon, Henry's standard bearer, and then, drawing his sword, started to hack a path through to Henry himself.

Warwick – a fairytale castle with a particularly nasty dungeon

Warwick WARWICKSHIRE

The dungeons of Warwick Castle The ghosts of a grim past haunt the forbidding walls and towers of Warwick Castle. Built for the Beauchamp family in the 14th century, it was immediately put to use housing French prisoners taken in the Battle of Poitiers, during the Hundred Years' War. The captives were thrown into dungeons in the brand new Caesar's Tower, with some left to die forgotten in a small cell appropriately known as the oubliette. The Beauchamps' seat had all the latest mod cons, including a parapet at the top of the tower designed for hurling stones, quicklime and boiling pitch on its attackers. The Caesar's Tower dungeon now houses a horrifying display of torture instruments. Among the castle's other treasures is the death-mask of Oliver Cromwell.

Another dungeon is tucked away under the town's county jail, where up to 50 prisoners could be shackled to a chain in a 21ft (6m)-square space, with only a narrow grating for air and light.

Acquitted but a pariah During the Warwick Assizes of 1817 a bricklayer called Abraham Thornton was indicted for the murder of Mary Ashford. He had talked to her during a May dance and offered to walk her home, after boasting to a friend that he would 'have connection with her though it cost me my life'. The next day, two sets of

footprints were discovered leading through a field to a spot where there were signs of a struggle and a pool of coagulated blood. From this spot a man's footprints and a trail of blood led to the edge of a pit, where some of the victim's clothes were found; her body was discovered lying at the bottom. Thornton's shoes were found to match the footprints, but he denied murder and to general surprise was acquitted. The victim's neighbours appealed to the Secretary of State and Thornton was taken into custody once more. When appeal proceedings began for a new trial, Thornton claimed the ancient right of 'trial by battle' (see right), but had no need of it: the judges dismissed his case. Shunned by the community, he tried to emigrate to America, but was turned away by the ship's company, who refused to carry a harbinger of bad luck.
LOCATION: 9 MILES SOUTH-WEST OF COVENTRY OFF A46

Whitley near Coventry WEST MIDLANDS
A desperate murder Young Mary Ann Higgins had the bad luck to take up with George Clarke, a ruthless and violent bully described in court as 'a most repulsive specimen'. Clarke beat her frequently and, when she became pregnant, refused to marry her unless she could come up with a dowry. Indeed, he threatened to leave her altogether, creating a desperate situation for a young mother-to-be in the 1830s. Mary pleaded with her uncle to give her the means and the blessing for marriage, but he turned her down, no doubt feeling that she was better off without the brute. At the end of her wits, Mary put two teaspoons of arsenic into her uncle's pea soup.

It took a jury only seven minutes to acquit Clarke and convict his lover of the murder. Mary Ann Higgins was taken to the scaffold in a cart, sitting on her own coffin. She was left hanging from the gallows for over an hour, during which time about 20 women were allowed to come forward and rub their necks with her hand, a supposed remedy for various ailments. Meanwhile George Clarke had been set upon by a mob and only just escaped; having fled to Rugby he was recognised and chased out of town and out of history.
LOCATION: SOUTHERN OUTSKIRTS OF COVENTRY OFF A444/A4082

TRIAL BY BATTLE

According to the archaic tradition of 'trial by battle', judges could fix a place and time for a hand-to-hand fight to decide the guilt or innocence of the accused.

On the appointed day, the judges would attend in their finery to watch the defendant throw down his glove and his accuser pick up the challenge. After taking oaths on the Bible, both would then get down to the rough stuff and carry on 'till the stars appeared in the evening'. If the defendant was beaten and unable to go on, he would be deemed guilty and hanged, the theory being that 'as well as if he were killed in battle, Providence was deemed to have determined in favour of the truth'. But if he killed his opponent or kept going from sunrise to dusk, he was let off. The accuser who didn't fancy his chances could appeal against trial by battle on the grounds that the defendant was under 14 or over 60, a woman, a priest, a peer, or a citizen of London – whose 'peaceful habits' apparently made them unfit to fight.

Wigmore HEREFORDSHIRE

Wigmore Castle Now ruined and overgrown, Wigmore Castle was once a formidable fortress guarding the Welsh Marches and occupied by Roger Mortimer, 1st Earl of March and lover of Queen Isabella. The ambitious Mortimer had his eye on the crown and played a part in the murder of Edward II, who had a red-hot poker thrust into his bowels. Mortimer's bid for power failed, and he was executed on Edward III's orders in 1330. Within a couple of hundred years the castle was described as 'utterly decayed', but continued to be used as a prison.

Archaeologists have excavated masses of evidence giving a vivid idea of life in a medieval castle. An inventory of its contents in 1322 included catapults for throwing stones or heavy metal arrows; crossbows ranging from simple wooden affairs to the deluxe variety complete with stirrup irons for winding up the bows; helmets 'for jousts and for real war'; lances, spears, suits of armour and coats of mail; an Irish axe and 'Saracenic bows and arrows'.

LOCATION: 8 MILES NORTH-WEST OF LEOMINSTER ON A4110

Willenhall (West Walsall) WEST MIDLANDS

Cholera epidemic During the Victorian era Willenhall was the centre of a thriving lock-making industry, profiting from the spread of urban life in the 19th century. But there was always a dark side to the commercial success of Victorian towns and cities, and the gardens known as Doctor's Piece bear testament to one of the common tragedies of the age.

Under the gardens is a mass grave of some 300 victims of cholera, a disease that swept like wildfire through the cramped streets and crowded slums of the day. Cholera is an infection of the intestine, usually caught by drinking infected water. At this time many households shared the use of one water-pump, which often drew its supplies from

The Commandery at Worcester, the Royalist headquarters for the disastrous battle of 1651

The King's flight at Worcester

the same rivers that carried away human sewage. The 300 souls lying under Doctor's Piece died from severe bouts of the disease with watery diarrhoea, vomiting and leg cramps. The sudden and rapid loss of body fluids would have caused dehydration, shock and death, possibly within a few hours of contracting the disease.

LOCATION: 8 MILES NORTH OF BIRMINGHAM OFF M6

Woodford NORTHAMPTONSHIRE

Unsolved mystery Woodford's Norman church has a strange item among its treasures: a preserved heart, found in the recess of one of the columns in 1860. The story behind this bizarre discovery is yet to be unravelled.

LOCATION: 2 MILES SOUTH-WEST OF THRAPSTON OFF A14

Worcester WORCESTERSHIRE

Carnage On 3 September 1651, Charles II stood in the tower of Worcester Cathedral and watched his troops being mauled by Oliver Cromwell's army. Cromwell's 'Essex trained bands' bore down on their enemies right into the cannon's mouth, then turned the guns round and fired on the city defences. By the end of the battle 6,000 men had been slain, and untold numbers wounded. Cromwell had secured his position and put back the Royalist cause for the best part of another decade.

Last burning for petty treason In the early 18th century Worcester was the scene of a private marriage between a 15-year-old servant and the son of her employer, a Warwickshire farmer. Within a few short years, young Catherine Hayes was destined to make history as the last woman in Britain to be burned at the stake for petty treason – that is, for killing her husband.

The relationship was tempestuous, involving many fights about money, and Catherine made frequent complaints about Hayes to her friends, remarking that it would be 'no more sin to murder him than to kill a dog'. During a heavy drinking session, she persuaded a Worcestershire man, Thomas Wood, and her son by another lover, Billings, to help her murder Hayes and share out his legacy of £1,500. The three issued a bet: that Hayes could not drink half-a-dozen bottles of mountain wine without getting tipsy. Hayes promptly drank himself senseless and, while he was lying unconscious on his bed, Billings and Wood bludgeoned him to death. The killers then sawed off his head with a knife, while Catherine held a bucket to catch the blood, and threw it into the river. The rest of Hayes' body was cut up and thrown into a pond. But the head was recovered and stuck on a pole, where it was recognised by a passer-by. Billings was hanged, and Wood died of fever in prison. Catherine Hayes was executed on 9 May 1726, taking three hours to be reduced to ashes.

LOCATION: 24 MILES SOUTH-WEST OF BIRMINGHAM OFF M5

WALES

History and myth are woven inextricably together in this beautiful, rugged country. The legends that were passed on by poets and story-tellers for centuries before they were finally written down probably contain an echo of the Iron Age, when Celts brought their vivid, complex and sometimes bloody way of life to the British Isles. Celtic trophies of war and slavery – elaborately worked swords, shields and shackles – have been dredged from the lake known as Llyn Cerrig Bach, on Anglesey, where they were probably thrown as gifts to the gods. This offshore island was the most sacred site of the druidic élite; according to the invading Romans, human sacrifices were common practice here. When conquering legionaries made it to Anglesey in AD 78 they slaughtered the druids and flattened their holy oak groves.

The coast at Rhossili, scene of a tragic shipwreck in 1887

From the 5th century the Welsh princes were kept busy fighting not only each other but the Picts, the Saxons and, later, the Vikings, who started plundering the coast in the late 8th century. While the Norsemen threatened the seaward boundaries, a good deal of territorial elbowing was going on inland. Offa, king of the formidable Mercian power in Central England, set his limits by digging a 167-mile (269km) ditch – which still more or less marks the border between England and Wales. Offa's Dyke, part defence system, part customs barrier, was a potent symbol of the enmity that would make the borderlands to each side of it a battleground for centuries to come.

War and magic

One of the most important sources of early medieval Welsh history is the collection of stories known as the *Mabinogion*, an account of the trials and adventures of various branches of Welsh and Irish royal families and other warring heroes such as King Arthur. Although wrapped in mystery and magic, these tales are believed to contain a thread of reality, and are always given precise geographical settings. They tell of a harsh and often violent world, divided into principalities which settled their disputes by the sword.

Storming Normans

William the Conqueror added fuel to the borderland fire by rewarding some of his followers with land and power along the Welsh Marches (borders). From here, the Marcher lords made repeated incursions into Wales, stamping their authority with a series of motte-and-bailey castles.

In the 13th century the last native prince of Wales, Llywelyn ap Gruffudd, united the country's territories by throwing his brothers – who were entitled to a share of the land – into prison. A disagreement between Llywelyn and Edward I over the payment of feudal dues led to an all-out English invasion and eventual conquest in 1284. Llywelyn was hunted down and killed (see Cilmeri, page 131), and Edward built an 'iron ring' of state-of-the-art fortresses to control this unruly land.

Dreams and dynasties

Early in the 15th century a minor noble, Owain Glyndwr, took his neighbour, Lord Grey of Rhuthun, to court and lost. Fuming at the English establishment, Glyndwr took matters into his own hands and stirred up a popular revolt, demanding Welsh independence. For over ten years rebel and royal troops fought battles, razed towns and massacred prisoners. Despite making powerful allies and calling his own parliament, Glyndwr was ultimately defeated, and went to ground in 1413, never to be seen again.

The dream of independence was kept alive by poets and propagandists throughout the Wars of the Roses, and when a Lancastrian claimant of Welsh descent, Henry Tudor, appeared on the scene, the Welsh rallied to his cause. Tudor took the throne as Henry VII and he and his successor, Henry VIII, set about unifying the Welsh and English administrative systems.

King Coal and beyond

The Industrial Revolution transformed parts of Wales. The country's mineral deposits had always been a coveted prize, but with new techniques came bigger enterprises, and by the 18th century slate quarries, ironworks and copper mines appeared all over the place.

When the race for coal began, as a fuel for industry, transport and homes, South Wales became a magnet for entrepreneurs, and collieries were set up throughout the valleys running from the Brecon Beacons to the coast. Settlements grew around them, covered in a permanent fog of coal dust and surrounded by black heaps of spoil or slag. Struggling to make a living in appalling conditions, the miners clashed frequently with their employers, and riots were not unknown. Rural life was no idyll, either: in the 19th century, aggrieved farmers vented their fury at the proliferation of road-tolls on the turnpikes and sometimes on the people who manned them.

The landscape was transformed again with the closure of the South Wales coalpits in the 1980s, leaving their communities to an uncertain future. In 1997 Wales took a new political step by voting to establish its own government assembly. Today the nation asserts its modern identity and expectations; but that identity is shaped by a long history – not only of legend and poetry, but of struggle, rebellion and bloodshed.

Abergavenny Castle, scene of a bloody betrayal

Aberdyfi (Aberdovey) GWYNEDD

The bells of Aberdyfi The story of the drowned cities of 'Cantre'r Gwaelod' has passed into Welsh mythology, but harks back to a time when the area now flooded by Cardigan Bay was still land. Its first written version dates from the 13th century, when it was recorded in the *Black Book of Carmarthen*. Details were embellished over the years, but essentially the story remains the same.

It tells of an ancient region, known as a 'hundred', which was made up of 16 thriving cities, ruled by King Gwyddno Caranhir. The area was protected from the sea – which, before the Iron Age, was still rising between Ireland and Wales – by an embankment and a series of sluice gates, operated by a guard called Seithennin. Disaster struck one evening after a raucous party, when Seithennin slumped into a drunken stupor and forgot to close the sluices. During the night the sea crashed in, destroying everything in its path and drowning the inhabitants of all 16 cities.

A romantic footnote to the story claims that you can still hear 'the bells of Aberdyfi' ringing from the deep on still nights; more solid evidence of the true basis of the legend can be seen when the tide is out, and the remains of ancient peatlands and tree trunks are revealed.

LOCATION: 4 MILES SOUTH OF TYWYN ON A493

Abergavenny MONMOUTHSHIRE

Bloody revenge Only a heap of ruins remains of Abergavenny Castle, scene of an infamous betrayal. Norman baron William de Braose had been nursing his wrath since the death of his uncle at the hands of the Welsh. In 1175 he hatched a plan for revenge. Under the pretext of reconciliation, he invited all the local lords to the castle for a Christmas feast. While they were tucking in, de Braose announced that his guests would be required to take an oath before leaving. They were to promise not to bear any bow or other kind of weapon on their travels. In those dangerous days, when every bush might hide a bandit, no self-respecting chieftain could agree to such terms and, as expected, everyone refused. At a word from the gracious host his guards drew their swords and killed the guests where they sat.

Vendetta was the name of the game in 12th-century Wales, and sure enough, eight years later, the sons of William's victims stormed Abergavenny Castle, burning everything in sight. They went on to attack Ranulf Poer, Sheriff of Hereford, as he supervised the building of another Norman castle. It was noted with some admiration that, despite having the veins and arteries of his neck and his windpipe 'separated with a sword', Ranulf managed to give his final confession before dying.

LOCATION: 9 MILES NORTH OF PONTYPOOL ON A40

Beaumaris ISLE OF ANGLESEY

Beaumaris Castle Edward I had Beaumaris Castle built in 1295 as one of his 'iron ring' of fortresses to intimidate the Welsh. Although it never saw much action, the castle is regarded as a near-perfect example of medieval military design, and gives a clear indication of the fate that would have lain in store for those reckless enough to attack it. The seaward gate was protected by 'murder holes' above; beyond these were portcullises, doors and more snipers' windows; and between the inner and outer walls any survivors would be exposed to a hail of crossfire from all sides.

In a later age another bully dispensed his own harsh brand of justice here when Judge Jeffreys set up one of his 'Bloody Assizes' at the courthouse. The jail still has its gruesome punishment cell and treadmill as a reminder of more brutal times.

LOCATION: 4 MILES NORTH-EAST OF MENAI BRIDGE ON A545

Beddgelert GWYNEDD

A faithful servant slain Prince Llywelyn's favourite hound, Gelert, was a gift from his father-in-law, King John. Llywelyn had no hesitation in leaving the faithful dog to guard his one-year-old son while he went hunting. One day, after returning to the castle, the prince found his son's cradle upturned and Gelert covered in blood. The child was nowhere to be found. Assuming that Gelert had turned on the baby and devoured it, Llywelyn drew his sword and ran his beloved hound through the heart. Immediately, he heard the sound of crying from under the cradle, and lifted it to find his child lying unharmed. It was only then that Llywelyn conducted a thorough search, and found the body of a wolf, killed by Gelert as it tried to attack the little boy. The broken-hearted prince buried his dog near the castle walls and had a stone cairn laid on the spot. Visitors still flock to Beddgelert ('Gelert's Grave') to see the dog's burial place, though it is probably only a couple of hundred years old, created to capitalise on the place-name and the ancient tale.

LOCATION: 14 MILES SOUTH OF CAERNARFON ON A4085

Betws DENBIGHSHIRE

Too many ropes Dick Hughes learned the art of petty theft at his home in Betws and soon graduated to a full career in burglary. He was caught twice, first receiving a whipping 'at the cart's tail', then obtaining a pardon having promised to go straight. But Hughes returned to his old ways, and was sentenced to hang in 1709. While he was being taken to the gallows his loving wife approached and asked him who was responsible for buying the rope. On learning that the sheriff saw to such things, she cursed her luck and admitted that she'd already spent tuppence on a rope. Dick reassured her that the money wouldn't go to waste 'for it may serve a second husband'. He was hanged with the state's rope and his body taken for dissection by medical students.

LOCATION: 8 MILES WEST OF LLANGOLLEN OFF A494

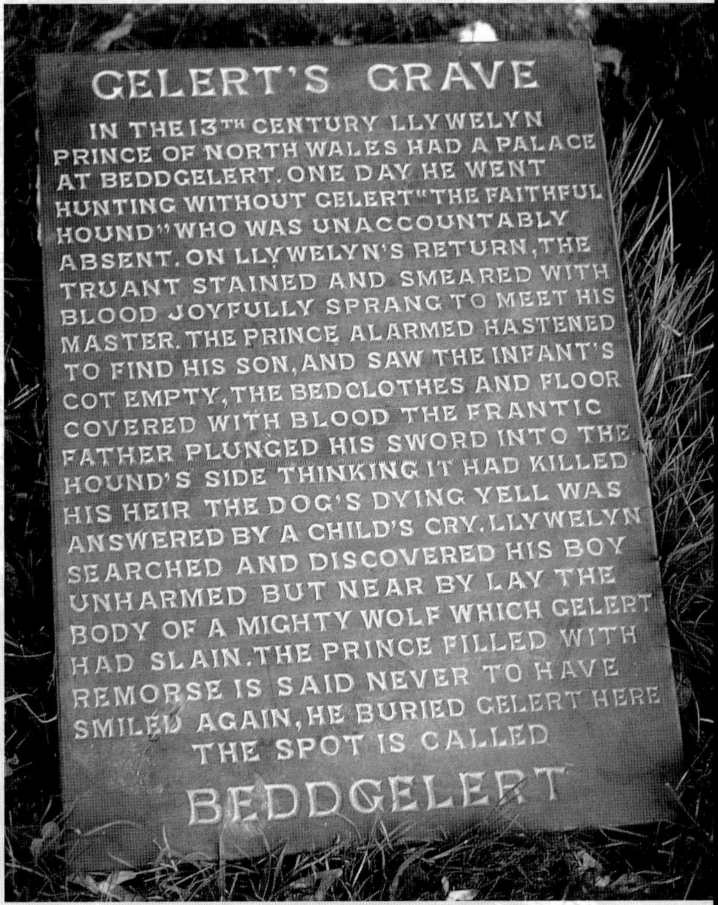

The grave of a wronged and faithful hound

The Big Pit at Blaenafon Torfaen

Blaenafon Torfaen (Blaenavon) GWENT

A vision of Hell The ruins of this ironworking community give little clue to the infernal conditions endured by inhabitants here in the early 18th century. Labourers lived in tiny, damp terraced cottages, backing on to a yard with communal toilets, and a huge chimney stack that belched out waste material from the furnaces.

Dominating the whole scene was a dramatic water balance tower, which contained a hydraulic lift to hoist materials to the top of a sheer cliff. Young girls – the lightest and most agile workers – had to climb to the highest point to empty the trucks. Exposed to the elements and balanced precariously on a narrow platform, many fell to their deaths.

Sidney Gilchrist Thomas made his name at the ironworks by devising a way of making iron ore into steel. But his hazardous experiments with the toxic ores cost him his health and, eventually, his life.

LOCATION: 5 MILES NORTH OF PONTYPOOL ON A4043

Caerleon NEWPORT

Nemesis invoked The Roman army established a legionary fortress on the Usk estuary in AD 75 and stationed 5,500 soldiers here. To keep the bored troops occupied, an impressive amphitheatre was added to the complex. Here they could while away the time watching gladiators mutilate and kill each other in a variety of challenging ways. A lead tablet found in the amphitheatre, which was excavated in the 1920s, reads: 'Lady Nemesis, I give thee a cloak and a pair of boots; let him who took them redeem them with his own blood.' The author, presumed to be a gladiator, was evidently promising the goddess of judgement the stolen gear, in return for delivering a hideous death to the thief in the arena.

LOCATION: 3 MILES NORTH-EAST OF NEWPORT ON B4236

Cardiff

The castle Despite its present appearance of Victorian mock-Gothic extravagance, Cardiff Castle has a long and bloody history. Its site was originally occupied by a Roman fort. In the post-Roman era the locals suffered terribly as fights raged between the Welsh and the Saxons, and marauding Vikings raided the coast. The defences were strengthened in the 10th and 11th centuries, and in 1112 the castle was captured by Ifor Bach, chief of Glamorgan, who held the occupants captive until he was paid off. A more gruesome episode involved Henry I's brother Robert, Duke of Normandy, who was blinded and imprisoned for 26 years in a tiny cell at the base of the entrance tower.

A rebel's death In 1306 the castle was taken over by the powerful and loathed Despenser family, who threw rebel Llywelyn Bren into a cell there in 1317, where he 'suffered a traitor's death' before being dragged through the streets. When Welsh rebel leader Owain Glyndwr passed by in 1410 he paused to take revenge for Llywelyn Bren's death, torching the whole area and razing Cardiff's many friaries to the ground.

Parading the severed head of Prince Llywelyn

Pirate son Llanrumney, in Cardiff, was the birthplace in 1635 of Harri Morgan. He was a notoriously bloodthirsty pirate who stormed the city of Porto Bello in Panama, using Catholic nuns and priests as human shields while his crew scaled the walls of the fort.

LOCATION: OFF M4

Carmarthen CARMARTHENSHIRE

Two memorable hangings Sex, death and religion attracted as much curiosity in the 19th century as they do in the age of the tabloid newspaper; when the three were combined in one story, they were irresistable. In 1817 a part-time minister was executed for poisoning his pregnant mistress. Over 10,000 people squeezed into town to watch him hang.

Twelve years later, onlookers at another Carmarthen hanging were treated to an extended spectacle when the cross-beam broke loose and David Evans fell to the ground with the noose still around his neck. Leaping to his feet, he yelled 'I claim my liberty!', but despite the loud support of the crowd, who demanded his release, the unfortunate man was put through the whole process again, and there were no further hitches.

LOCATION: 22 MILES NORTH-WEST OF SWANSEA ON A40

Chirk WREXHAM

Castle of doom Chirk Castle could be considered as being jinxed. Roger Mortimer, who had the place built in the 13th century, started out well enough as the Justice of Wales, but fell from grace and died in the Tower of London in 1326. No fewer than five other owners were executed as traitors, and several others fared equally badly on the battlefield.

The castle has been home since 1595 to the Myddletons, whose coat-of-arms incorporates a red hand, said to recall a dispute between two members of the family over their inheritance. They decided to settle the matter with a race: the first to swim across the castle lake and touch the far shore would win the legacy. But as one competitor was reaching out to the finishing line, his rival's crony sliced off his hand with a sword, and declared his opponent the winner.

LOCATION: 5 MILES NORTH OF OSWESTRY OFF A5

Cilmeri (Cilmery) POWYS

A prince's last stand Llywelyn, the last native prince of Wales, attacked and destroyed Builth Castle in 1260. Twelve years later he returned to whip up support against the English monarchy, but had to flee for his life after the castle's garrison refused to give him shelter from the King's troops. Llywelyn's favourite tactic for fooling his pursuers was to fit his horse with shoes facing the wrong way round. But his blacksmith betrayed him, and Llywelyn was tracked down by Stephen de Francton, who ran him through with his spear. Llywelyn's head was sent as a trophy to Edward I; a stone marks the spot near Cilmeri where he was killed.

LOCATION: 2 MILES WEST OF BUILTH WELLS OFF A483

All versions agree that the nine victims were butchered by Edward's army, who had them hanged, drawn, disembowelled, beheaded and quartered.

Conwy CONWY

Siege of Conwy Castle The magnificent 13th-century castle of Conwy was built by Edward I to subjugate the Welsh. The tables were briefly turned in 1401, during Owain Glyndwr's uprising. On 1 April, only two warders were on duty in the castle when a Welsh carpenter turned up for work. As they let him in, 40 of Glyndwr's soldiers burst through the gates, killed the guards and prepared to sit out a long siege. After three months, supplies were running low, and the impasse was broken by desperate means. In one version, nine heroic warriors surrendering their lives to the English in return for their companions' release. Another claims that they were ambushed by their comrades during the night, and offered up to the enemy. All versions agree that the nine victims were butchered by Edward's army, who had them hanged, drawn, disembowelled, beheaded and quartered.

LOCATION: 3 MILES SOUTH OF LLANDUDNO OFF A55

Cydweli (Kidwelly) CARMARTHENSHIRE

Complex loves An early tale of star-crossed lovers is associated with Cydweli Castle, home in the 12th century of Sir Elidyr Ddu. The love lives of Sir Elidyr's family was as complex as any modern soap opera. His daughter, Nest, and niece, Gwladus, both loved the same man – a Norman knight, Gwallter Mansel. Despite her father's disapproval, Nest was already conducting a passionate affair with her hero. Meanwhile her brother, Gruffudd, lusted after Gwladus, as did Gwladus's half-brother, Meurig. Plagued with jealousy, Gruffudd, Meurig and Glwadus concocted a murderous plot. As Gwallter arrived for his nightly tryst with Nest, they pounced, stabbed him through the heart and threw him into the river. Nest dived from a bridge to try and save him, but drowned in the waters of the Gwendraeth Fach.

Gruffudd and Meurig fled; in time, Meurig returned home. Fearing loose talk, Gwladus had him locked in a tower, but her dying prisoner managed to confess all to a priest who was

delivering the last rites. Gwladus, aware that the game was up, leapt from the tower to her death.
LOCATION: 7 MILES NORTH-WEST OF LLANELLI OFF A484

Deganwy CONWY

The yellow beast In the 6th century Deganwy was the seat of Maelgwn, Prince of Gwynedd, whose cruelty and depravity earned him the hatred of his people. When the Yellow Death, a deadly infection, swept through Europe in AD 547, Maelgwn was gripped with terror: the famous poet Taliesin had already predicted his death at the hands of a fearsome yellow beast. The prince shut himself and a few servants into his castle, but was tormented by voices calling his name. Eventually he couldn't resist looking through a spyhole in the gate, and with a scream of 'the yellow beast!' fell writhing to the floor, where he was left to die.

Noble sacrifice A later castle was built by the Normans at Deganwy and occupied by Robert, Earl of Rhuddlan. He met a brave end in 1088 when he rode out to the beach with only one other knight to challenge a band of raiders who had carried off some local hostages and were about to set sail. Predictably, both were shot to pieces by a hail of arrows from the raiders' boats.
LOCATION: 2 MILES SOUTH OF LLANDUDNO ON A546

Devil's Bridge CEREDIGION

Outside the law Devil's Bridge is a popular beauty spot, visited for the dramatic waterfall and three successive bridges across the steep, wooded gorge. In the 15th century this was a wild and remote area, with plenty of hiding places for those living outside the law. One notorious family of delinquents was known as the 'plant de Bat', or children of Bartholomew. Two brothers ensconced themselves in a cave near Devil's Bridge, accessible only through a hole in the roof. They lived by robbing passers-by, lying low while their sister brought them food. In one particularly savage attack the 'plant de Bat' killed a local man and left his gashed body near the bridge. This was the final straw: a posse of the victim's friends set out with their hunting dogs and traced the murderers to their cave, where they were found with their sister, surrounded by loot. The two boys were hanged for their crimes, and their sister burned at the stake.

A robber tricked Three centuries later, this was still an inhospitable part of the world. Many travellers found safety in numbers by teaming up with the cattle drovers who walked their livestock across country to the English markets. A sailor who jumped ship and headed for London with the drovers described their way of dealing with hold-ups. When a robber surprised them near Devil's Bridge, they handed over a jingling bag of 'coins' which were actually ox-shoes. As he rode away they fired at his head with a catapult and killed him.
LOCATION: 10 MILES EAST OF ABERYSTWYTH ON A4120

Dinas Emrys GWYNEDD

Ominous omen This Iron Age hillfort is mentioned in a 9th-century history of Britain as the site where British leader Gwrtheyrn (Vortigern) tried to build a castle. Gwrtheyrn had hired Saxon mercenaries to help him fight the Picts, and was reviled for allowing them a foothold on the island. According to chronicler Nennius, the building work was mysteriously taken apart every night. Druids advised Gwrtheyrn to sacrifice a virgin's son and sprinkle his blood on the foundations. The boy was found, but managed to distract the chief with a story of a white, Saxon dragon and a red, Welsh dragon asleep in a subterranean lake under the site. Gwrtheyrn had the lake drained and the two dragons engaged in a vicious battle, which the Saxon dragon lost. Dismayed by the omen, Gwrtheyrn fled. As for the boy, he turned out to be Emrys Wledig, the Welsh hero sometimes associated with Merlin himself.
LOCATION: 1 MILE NORTH-EAST OF BEDDGELERT OFF A498

The twin-towered gateway of Harlech Castle

Dylife POWYS

Thrown into a lead pit A skull and the iron frame of a gibbet were unearthed near Dylife in 1938, the only remaining evidence of one of Wales's most shocking murder cases. The skull belonged to a blacksmith, John Jones, who left Cardigan to find work at the lead mines in Dylife in the 18th century. His wife, Catherine, and their two children followed on, but by the time they arrived Jones was already embroiled with a local maid.

On 23 October 1719, he and his wife had a terrible argument and that afternoon Jones dumped Catherine and the children into a nearby lead pit, where they lay undiscovered until the following January. A rumour went around that one of the children had eaten its mother's breast before dying. Jones admitted his guilt, blaming 'some other woman and the Devil'. He was hanged and gibbeted near the pit where his family had perished.

LOCATION: 8 MILES NORTH-WEST OF LLANIDLOES OFF B4518

Fishguard PEMBROKESHIRE

French defeat The 1790s were a nervous time for the British. The French Revolution was causing waves all over Europe and beyond, and the authorities lived in fear of its radical ideas and of actual invasion. In 1797 some of their worst fears were realised when a small French fleet landed at Carreg Wastad Point near Fishguard. It was hardly an overwhelming force: the party consisted mostly of conscripted criminals, who seemed more intent on getting drunk than on overthrowing the government. During their brief stay they did cause considerable havoc, however. Some broke into a farmhouse and shot a grandfather clock whose ticking pendulum sounded in the heat of the moment like a cocked gun; others raped and shot a serving girl. A few were blasted by the locals' muskets, before the Fishguard women decided to sort things out once and for all. It is said that as they approached across the fields, the French mistook their traditional red cloaks and black stovepipe hats for British redcoats, and gave themselves up. Jemima Nicholas earned her place in history by personally rounding up 14 of them, armed only with a pitchfork.

LOCATION: 13 MILES NORTH OF HAVERFORDWEST ON A40

Gresford WREXHAM

Mine tragedy On 22 September 1934 locals were alarmed to see miners return from the colliery in total silence: it was immediately clear that some terrible catastrophe had occurred. The Gresford Colliery disaster, in which 266 miners died, was one of the worst of many mining accidents to hit Wales (see opposite). A painting in All Saints' Church commemorates the dead.

LOCATION: 3 MILES NORTH-EAST OF WREXHAM ON B5445

Grosmont MONMOUTHSHIRE

Bloody massacre Only a year after summoning his own parliament, Welsh rebel leader Owain Glyndwr was dealt a massive blow in 1405. The future Henry V routed Glyndwr's followers as they laid siege to 11th-century Grosmont Castle, massacring 800 men and putting paid to Glyndwr's ambitious plans.

LOCATION: 2 MILES SOUTH OF PONTRILAS ON B4347

Harlech GWYNEDD

The siege of Harlech Majestic Harlech Castle was the scene of a last, desperate siege in the Wars of the Roses. In 1461 Yorkist king Edward IV had all but obliterated the opposition, but Harlech, a defiant Lancastrian outpost, held out against a siege that would drag on for seven years. When his rival Jasper Tudor arrived to join forces with the 'Men of Harlech', Edward took drastic action. He sent his troops on a rampage through the local communities, burning, plundering and killing. Harlech finally surrendered and two of its garrison were executed; Tudor lived to fight another day.

LOCATION: 10 MILES NORTH OF BARMOUTH OFF A496

THE MINING LIFE

For thousands of years people have tried to take advantage of the rich mineral deposits that lie under Welsh land. Gold, coal, lead, slate and silver have all lured men and women under the earth in the hope of digging out a fortune.

Between the 18th and 20th centuries the mining industry was at its peak, and the valleys that run from the Brecon Beacon mountains to the southern coast were black with coal dust and slag heaps. For the families who moved there in search of work, it was a harsh and dangerous life. Miners worked long shifts for little reward in cramped, pitch-black passages, under constant threat from lethal gas, explosions, cave-ins and floods.

Accidents were an all-too-frequent occurrence, the worst in the history of British coal being at Senghennydd on 14 October 1913. Hundreds of miners were at work when a series of explosions tore through the mine, shooting one of the cages, their escape route, out of its shaft. The air being drawn underground through fans fuelled the fires, while some sections of the mine were cut off from the air supply by roof falls. By the time rescuers had finished their task, the death toll stood at 439. Some bodies were never recovered.

Even outside the mine, living conditions were dire. In 1893 a government report noted that human and animal excrement floated in the rivers, as well as the blood and guts from abattoirs and all sorts of other rubbish. In 1911 Aberdare, in the Rhondda valley, registered one of the nation's highest mortality rates – 213 children died per 1,000 births, almost twice the national average. Diseases such as cholera, diphtheria and typhus were common. For the miners themselves there were also occupational diseases such as miners' nystagmus, caused by bad light or noxious gases and leading to headaches, dizziness, intolerance of light and spasmodic movement of the eyeballs; or respiratory diseases such as phthisis or silicosis, caused by breathing in coal dust, discharged as 'black spit'. Other afflictions included 'beat knee', a swelling of the joint caused by kneeling in thin seams; or ankylostomlasis, a type of anaemia caused by a parasitic worm that hooks itself to the mucous membrane of the small intestine, causing internal bleeding. The parasite's eggs pass away in the host's faeces and survive in the warm humid atmosphere underground, ready to infect another victim.

In the early days of the mining industry, children as young as six were exposed to all these perils. A succession of parliamentary acts raised the minimum age, but by the 1860s children of 12 were still considered old enough to be sent 'down the pit' – a fact to keep in mind when musing that the younger generation is growing up faster than ever before.

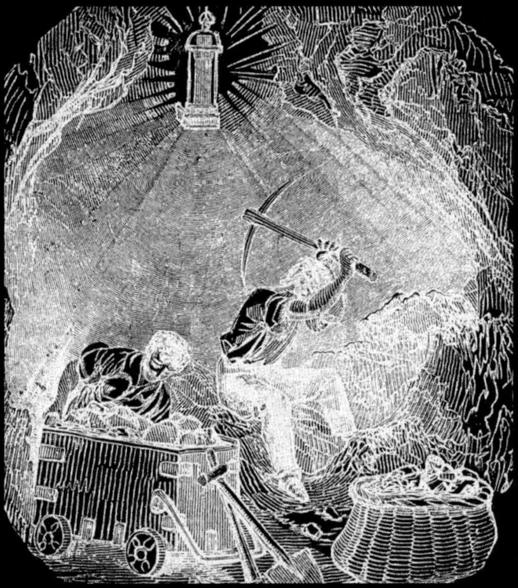

Digging for the 'black gold' was a hazardous occupation for all ages

THE PRISONERS' PESTILENCE

Even now, prison is no picnic, and the jails of past centuries were even grimmer. Being shackled in a small, dank, airless cell while awaiting some gruesome punishment was bad enough, but to top it all county jails were occasionally struck by the so-called 'jail fever', a mysterious and fatal ailment that spread among prisoners and anyone coming into contact with them. In one notorious case at Oxford in 1577, the judges, jurors and witnesses all died within 40 hours (see page 86), while the prisoners themselves were untouched. Various different theories were expounded, including witchcraft and poisonous gas, but the most widely held belief was that the disease had flourished in the filth and stench of the prisons, where, as one observer put it, 'the felons of this kingdom lie worse than dogs or swine, and are kept much more uncleanly than those animals are in kennels and sties'. Jail fever was one of the motives for reforms that introduced better sanitation and regular fumigation of the cells. It is now recognised that it was typhus, a feverish infection spread by lice. During World War I the wretched conditions in the trenches led to its recrudescence – as the dreaded trench fever.

'...the felons of this kingdom lie worse than dogs or swine, and are kept much more uncleanly than those animals are in kennels and sties...'

Hay-on-Wye POWYS

A wife-strangler George Price, a native of Hay-on-Wye, lived a quiet life there as a widow's servant. After seven years he left and married a barmaid, Mary Chambers, whom he presented to his family as the prospective heiress of an army officer's large fortune. The charms of this fantasy soon faded, however, and Price began seeing other women. One night in the 1730s George Price told his wife he had found her a job as a nursery-maid, and drove her into the countryside in a chaise. There he made three attempts to choke her with his whip-lash, finally succeeding when he pulled it so hard that it broke in his hands. Having disfigured and stripped her body, he left it under a gibbet. Price fled to his brother's home a few miles from Hay, but word spread that he had disposed of his wife, and eventually he gave himself up. He was sentenced to hang but died on 22 October 1738, of jail fever (see left).

LOCATION: 15 MILES NORTH-EAST OF BRECON ON B4350

Haverfordwest PEMBROKESHIRE

Black Bart, the pirate Bartholomew Roberts, otherwise known as 'Black Bart', was born in Haverfordwest in about 1682 and at the age of 37 embarked on a career of piracy in the Americas. He fought under a flag that showed him wielding a flaming sword and a dagger and standing on two human skulls; and Bart was equally formidable as a ship's captain. He insisted on the fair division of spoils; anyone trying to pocket too much had his nose and ears slit.

Black Bart's reign of terror came to an end off the coast of Africa, when he was blasted by grapeshot fired from a pursuing British warship.

LOCATION: 20 MILES WEST OF ST CLEARS ON A40

Holywell FLINTSHIRE

A brutal wooing Holywell is named after the curative springs whose origin is associated with Gwenfrewi, or St Winifrid, daughter of the 7th-century holy man St Beuno. Winifrid caught the eye of Prince Caradoc, an old-fashioned romantic who came after his beloved with a sword. Winifrid fled to her uncle for protection. Thoroughly annoyed, Caradoc followed and hacked off her head. The story goes that Holywell's springs bubbled to the surface on the spot where the head fell. St Beuno reunited Winifrid with her head, while Caradoc was swallowed into the earth.

Guard of honour During the 12th century this area was torn by conflict between Welsh and English. Medieval chronicler Gerald of Wales tells of a young Welshman who was killed by the King's army. His faithful greyhound guarded his corpse for eight days, forgoing food to fend off wolves and birds of prey. The English soldiers were so touched that they had the putrefying body retrieved and given a full Christian burial.

LOCATION: 14 MILES NORTH-WEST OF CHESTER OFF A55

Isle of Anglesey

Massacre of the druids Anglesey, or Ynys Môn, was once the main stronghold of Celtic druids, where, according to Roman invaders, human sacrifices were a normal part of the routine (see right). The first legionaries to reach the Menai Straits were terrified by the sight of long-robed druids waving torches from the opposite shore. Once the Romans had summoned up the courage to cross to the island, they conducted a wholesale massacre of this religious elite.

Wrecking Countless ships have foundered on Anglesey's treacherous shores, and the looting of shipwrecks was a well-established way of earning some extra cash. The law regarded personal theft as a crime and wrecks as a public domain, so the more unscrupulous made sure nobody survived to claim their goods. In 1774 wreckers used 'false' lights to lure the *Charming Jenny* on to the coast of Anglesey. Only the captain and his wife survived, and got ashore with 170 guineas between them. While they lay exhausted on the beach, the wreckers descended, dragged the captain away and cut the buckles from his shoes and his clothes from his body. When he staggered back to his wife he found her half naked and dead; the wreckers, meanwhile, had vanished into the night.

LOCATION: OFF NORTH-WEST COAST ALONG A5

SACRED SACRIFICE

Roman tales of druidic sacrifice may have been exaggerated to justify the destruction of this most powerful Celtic group. Early Christian propaganda also spread nasty rumours, particularly about the 'triple sacrifice', in which victims were drowned, stoned and speared all at the same time. But excavations suggest that sacrifices did take place, possibly as a way of communicating with the gods. The chosen ones were given herbs to induce hallucination before being bludgeoned, throttled and thrown into bogs, the gateways to a mysterious nether world.

Human sacrifice: druidic truth or Roman propaganda?

Knighton POWYS

The perils of Offa's Dyke Knighton is a good base for walks along Offa's Dyke, now a popular route for hikers, with wide views of the lovely borderland countryside. In the past, the borders were a perilous situation for any town, as is evident in the remains of Knighton's two Norman castles. As far back as the Iron Age the area was a hotbed of inter-tribal disputes. In the 8th century King Offa of Mercia marked the frontier of his kingdom with ditches and barricades, and after the Norman conquest there were frequent vicious skirmishes between the Norman Marcher (borderland) lords and their Welsh neighbours. As late as the 15th and 16th centuries, the dyke marked the point of no return for residents on either side. It was the custom for any Englishman found wandering to the west of the border to be seized and hanged; as for Welshmen venturing too far to the east, they came off relatively lightly: if caught, they had their ears sliced off.

LOCATION: 17 MILES NORTH-EAST OF LLANDRINDOD WELLS OFF A488

Llanddeusant ISLE OF ANGLESEY

The tale of a broken heart Fantasy and history are inextricably entwined in Welsh folklore. The ancient stories known as the *Mabinogion* give an outline of real historical events, with a heavy dose of poetic licence. One of the best known is the story of Bran, King of the Britons, and his sister, Branwen. A marriage had been arranged between Branwen and King Matholwch of Ireland, which was celebrated with a lavish feast. The British king's nephew, Efnisien, a man of superhuman strength, opposed the alliance, and made his feelings known by mutilating the Irish contingent's horses during the ceremony, slicing off their ears, lips, tails and eyelids. Matholwch immediately pulled out of the deal, but was won round again when Bran presented him with a magic cauldron capable of reviving the dead.

Branwen was duly taken to Ireland, where she gave birth to the King's son, but Efnisien's atrocities had not been forgotten, and she was beaten and abused. When the Welsh heard of this they sailed to Ireland, spoiling for a fight. Now it was Matholwch who sued for peace, inviting Bran and his party to the great hall to negotiate. Hanging on the pillars around the vast room were large, bulky sacks; when Efnisien pointed them out he was told that they contained meal. Feeling the contents, he realised that each sack actually contained an armed warrior, ready to ambush the Welsh. One by one, he moved round the hall and squeezed their heads through the sacks until they were a mess of pulped brain and bone. His finishing touch was to seize Matholwch and Branwen's infant son and hurl him into the fire. All hell broke loose. The armies fell on each other, but as quickly as the Irish were killed, they were piled into the magic cauldron and brought back to life. Seeing the Welsh cut to pieces, Efnisien finally had a twinge of conscience. He flung himself into the cauldron, stretched to the limits of his strength and cracked it in two, bursting his own heart in the process. It was too late for Bran, though, who with his dying breath ordered that his head be cut off and carried to London, where it was buried on the spot now occupied by the Tower.

Branwen sailed home, and as she arrived at Llanddeusant gave a great cry of grief and died. In 1813 farmers were taking stones from a mound known locally as Branwen's Cairn when they found, buried under the earth, a stone chest. Inside were the ashes and burnt bones of a woman. A single stone now marks the place where Branwen broke her heart.

LOCATION: 5 MILES NORTH-EAST OF HOLYHEAD OFF A5025

Llandeilo CARMARTHENSHIRE

A grisly bequest For hundreds of years, sufferers of the whooping cough would travel to Llandeilo's small church to drink from the restorative stream beside it, scooping the water up with a human skull. The unconventional drinking vessel had once belonged to St Teilo, bishop of

Llandaff, whose dying wish had been that his skull be brought here for this purpose. It was still in use until the beginning of the 20th century.

LOCATION: 14 MILES EAST OF CARMARTHEN ON A40

Llandrindod Wells POWYS

Kill or cure? A saline spring, discovered in 1696, and a stinking sulphur spring, found in 1736, made Llandrindod a fashionable centre during the heyday of the British spas. Visitors drank cups full of the bitter water hoping to cure their gout, an inflammation of the joints with hard, yellow lumps just beneath the skin. This painful condition is caused by high levels of uric acid in the blood.

LOCATION: 7 MILES NORTH OF BUILTH WELLS ON A483

Llandybie CARMARTHENSHIRE

Redhand's gang A cave near Llandybie served as a shelter during the 14th century for a gang that terrorised locals. Its leader was Owain Lawgoch, or 'Redhand', who earned his name when an indomitable old woman spotted his arm reaching through her larder window to snatch food, and hewed at it with her carving knife until the hand was severed. After enduring years of thuggery, the people of Llandybie banded together to deal with their persecutors. When the gang had gathered in its cave, they rushed towards it, some firing arrows into the darkness while others piled boulders against the entrance. There was no way of shifting the rocks, and after months had gone by it was assumed that the outlaws had starved to death.

In 1813 workers in a new limestone quarry discovered the bones of several men in the recesses of the cave. But some said the gang itself had escaped through a secret passage, and that the walled-in victims were actually innocent hostages, left to a slow and dreadful death.

LOCATION: 9 MILES EAST OF CARMARTHEN ON A483

Llanefydd CONWY

Woman of substance Katheryn Tudur (1534–91) was a survivor, who saw off four husbands, had a large brood of children and became one of the richest women in Wales. She lived at the mansion of Berain in Llanefydd, where she was rumoured to have got up to all kinds of mischief. One story was that she attacked her second husband, Sir Richard Clough, in a violent frenzy, spattering his blood over the wall of the bedroom. Others alleged that she had murdered seven or eight lovers by pouring molten lead down their ears, and that the evidence was buried in the orchard, if anyone dared look for it.

LOCATION: 5 MILES SOUTH OF RHYL OFF B5382

Others alleged that she had murdered seven or eight lovers by pouring molten lead down their ears, and that the evidence was buried in the orchard, if anyone dared look for it...

HIGHWAY ROBBERY

There's no shortage of popular highwaymen in folk history. Romantic heroes who charmed the ladies and spared the passengers' lives may have existed here and there, but generally the masked robber armed to his teeth was someone to avoid.

From the 17th century, hand-guns became available and the average highwayman prepared himself for a night's work with six or seven pistols. Far from living up to their reputed chivalry, some robbers singled out lone women to rob and rape. But it was the fact that highway robbery targeted the affluent that made it such a harshly punished crime. Hanging in chains was a common penalty; usually the victim was executed first, but in some cases he was suspended alive, and left to starve to death.

The 'gentleman highwayman' became the stuff of popular legend

Llanfabon RHONDDA

The Devil's instructions Edward Morgan was hanged in chains at Glamorgan on 6 April 1757, for a hideous multiple murder. He had been spending the Christmas holiday with his cousin, Rees Morgan, at Llanfabon, and after a day of festivities retired to the bed that he was sharing with the apprentice. During the night Morgan heard the Devil instructing him to kill the occupants of the house. He began his task by attacking the apprentice, who managed to get away and hide. Undeterred, Morgan armed himself with a knife, even taking time to sharpen it on a grinding stone. He then crept into his cousin's room and cut first his throat and then his wife's. His final victim was the couple's daughter, who was asleep in the next bed. Before fleeing he set the house and its outhouses on fire to cover his tracks, but the apprentice survived to tell the grisly tale, and Morgan eventually made a full confession.

LOCATION: 3 MILES NORTH-EAST OF PONTYPRIDD OFF A4054

Llantrisant RHONDDA

Home burial Dr William Price, physician and self-proclaimed arch-druid, led an eventful life. In his youth he had to escape to France after playing a leading role in the Chartist riots. By the time he was in his 80s Dr Price was happily settled in Llantrisant with his 30-something lover, Gwenllïan Llywelyn. The neighbours were used to his eccentric ways: his long, white beard and robes, and a habit of practising moonlit rites wearing a dead fox on his head went largely unremarked.

But one night in January 1884 they were puzzled to see the old man chanting over a home-made funeral pyre. As a crowd gathered, it became apparent that a child's half-cremated body was lying on the heap. The body was pulled from the flames and Price was taken into custody, suspected of murder. A tragic story unfolded: the child was Price and Llywelyn's son, Iesu, who had died a natural death; Price had been conducting his own choice of funeral rites. Unfortunately, cremation was then illegal, and the doctor was put on trial, but his eloquent self-defence led to an acquittal, and subsequently to the acceptance of the practice of cremating bodies. The arch-druid had two more children with Gwenllïan before his death at the ripe old age of 93.

LOCATION: 4 MILES SOUTH OF PONTYPRIDD ON B4595

Llanwynno RHONDDA

Morgan the runner Llanwynno's most famous son was Gruffudd Morgan, known as Guto Nyth Brân after the farm where he grew up. Guto was an outstanding and dedicated runner, who chose to sleep on the dungheap in the belief that it gave more strength to his legs. After he had won a race against a man on horseback the challenges came thick and fast, and Guto couldn't turn them down. In 1737 a small fortune was bet on his winning a race from Newport to Bedwas, a distance of about 12 miles. Despite the dirty tricks of his opponents, who sprinkled broken glass on the track to shred his feet, Guto covered the distance in 53 minutes. As he crossed the finishing line, his feet were bleeding, his lungs strained to their limit and his heart swollen with effort. His admirers rushed to congratulate him, slapping him on the back, but Guto's body could take no more. His legs buckled and his outsize heart blew apart. Before he could celebrate his greatest triumph Guto crumpled to the ground, dead at the age of 37.

LOCATION: 5 MILES NORTH-WEST OF PONTYPRIDD ON MINOR ROAD

Llanymddyfri (Llandovery) CARMARTHENSHIRE

Twm Siôn Catti Catti was the Welsh version of Robin Hood, known less for his charity to the poor than for the tricks and disguises he used in the course of his career as thief and highwayman. Born in 1530, Thomas, son of 'Catti' or Catherine Jones, may have been the bastard son of Sir John Wynne, head of a powerful North Wales family. Innumerable ripping yarns have been linked to the 'gentleman thief', most of them celebrating his humour and narrow escapes. But the background to his marriage hints at another side to the outlaw's personality.

Twm robbed a squire and his daughter who lived near Llanymddyfri, and fell for the girl. He bombarded her home with messages but to no effect. Finally, he seemed to give up hope and begged to be allowed one last secret visit to the manor to kiss her hand. The girl agreed, and was ready at the window at midnight, extending her arm to receive his farewell kiss. Quick as a flash, Twm seized her hand and announced that he would take that, at least, whether she liked it or not. To ram home his point he produced his sword and drew the blade across her arm. The sight of blood pouring from the gash convinced the squire's daughter of his affections, and she hastily accepted his proposal. Twm's unusual courtship paid dividends: his scarred bride managed to wangle him a general pardon, and he lived out his days as a magistrate and pillar of respectability.

LOCATION: 17 MILES WEST OF BRECON ON A40

Llyn Idwal near Nant Ffrancon Pass GWYNEDD

Death by drowning High in Snowdonia, below the main precipice of the Glyder Fawr, lies the eerie lake (*llyn*) of Idwal, named after the victim of a cold-blooded murder.

Idwal was the son of Owain, 12th-century Prince of Gwynedd. During a series of wars against the kingdom of Powys, the prince left his child in the care of a distant relative, Nefydd, in the wilds near Capel Curig. Nefydd's own son, Dunawt, was no match for the handsome and talented Idwal, and his jealousy festered as the two grew up together. It reached its terrible climax when he was sent to show his foster brother the route to the secret mountain lake. Dunawt led his trusting companion along the western shore, where sheer, dark cliffs overhang a fissure known as Twll Du (Black Hole), where the lake is at its deepest. Here the treacherous guide pushed Idwal into the water and watched as he drowned.

Prince Owain suspected Nefydd of encouraging his son in the evil deed, but without evidence could do no more than demote the family from baronial status to that of bondsmen. Legend has it that since Idwal's death no bird has ever flown across the black waters of the lake.

LOCATION: SOUTH-EAST OF BETHESDA OFF A5

Llyn Llydaw near Llanberis GWYNEDD

Arthur's last battle At the top of the Llanberis Pass, above the waters of Llyn Llydaw, King Arthur fought his last battle. There are many versions of Arthur's last stand; one has the traitor Mordred arranging a meeting of rival armies to overpower the British warlord. Local legend tells of Arthur leading his followers up the steep valley under Snowdon's central peak, negotiating the craggy slopes with difficulty in the winter mist. When the two forces met the battle was long and desperate. Blades sliced through armour and axes smashed into skulls; the clash and screams of battle rang through the valley from dawn till dusk. By the time darkness fell, Arthur had forced his enemies to the precipice between Snowdon and Lliwedd. Here, at the spot now known as Bwlch y Saethau, or 'Arrows' Pass', an arrow thudded into his heart. Before dying Arthur summoned the strength to plunge his sword into Mordred's brain. The dead king was carried back down to the lake and placed in a boat, which sailed across Llyn Llydaw and into mythology.

LOCATION: 6 MILES SOUTH-EAST OF CAERNARFON ON A4086

Mallwyd GWYNEDD

Thr Red Bandits The Brigands' Inn in Mallwyd recalls a gang that caused havoc in this area in the 15th and 16th centuries. Many of the 'Red Bandits', so-called because of their red hair, were related to each other, and their close-knit group evaded capture for many years, during which time the community lived in dread of their casual violence. As late as the 19th century, some houses still had scythe blades in their chimneys, kept there to protect the household in the event of an attack. In 1554 the High Sheriff of Meirionydd, Baron Lewis Owen, finally rounded up over 80 gang members, and sentenced them to die on Christmas Eve. The mother of one outlaw, whose pleas for mercy had gone unheeded, swore that her other sons would take their revenge and wash their hands in the baron's blood. Nevertheless, the Red Bandits were hanged and buried in a mass grave east of Mallwyd village. A year later, Baron Owen was returning from the assizes at Welshpool when he was ambushed and stabbed to death at a place now called Baron's Gate. Remembering the mother's curse, one of the murderers returned to the scene to smear the victim's blood over his hands. But the bandits' days were numbered; after this incident the authorities had every remaining male member of the family executed.

LOCATION: 10 MILES NORTH-EAST OF MACHYNLLETH ON A470

'all kinds of dreadful sounds' and a 'mountain of dross … with its terrific glare'.

Merthyr Tydfil MERTHYR TYDFIL

Mob violence Tydfil the Martyr, daughter of Chief Brychan, was murdered here by Saxons in the 5th century, hence the town's name. The small settlement that grew around her shrine was transformed in the 18th century, when a series of ironworking enterprises turned it into the world's largest iron-producing town. The flames and scalding fumes of its furnaces made a deep impression on visitors such as George Borrow. The workers' dwellings were, he said, 'of a gloomy horrid Satanic character'; Merthyr had the worst public health record in Britain. Not surprisingly, there were sometimes angry demonstrations. In 1831 a mob took over the town, and a troop of soldiers sent to restore order opened fire. Over two dozen workers and 16 soldiers were killed and hundreds wounded in the ensuing skirmish. Merthyr found a second martyr in Richard Lewis, or Dic Penderyn, who was charged with wounding a soldier and hanged in Cardiff jail. In the 1870s a Welshman living in America confessed to the crime for which Richard had hanged.

LOCATION: 21 MILES NORTH-WEST OF CARDIFF ON A470

Far left: Sweeping mountains above Llyn Idwal

Moelfre ISLE OF ANGLESEY

Shipwreck disaster The *Royal Charter* was one of many ships to be defeated by the rocky shores of Anglesey. Towards the end of its journey from Australia in 1859 it was caught in a fierce storm and smashed to pieces. Gold bullion and £400,000 worth of valuables were washed ashore, but 460 passengers and crew were drowned or pounded to pieces against the lethal rocks.

LOCATION: 6 MILES SOUTH-EAST OF AMLWCH OFF A5025

Mold FLINTSHIRE

The bard's revenge A convoluted chain of events and grievances led to disaster and mass murder at Mold in the 15th century. It began when renowned bard Lewis Glyn Cothi opened a shop in Chester without the mayor's permission, and was unceremoniously kicked out of town. Fuming with indignation, the bard penned a verse heaping insults on Chester, and suggesting that Flintshire chieftain Rheinallt ap Gruffudd ap Bleddyn might fancy a spot of plundering and torching. Rheinallt obliged, but to avoid inconvenience, waited until the mayor of Chester and a crowd of other townspeople were at the Mold fair. To general consternation, Rheinallt and his warriors burst into Mold, attacked the passers by, locked the survivors in the tower and set it on fire and, as a finishing touch, hanged the offending mayor.

LOCATION: 11 MILES NORTH-WEST OF WREXHAM ON A541

Montgomery POWYS

The Robber's Grave In a plot known as the Robber's Grave in Montgomery churchyard lies John Newton, executed in 1821 for a crime which he denied to his last breath. Two years before his death, Newton had been appointed bailiff to a wealthy widow at Oakfield Farm. His success there, and particularly with the widow's daughter, went down none too well with two rivals, Robert Parker and Thomas Pearce. In November 1821, while Newton was in Welshpool, the two committed a robbery and made sure the bailiff got the blame. As he stood on the scaffold with the noose around his neck, John Newton cursed both men, and announced that, as proof of his innocence, no grass would grow on his grave for a hundred years – a prophecy that, by all accounts, held true. As for the conspirators, Pearce turned to drink and was later killed in a quarry explosion, and Parker developed a wasting disease and suffered a lingering decline and death.

LOCATION: 7 MILES SOUTH OF WELSHPOOL ON B4385

Narberth PEMBROKESHIRE

A princess's penance One of the most famous stories of early medieval Wales revolves around the royal family of Dyfed. Prince Pwyll and his wife, Rhiannon, held court at Narberth Castle,

. . .'mixing with human bodies, with a purple c

where their first son was born. As the mother and new-born child slept, six ladies-in-waiting kept watch over them in the chamber. One night all six women fell asleep. To their horror, when they woke the child had vanished. Knowing that they would be savagely punished for their negligence, they concocted a plan. One of the women snatched a pup from a hound's litter in the next room, killed it and laid its bones on the lap of the sleeping princess. The others smeared its blood over her clothes and hair. Then they raised the alarm, claiming that Rhiannon had used witchcraft to paralyse them while she ate her own child. Despite her protests, Rhiannon was ostracised, and sentenced to sit at the castle gate, telling her story to visitors before carrying them to the castle on her back.

Meanwhile, a new-born baby wrapped in expensive linen was found by a farmer outside his stable at Gwent Is-Coed. He brought the child up as his own son, until rumours of his resemblance to the prince reached the court some years later. Pwyll and Rhiannon were finally reunited with their child, aptly re-named 'Pryderi' ('worries'), and the princess was released from her penance.
LOCATION: 9 MILES NORTH OF TENBY ON A478

Nant Gwrtheyrn near Llithfaen GWYNEDD
Vortigern's leap Britain was a troubled land in the 5th century, abandoned by the Roman army and torn apart by war between the remaining political factions. Gwrtheyrn, or Vortigern, the founder of the Kingdom of Powys, hired Saxon mercenaries to help him fight the Picts and did a deal, giving them a big slice of land. Exploiting the unstable situation, the Saxons brought in thousands more of their countrymen and set about conquering additional territory.

Contemporary accounts describe them driving the British to the coasts, where the sea drove them back again. People were 'mown down together', reports 6th-century historian Gildas; towns were battered to pieces and towers brought crashing into the streets, 'mixing with holy altars and fragments of human bodies, as though they were covered with a purple crust of clotted blood'.

ly altars and fragments of
though they were covered
ist of clotted blood'.

Gwrtheyrn himslef fled, first to Dinas Emrys and then to a clifftop site on the Llyn Peninsula called Nant Gwrtheyrn, or Vortigern's Stream. From a spot still known as Leap Rock he jumped, maybe under duress, to an agonising death among the rocks and lashing waves below.

Entombed bride Tradition has it that the village was cursed by Christian missionaries, who swore that no two lovers would ever marry there. It was fulfilled when a young bride-to-be, Meinir, was observing an old custom by hiding from her fiancé on the way to church, and got hopelessly stuck in a hollow tree-trunk. Many years later the tree was split apart by lightning and her skeleton tumbled out, still in its mouldering bridal dress.
LOCATION: 4 MILES NORTH-EAST OF NEFYN ON B4417

New Radnor POWYS
Silver John The youth of New Radnor were taunted for generations in a song recalling the foul murder of Dr John Lloyd in 1814. Known as Silver John for the buttons on his dandy waistcoat, Dr Lloyd belonged to a family of medics, and had made a name for himself as a bone specialist. He was mugged, according to the ditty, by 'the Radnor boys', who 'pulled out his eyes', and stole the fee-money he was carrying, as well as the famous silver buttons. Silver John's body was eventually found floating under the frozen surface of Lake Hilyn.
LOCATION: 6 MILES NORTH-WEST OF KINGTON OFF A44

Peaceful Newport, where 22 Chartists died in a demonstration of 1839

Newport NEWPORT

Chartist demonstration On a wild, stormy night in November 1839 a vast and angry crowd marched into Newport from the industrial valleys, demanding political reform and a say in government. These were supporters of the Chartist movement, which had unsettled the authorities throughout the country, and awaiting them was a detachment of soldiers and special constables, holed up in the Westgate Hotel. As the demonstrators moved towards the building and threatened to break in, the soldiers opened fire from its windows. In all, 22 people were shot dead. The three leaders of the march were sentenced to be hanged, drawn and quartered, but the penalty was commuted to transportation.
LOCATION: 10 MILES NORTH-EAST OF CARDIFF OFF M4

Painscastle POWYS

Grim reprisal Marcher lord William de Braose had a full schedule. When not busy murdering Welsh chieftains (see page 128), he was fending off attacks by incensed relatives of his many victims. Gwenwynwyn, Prince of Powys, laid siege to de Braose's base at Painscastle, hoping to exact revenge for the treatment of his cousin Trahaiarn, who had been dragged through Brecon at the tail of a horse and then beheaded, at the Norman's instigation. Gwenwynwyn's siege failed, and de Braose lived up to his reputation by arranging a grim reprisal. He summoned southern Welsh and Norman warlords to the castle, where they formed an uneasy alliance before being set loose to massacre the menfolk of Powys.
LOCATION: 5 MILES NORTH-WEST OF HAY-ON-WYE ON B4594

Pembrey CARMARTHENSHIRE

Shipwrecked on sand The village of Pembrey sits on a wedge of land between two estuaries on the Gower Peninsula, a perilous spot for seafarers through the ages. A memorial in its churchyard commemorates the crew and passengers of the French sailing ship *Jeanne Emma*, which ran aground on the sands of the Tywi estuary in 1828.

Pile-up Forty years later, 19 ships set out from the port of Llanelli, having waited for ferocious January gales to die down. Unfortunately the treacherous underwater swell had not abated, and as the convoy left the Burry Estuary it started to drift, and was buffeted against the sands. Water cascaded into the hulls of some vessels, which quickly began to sink; others were driven onto the beach and smashed apart by the waves. As they lost control, some of the ships collided. Darkness fell, and cries for help could be heard from sailors clinging desperately to the hulls. The following morning, wreckage and bodies were discovered strewn along the Llanmadog and Broughton sands. In all, 18 people died in this 19th-century pile-up.
LOCATION: IMMEDIATELY WEST OF BURRY PORT ON A484

WELSH WARRIORS

William de Braose may have had a habit of killing Welshmen, but he had a grudging respect for their fighting skills nonetheless.

In his 12th-century accounts of Welsh archery, he describes the techniques and weapons that would be put to devastating effect on the battlefield at Agincourt 300 years later. The bows used in Wales were, de Braose noted with interest, made of unpolished wild elm, rather than the more usual and more flexible horn, ivory or yew. This provided strength as opposed to elasticity: designed not so much to fire arrows over great distances as to inflict severe wounds at close range, the ideal method for guerrilla-style raids and ambushes. The weapon's success was underlined in his description of an attack on one of his Norman soldiers: the arrow, de Braose claimed, passed right through the unfortunate man's armour, his thigh and his leather saddle, killing his horse beneath him. Another had his hip shot through to the saddle on one side and, turning to escape, suffered the same fate on the other side, ending up stapled to his steed.

The warriors of South Wales excelled in their use of the bow, but in North Wales the lance was the weapon of choice. According to de Braose, the toughest suit of armour available was as butter to a hefty lance hurled by one of these fighting men.

The warriors seen by de Braose would have been dressed in simple linen shirts and trousers, with no more protection than a woollen cloak. Some were said to fight wearing only one shoe, so that they could get a better grip on the rugged Welsh terrain. As well as their lances and bows, they had a varied range of lethal weapons including javelins, axes and heavy clubs with metal heads bristling with spikes. Most Welsh armies were made up of the princes' feudal retainers, led by the *teulu* or family of knights, who fought on horseback wearing helmets and chainmail, and generally used lances and javelins. Many confrontations began with full-out assaults by the spearmen, sending a cloud of javelins into their enemies' ranks, followed by a false retreat, to draw the opposition into a trap. This was when the close-range bowmen came into their own, emerging from hiding places to power their arrows into bodies and faces.

There were few heavy-duty weapons among the fighting forces. When they assaulted a castle, the Welsh showed no inclination to batter the doors down or storm the walls. Instead, they relied on the intimidating presence of their troops to keep the occupants sealed up in their fortress. They made sure no supplies were allowed through, forgoing the satisfaction of sending pointed steel into skulls, and opting instead to starve the enemy slowly to the point of surrender or death.

William de Braose detailed the skills of the Welsh archers in the 12th century

Pembroke PEMBROKESHIRE

Deadly lottery Pembroke was the scene of stubborn resistance during the final years of the Civil War. The town's mayor, John Poyer, was originally a Parliamentarian, but he and his comrades Rowland Laugharne and Colonel Powell were aggrieved at their thin salaries, and fed up with paying their soldiers from their own pockets. The three switched sides, and on 24 May 1648, Cromwell brought his forces into town, demanding that Poyer hand over the castle's keys. Poyer's response was to fire on the army, blasting 16 men. For six weeks he and his companions held fast while Pembroke was battered by Cromwell's troops. Finally, on 11 July, they surrendered. After their conviction for treason, it was announced that only one of the ringleaders would be shot. A child was sent into the prison with three pieces of paper: one blank, and two bearing the words 'Life granted by God'. Poyer drew the blank, and was shot by a firing squad in 1649.

LOCATION: 29 MILES SOUTH-WEST OF CARMARTHEN ON A4075

Pen y Fan near Brecon POWYS

Lost on the moors An obelisk high up on the barren slopes of the Brecon Beacons is a grim reminder of the dangers of these wild mountain moors. It marks the spot where five-year-old Tommy Jones's body was discovered in 1900.

Tommy and his brother had been waiting for their father at an inn in the valley below. Growing impatient, Tommy slipped away and set off to meet his father, who was only a short walk away. In the mountain mists, the boy became disorientated, and wandered further and further away. Despite the desperate efforts of a search party, it was four weeks before Tommy was found. He had died of exposure.

LOCATION: 14 MILES NORTH OF MERTHYR TYDFIL ON A470

Pendine CARMARTHENSHIRE

High-speed death Speed was the obsession of the 1920s, as the sleek new cars and motorcycles were pushed to their limits. The broad, flat sands of Pendine were turned into a motoring speedway as Sir Malcolm Campbell and J Godfrey Parry-Thomas raced against time and broke more than one landspeed record.

Background: Pen y Fan, site of a tragedy in 1900

Right: The memorial to young Tommy Jones

Campbell registered 174.8mph in 1927, but in trying to beat that Parry-Thomas crashed his aero-engined vehicle, *Babs*, and was killed. The car remained where it was for 40 years, but was finally dug out of the dunes and salvaged.
LOCATION: 5 MILES WEST OF LAUGHARNE OFF A4066

Pilleth POWYS

Slaughter of the English Pilleth was the site of a military triumph for Owain Glyndwr, leader of the 15th-century movement for Welsh independence. In 1402 his forces clashed with an army commanded by Edmund Mortimer, Lord of Wigmore, on Bryn Glas Hill. The slaughter that followed ended with the utter devastation of the English troops. Mortimer himself was captured and, seeing how the wind blew, changed sides, even marrying Glyndwr's daughter.
LOCATION: 3 MILES SOUTH-WEST OF KNIGHTON OFF B4356

Plas Newydd ISLE OF ANGLESEY

Waterloo hero The most celebrated occupant of this stately home was the 1st Marquess of Anglesey, Henry William Paget, a dashing chap who had two wives and 18 children. Perhaps his finest hour, though, came during the Battle of Waterloo in 1815, when he was hit by grapeshot, which blew away one of his legs. Looking down, he is said to have remarked to the Duke of Wellington, who was standing near by, 'By God, sir, I've lost my leg!', to which the Duke replied, 'By God, sir, so you have!' Undaunted, the Marquess had himself fitted with the world's first articulated wooden leg, and lived to the robust old age of 86.
LOCATION: 1 MILE SOUTH-WEST OF MENAI BRIDGE ON A4080

Presteigne POWYS

Robbing the famous Welshman Davy Morgan fled to Presteigne after committing a series of robberies in London, during which he broke into the house of Titus Oates, whose fabricated allegations about a 'Popish (Catholic) plot' led to the execution of 35 people. Morgan was clearly well aware of his victim's background; after tying him by the neck and heels, he crammed his mouth with a gag, commenting that if this had been done years before many lives would have been saved.

Morgan continued his trade in Presteigne, stealing the church communion plate and finally breaking into the home of Edward Williams, 'whom he barbarously murdered'. For this Morgan was executed in April 1712 and his body suspended in chains.

LOCATION: 5 MILES SOUTH OF KNIGHTON ON B4355

Pumlumon (Plynlimon) CEREDIGION

Welsh revolt By the summer of 1401 Owain Glyndwr's Welsh revolt was going well. Since raising the banner of independence the previous September, he had burned down several English settlements in the northern borderlands. Now he was on his way south with 120 followers to do more of the same.

A force of 1,500 royal soldiers was sent to stop him, and the two sides met on the bleak uplands of Pumlumon. Armed with bows, billhooks, axes, pikes, spears and swords, the heavily outnumbered Welshmen employed their favourite tactics of ambush and false retreat, and inflicted a terrible death toll, sealing Glyndwr's heroic reputation among the Welsh.

LOCATION: 10 MILES WEST OF LLANIDLOES, NORTH OF A44

Heavily disguised 'Rebecca rioters' attack a turnpike

Rhaeadr (Rhayader) POWYS

Attack on a tollgate Turnpikes were installed on thousands of miles of roads in the 18th and early 19th centuries, imposing tolls to pay for repair and maintenance. It meant a heavy financial burden for the farmers of rural Wales, who relied on transporting their produce to market. In the 1840s groups of protestors dressed in women's clothes started vandalising the tollgates at night. They called themselves 'the daughters of Rebecca', after a Biblical verse: 'the seed of Rebecca shall possess the gates of her enemies'.

On 9 October 1843, about a hundred Rebecca rioters attacked the tollgate at Bodtalog, near Rhaeadr. The elderly woman guarding the tollgate recognised the men, and one attacker pointed his gun into her face and pulled the trigger, blinding her in both eyes. Fearing reprisals, she refused to give evidence against her assailants, and within a

month they had entered Rhaeadr itself, destroying four of the six tollgates.
LOCATION: 11 MILES NORTH OF BUILTH WELLS ON A470

Rhossili SWANSEA

A tragic drowning The wooden ribs of the *Helvetia*, shipwrecked in November 1887, still jut from the sands at Rhossili Bay. The captain and crew managed to abandon the ship in time, but the incident set off a chain of events that ended in tragedy. For weeks, salvagers sailed into the shallow bay waters to collect the vessel's wood for sale. The steamboat *Cambrian* was busy loading timbers when it was tipped sideways by a sudden swell. The coastguard managed to help right the boat, and the crew sailed to safety, but some returned later to collect the anchor, which had broken adrift. As they dragged the anchor on to their own boat it capsized, and five of the six crew were drowned in the icy Atlantic.

In Rhossili's church of St Mary the Virgin, a memorial pays tribute to local man Petty Officer Edgar Evans, one of the explorers to die on Captain Scott's ill-fated Antarctic expedition in 1912.
LOCATION: 5 MILES SOUTH-WEST OF KNELSTON ON B4247

Rhuthun (Ruthin) DENBIGHSHIRE

Huail's Stone A boulder in St Peter's Square, Rhuthun, is known as 'Maen Huail' (Huail's Stone). It is said to mark the spot where Huail, a 6th-century warlord and brother of Gildas the historian, had his head hacked off on the orders of King Arthur, as the penalty for stabbing his own nephew, Gwydre, to death.

An alternative, more fanciful version of the story describes a love triangle made up of Huail, Arthur and one of Arthur's mistresses. After a fight over the woman, Huail wounded the king in the knee but was pardoned on condition he never mention the injury. Arthur then disguised himself as a woman, tricked his rival into commenting on his limp, and seized the opportunity for a spot of decapitation.

Owain's revenge In a later age, Owain Glyndwr took his own revenge here against his arch-enemy Lord Grey, who lived in the castle. Grey had tried to get his hands on Glyndwr's lands, and it was the ensuing court case, and Glyndwr's fury at losing it, that first propelled him into revolt against the Crown.

In 1400 he saw his chance to get even. A fair was in full swing and many English traders had come into Rhuthun. Glyndwr appeared with his henchmen and ran amok, cutting down the screaming fair-goers as they tried to escape and plundering the town before setting the whole place on fire.
LOCATION: 7 MILES SOUTH-EAST OF DENBIGH ON A494

Golden sands at Rhossili

Strata Florida near Pontrhydfendigaid
CEREDIGION

Partial drowning The ruined 12th-century abbey of Strata Florida, set in beautiful and remote mid-Wales countryside, is best known as the site where medieval poet Dafydd ap Gwilym is buried. But there's another intriguing grave near by, where part of a thigh and an entire left leg have been laid to rest. Their owner was Henry Hughes, a cooper, who had his amputated bits interred on 8 June 1756. Their loss was evidently no impediment, as he went on to start a new life in America.

LOCATION: 5 MILES NORTH-EAST OF TREGARON ON B4343

Swansea SWANSEA

Air raids During World War II the industrial ports of South Wales were badly hit by German air-raids. Swansea received the worst pounding; in the course of three February nights in 1941 its centre was pretty well obliterated. The glow from fires raging in the city could be seen from Cardiff, 35 miles away. Well over 11,000 houses suffered bomb damage, and 282 were demolished altogether. Some 387 people were killed, and many hundreds more were injured in the raids.

LOCATION: 35 MILES WEST OF CARDIFF OFF M4

Tonypandy RHONDDA

Miners' riot In 1910, when miners working at Thomas's Cambrian Collieries in the Rhondda refused to accept the meagre pay offered per ton of coal, some were locked out of their pit. This sparked off a strike by all 12,000 employees, and by November of that year there were 30,000 miners on strike. On the night of 7 November a dispute between strikers and strike-breakers escalated into a violent riot on the streets of Tonypandy. Police were drafted in and a fierce battle raged for several hours. Stones were hurled into the police ranks by a huge mob which was in turn driven back by what the *South Wales Daily News* called 'a sanguinary baton charge'. Later in the night the demonstrators marched through Tonypandy smashing windows and looting shops. Elsewhere in the Rhondda other

Stones were hurled i ranks by a huge mo in turn driven back b South Wales Daily New 'a sanguinary baton c

riots broke out: a fire was started at Aberaman, and some of the crowd were shoved by a police charge into the local canal.

The next morning Home Secretary Winston Churchill sent in cavalry and infantry detachments, who patrolled the Rhondda until the following January, at one point threatening locals with fixed bayonets after police had been stoned. By the time the violence subsided, it had claimed one life: Samuel Rays of Tonypandy died after his skull was smashed during the worst of the riots.

LOCATION: 5 MILES NORTH-WEST OF PONTYPRIDD ON A4119

o the police
vhich was
vh at the
called
rge’.

Usk MONMOUTHSHIRE

A martyr hanged Usk had a bad time of it during Owain Glyndwr's independence campaign. On both his visits there the rebel leader torched the town. A couple of centuries later, the country was in a panic about the so-called Popish Plot, largely an invention of informer Titus Oates (see page 150). In 1679 David Lewis, a Catholic priest arrested for saying mass, was examined by Oates and accused of being part of the conspiracy. On 27 August he was taken to Usk to be hanged, drawn and quartered; he was canonized in 1970 and is regarded as the town's own martyr.

LOCATION: 9 MILES NORTH-EAST OF NEWPORT OFF A449

Wrexham WREXHAM

Monastic murder A monastery that once stood at Bangor-is-y-Coed, near Wrexham, was the scene of a terrible atrocity in the 7th century. Ethelfrid, the pagan king of Northumbria, set his warriors loose to massacre the 1,200 monks who lived here. When the last victim had been despatched, they destroyed the monastery itself. Ethelfrid justified the outrage by claiming that those who prayed against him caused as much damage as those who fought against him. A few survivors escaped the bloodletting and found their way to the remote island of Bardsey, still home to monks today.

The Golden Farmer Wrexham was the birthplace in the early 17th century of William Davis, known as the Golden Farmer because of his habit of paying debtors in gold. Davis was, to all appearances, an honest and respectable man, married to the daughter of a rich innkeeper, father of 18 children and devoted to his farming trade. But the Golden Farmer had a secret: for 42 years, without arousing the least suspicion, he made his pocket-money as a highway robber. Despite some dramatic escapades, including a gunfight in which he wounded a postilion, a coachman and two footmen before wrenching the diamond rings from the fingers of the Duchess of Albemarle, Davis maintained his double life. He even robbed an acquaintance of his, a Justice of the Peace living in Bristol, after shooting his horse from under him. As his exploits grew more reckless, Davis found the authorities on his heels, and he was finally caught and hanged in chains in 1689, at the age of 64.

LOCATION: 11 MILES SOUTH-WEST OF CHESTER ON A483

NORTHERN ENGLAND

Two themes dominate the bloodier aspects of history in the north of England. The first is the region's strategic location on the border with Scotland. The second is the impact of the Industrial Revolution, which transformed its landscape and overwhelmed its traditional communities.

The church at Seaham is one of many with a memorial to miners who died in the course of their work.

Until the middle of the 18th century, if the Scots were not invading in their own right, their armies were south of the border doing someone else's bidding, as Royalists, as Jacobites, as Protestants or as defenders of the Catholic faith. In the counties which actually faced the border – Cumbria and Northumberland – the constant cross border raiding by the terrifying steel-bonneted reiver families kept inhabitants on a high state of alert. There are very few grand houses here, for every great home had to be a castle; the strongholds at Naworth, Alnwick, Berwick, Carlisle and Lancaster are still standing today.

Battles of Britain

Some of the most important battles in British history took place on northern soil. Towton, in Yorkshire, where a chapter in the Wars of the Roses came to a bloody conclusion, claimed the lives of over 28,000 men in 1461 – a frightening prospect when you consider England's total population at the time was only a few million. At Flodden in 1513 much of the Scottish ruling class fell to the billhooks wielded by the northern English loyal to Henry VIII. The Civil War of the 17th century brought more bloodshed, especially in Lancashire and Yorkshire; the Parliamentarian siege of York was bitter, the Royalist occupation of Bolton verged on the criminal.

In the 18th century, the northern counties were the last in England to experience full-scale war with formal opposing armies. In 1715 and 1745, forces supporting the Stuarts' claim to the throne invaded from the north and were met by Hanoverian armies in Cumbria and Lancashire. The defeated Jacobites were cruelly punished and the dead bodies of their soldiers hung on northern city gates for many years to come.

The rise of industry

In later centuries, conflict was replaced by industry as the biggest threat to life and limb. The Industrial Revolution transformed the relatively poor, agriculturally backward region into a commercial powerhouse. Its natural resources – coal, iron, water – became the raw ingredients of a new era of unparalleled economic and urban expansion. But to begin with, conditions for the workers in the mills, mines and factories were as primitive as those they had left behind on their meagre farmsteads. The scale of death and injury caused by a millfire, a burst dam, or a colliery explosion, was not on the same level as the horrors of warfare, but because these events are more recent, their circumstances seem less remote, more tragic, to the modern reader, than the battles of old.

Coal mining, in particular, was a dangerous occupation. The handful of accounts illustrated here barely do justice to the sacrifices made by workers all over the north of England in the pursuit of 'black gold'. Stories of children as young as six working underground and being crushed by the wheels of a loaded wagon are not uncommon.

The conflicts now changed from the political fights of kings and rulers to more modern concerns. The wool croppers and shearers of the Yorkshire Pennines rebelled against the introduction of machinery which would take their jobs. Their 'Luddite' protests might end in the murder of mill owners, and their ringleaders hanging on the gallows at York. Over the Pennines in Manchester, political unrest included Irish nationalists, some of whom were the last ever to be hanged in public in this country, in 1868. Ordinary criminals met with equally brutal treatment.

Transport network

The new industries demanded a new transport infrastructure, and without the benefits of modern construction machinery, the canals and railways, which were to enmesh the whole region, had to be built by hand. The death toll amongst the navvies and their families living in insanitary shanty towns was high. Many towns throughout the north have memorials to those killed bringing routes through the mountains and across steep valleys. Later, those same mountains would prove fatal obstacles to wartime flyers, young men searching for their home airfields in the swirling mist and rain.

Visiting these bloody sites today, it is easy to forget how cruel life could be in days gone by. A ride on the beautiful Settle-to-Carlisle railway gives no hint of the loss of life involved in its construction, nor of the death and injury caused to passengers in a time when rail safety was still a hit and miss affair. In lonely Northumberland, you may sense the ghosts of the Border reivers, or of their victims. Many of the mines, mills, city walls and battle sites have vanished under homogenous modern developments and for many tragedies only a solitary stone memorial remains.

Ais Gill CUMBRIA

Settle-to-Carlisle railway In the years before World War I, the Settle-to-Carlisle railway line which traverses the lonely landscape of the Yorkshire Dales, became a notorious black spot for travellers. On Christmas Eve 1910, 12 people were killed when the midnight express from St Pancras smashed into the back of a slow engine emerging from Moorcock tunnel. A gas lighting pipe was shattered and the wreckage engulfed in a terrible fireball. Three years later, at a spot near by, an Edinburgh express train ploughed into the back of the Stranraer sleeper which had stalled on the gradient. Again, there was a fire and 16 passengers were incinerated.

LOCATION: AIS GILL SUMMIT ON SETTLE-TO-CARLISLE RAILWAY LINE, 7 MILES SOUTH OF KIRKBY STEPHEN

Atherton GREATER MANCHESTER

Mining disaster Conditions in the Lancashire pits were amongst the most dangerous in the country, and when things went wrong the results were horrific. Perhaps the worst pit disaster was at the Hulton Colliery, known as Pretoria Pit, between Atherton and Westhoughton. About 900 miners clocked on for the morning shift on 21 December 1910. A roof collapsed, causing a build up of gas, and a faulty lamp was all it took to ignite the deadly mix. In the explosion that followed 344 miners lost their lives.

LOCATION: 5 MILES SOUTH-WEST OF BOLTON

Ashton-in-Makerfield GREATER MANCHESTER

Hand of a martyr St Oswald's Roman Catholic Church in Ashton preserves the hand of Edmund Arrowsmith, a priest from Haydock who was executed at Lancaster for his Catholic faith in 1628. Arrowsmith toured Lancashire on horseback, serving his communicants, before he was betrayed outside the old Blue Anchor Inn at Brindle. At Lancaster the hangman refused to carry out the sentence of the court, so it was left to an army deserter to hang him and draw out his entrails. The quarters were hung on John O'Gaunt's Tower, but some parts were rescued and kept as holy relics.

LOCATION: 5 MILES SOUTH OF WIGAN ON A49

Barley LANCASHIRE

Pendle witches Belief in witchcraft came to a head in north-west England during the reign of James I (1603–25). In 1612, 19 suspected witches were tried at Lancaster, many of them from the Pendle district. Prominent among them was Elizabeth Southerness of Malkin Tower, known as Old Mother Demdike, who was thought to have sold her soul to the devil. Anne Whittle (aka Old Chattox) was one of her acolytes, but their families fell out and they became sworn enemies. There's no doubt that the area suffered under the influence of these devilish clans, but other women too, who were merely independent of spirit, were branded witches. Amongst these was poor Alice Nutter of Rough Lee Hall, who was hanged on the testimony of the Demdikes. Elizabeth Southerness escaped

Berwick has changed hands many times in the border struggles

the fate of her fellow accused and died in her cell of natural causes.

LOCATION: 5 MILES NORTH OF BURNLEY

Berwick-upon-Tweed NORTHUMBERLAND

Rebel town Berwick's prominence in Anglo-Scottish affairs has left a bloody legacy. In 1296, the English King Edward I led an army into the town, his troops ruthlessly killing almost every inhabitant. It is claimed Edward only put a stop to the massacre when he saw a woman being hacked to death as she gave birth. In 1305 the leg of the Scottish rebel leader William Wallace was nailed above the gatehouse leading to the old town bridge. Wallace had been hanged, castrated, disembowelled and beheaded in London.

LOCATION: ON A1167, 64 MILES NORTH OF NEWCASTLE-UPON-TYNE

Bolton GREATER MANCHESTER

Bolton Massacre James, Earl of Derby, spent the last night of his life at the Man and Scythe Inn on Churchgate in Bolton. The next day, 15 October 1651, he was beheaded in front of a small crowd, for what we would call a 'war crime'. Seven years earlier, in May 1644, he had led Royalist troops into the staunchly Puritan town. The defenders were given no quarter and as many as 1,500, it is claimed, were run through with swords as they offered their surrender. Parliamentary justice caught up with the Earl after the Royalist defeat at Worcester. He was tried for treason at Chester and sentenced to death.

LOCATION: 11 MILES NORTH-WEST OF MANCHESTER

Mel Gibson portrayed rebel leader William Wallace in the Holywood version of the story, 'Braveheart'

Burnden Disaster An FA Cup tie turned to tragedy on 9 March 1946, when 67,000 fans crammed into Bolton Wanderers' old Burnden Park stadium to watch the sixth round, second-leg match against Stoke City, whose team included the legendary Stanley Matthews. Just before kick-off, densely packed fans in the north-west corner of the ground began to sway and two crush barriers gave way under the strain. As the crowd surged forwards, many tripped and fell on those in front of them. As the spectators spilled on to the pitch, 33 football fans lay dead on the terrace, asphyxiated by the horrendous pressure of the crush. Over 100 more were seriously injured.

LOCATION: SITE OF FORMER GROUND OFF A666, JUST SOUTH OF TOWN CENTRE

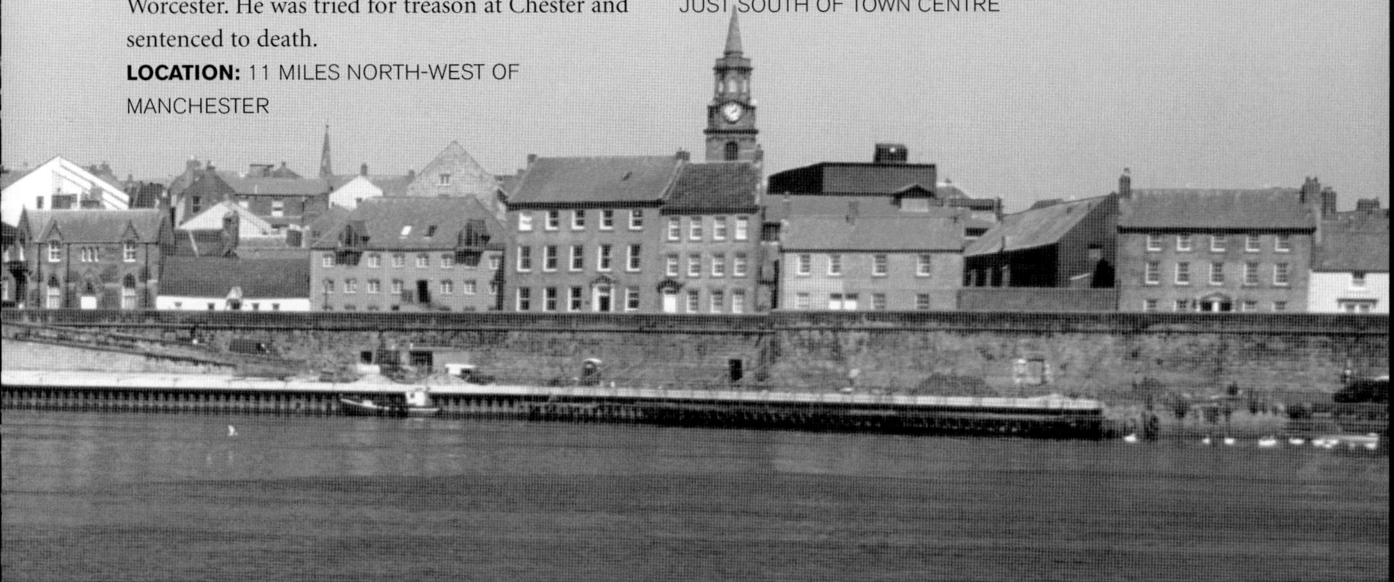

Above: The picturesque Strid has claimed many victims over the centuries

Above right: On the ramparts of Carlisle Castle

Bolton Abbey NORTH YORKSHIRE

The Strid In the woods to the north of the priory, the River Wharfe churns through a rocky cleft known as the Strid. It looks narrow enough to jump across, which is exactly what Romilly, 'the Boy of Egremont,' tried in the 12th century. Sadly his greyhound thought better of the leap and stayed put. The leash dragged Romilly back into the foaming water and he was never seen again. In more recent centuries, this notorious spot has been known to take several days to release the body of any unfortunate victim.

LOCATION: 6 MILES NORTH OF ILKLEY ON B6160

Burnley LANCASHIRE

Jacobite relic Towneley Hall was the home of the defiantly Catholic Towneley family. In 1745 Francis Towneley led the Manchester Regiment for Bonnie Prince Charlie's Jacobite army. He was captured at Carlisle, taken to London and hanged, drawn and quartered. His head was eventually returned to Burnley, where the family kept it in a basket in the drawing room at Towneley Hall for many years. Later it was moved to a cavity in the chapel, but it had to be moved again after it was damaged by nearby waterpipes. In 1947 the disembodied skull was transferred to a family grave in St Peter's Church.

LOCATION: JUST SOUTH OF BURNLEY OFF A671

Carlisle CUMBRIA

Lots for execution It's difficult to imagine the squalor of the cells below Carlisle Castle, when in 1746, after Bonnie Prince Charlie's defeat at Culloden, they were filled with over 400 Jacobite prisoners awaiting trial. Many of the prisoners were Highlanders who did not speak English. The youngest was William Crosby, aged seven, who joined the Manchester Regiment of Francis Towneley (see Burnley) with his father, an Irish weaver. He died sometime in 1746 in the fetid dungeon. The prisoners were asked to draw names from a hat to decide who should be executed and who merely transported or conscripted. In the end 21 were dragged through the city on hurdles to Harraby Hill where they were hanged, drawn and quartered. The rebel's heads were still displayed on the city's gate over 30 years later.

LOCATION: CASTLE OFF A595, ½ MILE FROM CITY CENTRE

Carter Bar NORTHUMBERLAND

Feuding families Feuds between the border families were often bloody and treacherous. During Elizabeth I's reign (1558–1603) Parcy Reed of Troughend was made Keeper of Redesdale and arrested a Crozier from Liddesdale for banditry. The Croziers swore revenge and enlisted the help of the 'fause-hearted' Halls of Girsonfeild, deadly enemies of the Reeds. They took Parcy hunting on the fells and, after a long day in the saddle, rested in the Bateinghope Valley near Carter Bar. But whilst Parcy dozed, the duplicitous Halls disarmed him and crept away. The Croziers were awaiting the signal, and mercilessly fell on the Keeper, hacking off his hands and feet before delivering the deadly blow. Parcy's remains were returned to Troughend in a sack, and his ghost is still seen in the valley.

LOCATION: ON A69, 15 MILES NORTH-WEST OF OTTERBURN

Chipping LANCASHIRE

Jilted Lizzie Young Lizzie Dean worked in the Sun Inn, across the road from St Bartholomew's Church in the 18th century. Hearing wedding bells she joined the happy crowd of onlookers, only to see her fiancé lining up as the groom to marry another woman. In her grief at this betrayal she hanged herself, asking that her body be buried under the pathway to the church door, so that her beloved would have to walk across her grave every time he went to church. The vicar couldn't agree to this and put her in a corner under the yew tree. Denied even her dying wish, she is said to haunt the pub still.

LOCATION: 5 MILES NORTH OF LONGRIDGE

Colne Bridge WEST YORKSHIRE

Fire at the mill Tragedy struck on Valentine's Day 1818 at Atkinson's Mill. Discipline had been a problem, and overseers had taken to locking their young mill hands in, to prevent them leaving before their shifts ended. Unfortunately the new textile mills were dangerous places and fire safety measures were sacrificed to the ever-growing demand for productivity. So it was that when a fire did break out 17 young girls between the ages of 9 and 18 found they could not escape the flames because the doors were bolted. They all perished and there was a public outcry. A monument in Kirkheaton churchyard records their 'dreadful fate'.

LOCATION: OFF B6118, 3 MILES EAST OF HUDDERSFIELD

...when a fire did break out 17 young girls between the ages of 9 and 18 found they could not escape the flames because the doors were bolted. They all perished...

CHILD LABOUR

In the first half of the 19th century, parliamentary committees investigated the use of children in factories and mines. The tales of the witnesses they called make gruesome reading. In Wolverhampton a nine-year-old boy was one of many to have his fingers chopped off in a nail making machine. Another had his ears nailed to a bench for producing poor work. The factory owner suggested the injuries were caused by 'sheer carelessness'. In the collieries, boys and girls as young as eight would be used to haul coal through the narrow workings. Often below ground for over 12 hours at a time, they would strip to the waist to stay cool, and allegations of rape were not unusual.

Coxwold NORTH YORKSHIRE

A familiar corpse This North Yorkshire village is best known as home to Laurence Sterne (1713–68), author of *Tristram Shandy* and one time resident of Shandy Hall. The writer's body was re-buried in the village in 1969 after building work in London disturbed his grave, but this was not the first time the corpse had been moved. In 1769, a professor of anatomy at Cambridge University was shocked to recognise his celebrated writer friend in the cadaver delivered to him for public dissection. He returned it to St George's graveyard in Hanover Square, London, from where it had been stolen a few days previously.

LOCATION: SHANDY HALL, COXWOLD, 7 MILES SOUTH-EAST OF THIRSK

Croglin CUMBRIA

A vampire strikes When Bram Stoker wrote *Dracula* in 1897 he may have had a gruesome local tale in mind. In the summer of 1874, young Amelia Cransworth and her two brothers were holidaying in a remote farmhouse in the Eden Valley. It was a warm night and, retiring early, Amelia was awoken by scratching at her window and two eyes peering in. In panic, she could not open her bedroom door. An animal in human form broke in, pushed her back on the bed and bit her neck, before escaping through the open window. Traumatised by the ordeal, the wealthy Australian family decamped to Switzerland, but returned in March 1876. One night Amelia again heard the scratching. She screamed as her shuttered windows were ripped open. Her brothers arrived on the scene and one fired shots at the creature before chasing it across the fields. It disappeared in the small churchyard in Croglin. At dawn the churchyard was searched. In a disturbed tomb they found a mummified figure with a fresh bullet wound. The corpse was exhumed and cremated.

Planes crash At least four planes have crashed into the fells above Croglin in poor weather, including a Hawker Hurricane and a Bristol

Vampires were believed to suck the blood of the living – both men and women

Beaufighter in the spring of 1943. The crews of both planes were killed on impact, and some wreckage can still be traced.
LOCATION: 12 MILES NORTH OF PENRITH ON B6413

Darlington COUNTY DURHAM
Railway tragedy The Mothers' Union from Hetton-le-Hole in East Durham's coalfield had been on a day trip to Scarborough when their train approached Darlington's Bank Top station at around 10.45pm on 27 June 1928. Ahead, an inexperienced driver was shunting another train out of the station and into their path. The excursion express smashed into its rear at 45mph, driving it back 1,800yds (1,642m) up the line. As the carriages were crushed, 25 passengers lost their lives, including 14 from the close-knit Hetton-le-Hole group. The disaster created four widowers on the same street.
LOCATION: DARLINGTON (BANK TOP) STATION, NEAR TOWN HALL

Durham COUNTY DURHAM
Norman defeat In 1069 the Norman nobleman Robert de Comyn arrived in Durham to claim the Earldom of Northumberland, granted to him by William I. Despite a warning from Bishop Egelwin that his presence would be met by local resistance, Robert and his 700 followers took over the city, plundering and murdering any inhabitants who stood in their way. But as the Normans celebrated, the Northumbrians counter-attacked, breaking open the city gates and slaughtering the newcomers in the streets. Comyn took shelter in the Bishop's Palace which was then set alight by the angry mob. As snow settled on the Norman corpses the next morning, the few left alive fled south to give word of the massacre to their king.

Serial killer Mary Ann Cotton's mistake was to send her eight-year-old stepson Charles to the chemists for arsenic; the chemist refused to sell to a minor, so a neighbour bought it instead and remembered the incident. When the boy died a few months later, suspicions led to a post-mortem and a particularly grisly discovery. It became apparent that Mary had left a trail of dead children in her wake as she moved around the north-east, marrying and re-marrying, and always claiming the insurance money. Some 17 people had died from 'gastric fever' traced back to her poisonous tricks, 13 of them children. She was tried and hanged at Durham in 1873.

Piper's lament St James's Chapel on Elvet Bridge retains traces of the old county jail, in use until 1819. Northumbrian piper and horse stealer Jimmy Allen was detained there in 1803 to await transportation to the Colonies, but the transport never came.

After seven years of waiting he was pardoned by the Prince Regent, but Jimmy was an old man and he died the day the pardon arrived. It is said his pipes can still be heard if you stand on the bridge at night.
LOCATION: 15 MILES SOUTH OF NEWCASTLE-UPON-TYNE

Pele tower in the isolated village of Elsdon

Elsdon NORTHUMBERLAND

Pagan sacrifice In 1837, workmen repairing the bell tower of St Cuthbert's Church unearthed the skulls of three horses, laid in ceremonial array. It is thought that they may have been put there when the church was first built as a reminder of the pagan practice of sacrificing valuable animals to ensure the solidity of the new church. Elsewhere in the church there are sword marks on a pillar near the entrance where the local Redesdale men sharpened their weapons before going out to fight, and under the north wall is the mass grave of many men killed in the battle of Otterburn in 1388.

The Winter Gibbet On a nearby hill, by the old Steng Cross boundary stone, stands the Winter Gibbet. Here the body of William Winter hung for many years after his execution for the murder of an old lady at Raw Bastle in 1792. It was believed criminals should hang within view of their victim's homes. The corpse became a local attraction, with onlookers coming from all around the area, but after several years it was considered unsanitary and a dummy replaced the corpse. This later lost its body, leaving just the head to remind visitors of the awful crime.

LOCATION: 3 MILES EAST OF OTTERBURN ON B6431

Flamborough Head

EAST RIDING OF YORKSHIRE

Shipwreck The north-east coast of England has claimed many ships and many lives. The cliffs of Flamborough Head have taken more than their fair share including the crew of the *Princess*, carrying ore from Bilbao to Sunderland. At 2am on a grim November night in 1893, she rounded the headland only to confront a hurricane force north-easterly. Swamped by monstrous waves the steamer battled against the icy onslaught but was slowly driven back. She struck the rocks in Thornwick Bay and broke up within minutes, despatching all 19 of her crew to watery graves.

LOCATION: THORNWICK BAY, ½ MILE NORTH-WEST OF NORTH LANDING. FLAMBOROUGH, OFF B1255

Flodden NORTHUMBERLAND

The Flowers of the Field

Over 10,000 Scottish and French soldiers died in the bloody battle of Flodden in September 1513. Despite their strong position at the start, the Scots invaders found themselves reduced to bitter hand-to-hand

A cross on Pipers Hill, near Branxton, marks the battlefield of Flodden

fighting in which their long pikes and artillery were useless against savage English billhooks. Along with the cream of the Scottish aristocracy, King James IV was also slain, his mutilated body found amongst the piles of dead. The English, under the command of the aged Earl of Surrey, lost barely 2,000 men.

LOCATION: NEAR BRANXTON, OFF A697 5 MILES WEST OF COLDSTREAM

Freckleton LANCASHIRE

Bomber disaster When *Classy Chassis II*, a B-24 Liberator bomber, left the USAAF's huge refurbishment base at Warton in August 1944, pilot John Bloemaendal flew into a violent storm. Five minutes into the flight he steered his 24-ton plane around to return to base, but a wing tip snagged a tree and the Liberator ploughed into the ground. Tragically, its crashing path took in three houses, the 'Sad Sack' snack bar and the infants wing of Freckleton Holy Trinity School. Sixty-one people perished, including the aircrew, four RAF personnel taking breakfast in the café, and 38 children.

LOCATION: 5 MILES WEST OF PRESTON ON A584

Gateshead TYNE AND WEAR

The first 'Prince Bishop' William Walcher of Lorraine was the first Norman bishop of Durham. In 1079 he was made Earl of Northumberland too, giving him unprecedented powers as the first of the 'Prince Bishops'. In 1080 two of his men murdered Liulf of Lumley, a Northumbrian nobleman. It caused considerable unrest, and Walcher went to Gateshead to address the furious locals, but his speech was drowned out by the mob. He took refuge with his men in the church, then offered to hand over the murderers. As they emerged, they were cut down and the church set alight. Fleeing for his life, Walcher was slain by a spear through the heart. His corpse was found by monks from Jarrow, 'naked, mangled and insulted'.

LOCATION: 1 MILE SOUTH OF NEWCASTLE-UPON-TYNE

BORDER REIVERS

The borderlands between England and Scotland were notoriously lawless before the two kingdoms were united under James VI/I in 1603. Endless feuds between clan-like families, who also pillaged and burnt communities from Edinburgh to Yorkshire, were a constant source of worry. The responsibility of keeping the 'reivers', as the families became known, in order was given to the Wardens of the Marches, based in the great castles such as Carlisle, Naworth, Warkworth and Hermitage.

The stealth and speed of the reivers made them notorious throughout the 16th century when the Armstrongs, Littles, Bells, Grahams and Scotts brought terror to the border valleys. Night after night they would plunder cattle and destroy property. One March Warden on finding his quarry had escaped justice yet again by slipping over the border exclaimed 'they are people that will be Scottishe when they will and English at their pleasure.' One of their specialisms was extortion. The local word for tribute money was 'mail', and the reivers' racketeering fees became known as 'blackmail'.

Recruited to English, Scottish and French armies for their horsemanship and skirmishing abilities, the borderers sometimes confounded all sides by putting family loyalty above nation. At the Battle of Flodden it is claimed the reiver contingents from both camps spent more time killing and robbing enemies on their own side than engaging with the supposed foe.

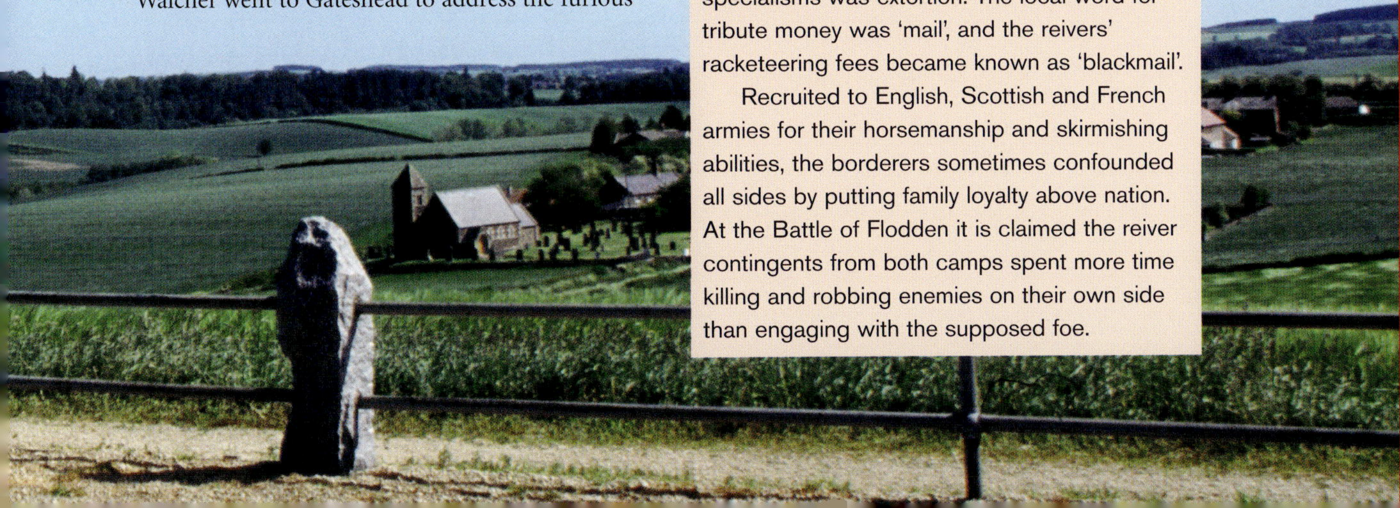

Goswick NORTHUMBERLAND

A pair of accidents Coincidences often have the most gruesome overtones. In October 1947, the *Merrie Hampton* pulling the 'day Scotsman' train south from Edinburgh overshot the points near tiny Goswick Halt and rolled into a ditch at 60mph. As the coaches disintegrated with the force of the impact, 28 passengers were killed. The accident may have been caused by the presence of an amateur train enthusiast on the footplate, smuggled in by the train's crew. In this same ditch, 40 years previously, a driver and fireman had also lost their lives when their engine overran the crossover track and smashed into the gully.

LOCATION: 6 MILES SOUTH-EAST OF BERWICK-UPON-TWEED OFF A1

Halifax WEST YORKSHIRE

From Hull, Hell or Halifax Five hundred years before Monsieur Guillotine's device sanitised judicial murder in the French Revolution, the residents of this West Riding wool town were already familiar with the swish of the falling blade in a frame. The 'Halifax gibbet' was a fairly primitive affair, but proved very effective in cutting off the heads of felons caught within the scope of 'Halifax Gibbet Law'. This stated that any thief caught with more than 13½ pence worth of goods should be tried before a jury of 16 local residents. No judges or lawyers were involved and there was no appeal. If found guilty, the condemned would be held until market day (Saturday), then taken to the scaffold. The blade was attached to a long rope stretched out into the crowd. If the throng agreed with the judgement they would pull the rope and the blade would fall. If the prisoner had stolen an animal, then the rope would be tied to its halter and the animal would dispense the justice.

Oliver Cromwell finally put an end to the practice in 1650, after which executions were carried out at gaols. A replica was erected on the original gibbet mound in 1974 .

LOCATION: CORNER OF NEW BRUNSWICK STREET AND GIBBET STREET

Pillory Not content with their terrible gibbet law, the people of Halifax also had a pillory at the junction of Old Market and Northgate where more minor wrongdoers were exposed for public humiliation. Women had their own form of punishment in the ducking-stool by the river. So-called 'ale wives' accused of gossip, drunkenness, lewd or rowdy behaviour, were strapped to a chair stool pivoted on a long pole. The chair would drop them into the water, completely submerging them, before being lifted again to the jeers of the crowd. The number of duckings varied with the severity of the misdemeanour.

Mill fire The deaths of five young girls at Wellington Mill on Wade Street in the winter of 1873 were a tragic reminder of the price of industrial progress. The new gas lighting had been

So-called 'ale wives' accused of gossip, drunkenness, lewd or rowdy behaviour, were strapped to a chair stool pivoted on a long pole. The chair would drop them into the water, completely submerging them, before being lifted again to the jeers of the crowd. The number of duckings varied with the severity of the misdemeanour.

The lonely slopes of Hlevellyn

causing problems. A meter required replacing, but the supply couldn't be turned off because it lit the whole mill. Instead the pipe was temporarily plugged, but the plug gave way, followed inevitably by an explosion and fire.

Most workers escaped across a gangway to a neighbouring building, but when the debris settled the heart-rending death toll was revealed. Five girls, aged between 8 and 18, had been caught in the initial blast. They were buried together in Stoney Royd Cemetery.

LOCATION: WADE STREET, NEAR PIECE HALL

Hebden Bridge WEST YORKSHIRE

Express crash The Liverpool-to-Leeds express which left Rochdale at 2.45pm on 21 June 1912 was pulled by tank engine No.276 as usual. As it steamed towards Hebden Bridge it entered the notorious S-shaped Charlestown curve. Perhaps the driver braked too slowly, but the train began to rock from side to side and then jumped the track. As the engine screamed to a halt in the cutting, the front two carriages were smashed to pieces, killing four passengers outright. As the other carriages toppled, many others were injured. Between the two front carriages had been a short van carrying a coffin. So a fifth corpse was laid out in the Calderside signal box to await the undertaker.

LOCATION: 1 MILE WEST OF HEBDEN BRIDGE

Helvellyn CUMBRIA

A poetic commemoration The lonely death of an angler rarely merits a place in literary history, but Charles Gough's demise on the slopes of England's third highest mountain inspired both William Wordsworth and Walter Scott.

In 1805, Gough, a Quaker from Manchester, was walking from Patterdale over Helvellyn to Wythburn, with his fishing poles and his terrier, Foxie. Caught in a snowstorm, Gough slipped and fell 1,000ft (308m) into the corrie of Red Tarn. His body was not discovered for three months, and when finally a shepherd came upon the scene, next to the withered corpse sat Foxie, emaciated but loyal to her dead master.

LOCATION: MEMORIAL ON SOUTH-EAST SIDE OF SUMMIT OF HELVELLYN, 3 MILES SOUTH-WEST OF GLENRIDDING

Hexham NORTHUMBERLAND

The wrong man hanged The Northumberland market town frequently suffered the indignity of cross-border attacks and boasts England's first purpose-built jail, constructed in 1330, to hold men found guilty of cross-border banditry.

But the most notorious incident in the town's history came in March 1761 when a crowd of 5,000, many of them lead miners from nearby Allendale, gathered to protest against conscription to the militia. When they failed to disperse, magistrates ordered troops to open fire on the crowd. In the panic that followed, 40 were shot dead and over 400 injured. Later that year an old man was arrested and convicted for his presence at the 'riot'. He was hanged, though it was later found he had not even been in Hexham that day.

Heavenfield

A nearby section of Hadrian's Wall is said to have been the site of the battle of Heavenfield, where the Northumbrian prince Oswald routed a much larger Welsh army under Cadwallon in AD 633. Bones and weapons found near the site have been claimed to have belonged to the defeated Gwynedd men who were butchered as they fled from the field of battle.

LOCATION: ON A69 25 MILES WEST OF NEWCASTLE

Holmfirth WEST YORKSHIRE

Dam break Holmfirth is the heart of 'Last of the Summer Wine' country, but in February 1852, the valley made famous by Compo, Foggy, Clegg and Co, was in the news for far more unpleasant reasons.

Heavy rains over the previous weeks had put great strain on the dam holding the Bilberry reservoir at the head of the Holme Valley. At 1am on 5 February it gave way, unleashing a wall of water on the unsuspecting dale. Over 60 perished in the onslaught, mostly mill workers and their children. Bodies were still being recovered from the river three months later, as far down stream as Castleford, some 30 miles away.

LOCATION: 6 MILES SOUTH OF HUDDERSFIELD ON A6024

Huddersfield WEST YORKSHIRE

Murder of a mill owner The junction in Crossland Moor where William Horsfall was gunned down has changed greatly since that bloody April evening in 1812. It would have been a rural spot when the unpopular mill owner was making his way home along Blackmoorfoot Road. At the junction with Dryclough Road, he was shot twice from behind a drystone wall. He died the next day at the Warren House Inn, now a corner shop ½ mile towards Huddersfield. Three men, George Mellor, Thomas Smith and William Thorpe, all prominent Luddites, were convicted for his murder on circumstantial evidence, though all three had alibis. They were hung and dissected at York castle the following October.

LOCATION: 2 MILES WEST OF TOWN CENTRE

Hyde GREATER MANCHESTER

Contract killing As 22-year-old Thomas Ashton returned to the large cotton spinning mill which his family owned at Apethorn, he was ambushed and shot twice. The first bullet pierced his heart, the second shattered his spine and he died on the spot, in the dark and narrow Apethorn Lane, barely ten minutes walk from his home. A joiner from the mill found his body, lying on its back, the face splashed with blood and froth.

Although no one witnessed the murder, James Garside finally confessed to having been paid £10 by persons unknown to do the deed, along with the brothers William and Joseph Morley. Although each claimed they

Far right: The severed remains of the Earl of Carlisle lie buried at Kirkby Stephen

didn't fire the fatal shots, all three were hanged for the crime.

LOCATION: OFF A560 STOCKPORT ROAD

Kingston upon Hull

EAST RIDING OF YORKSHIRE

Bombed out Hull was singled out for particularly ferocious air attacks during World War II. Perhaps the saddest episode was when a parachute mine landed on a public shelter in Ellis Terrace in April 1941. Sixty people were killed, including three generations of some families. The following May, incendiary bombs engulfed the heart of the city, spectacularly destroying Hammonds department store among others. It is claimed the fires could be seen in Denmark. Over 1,200 died in the bombing, and of the city's 92,000 homes, fewer than 6,000 survived untouched.

Kirkby Stephen CUMBRIA

Gathering the quarters It would have been difficult for the de Harcla family to recover the body of Andrew de Harcla, Earl of Carlisle. The Earl was executed in 1323 after Edward II blamed him for a defeat by the Scots at Byland Abbey in the previous year. He was hanged, his heart and entrails removed and burnt, his body cut into quarters to be displayed at Carlisle, Newcastle, York and Shrewsbury and his head was stuck on a spike on London Bridge. But Edward III was a magnanimous monarch and he decreed that the various parts be returned to Andrew's sister for proper burial in 1337. A brass plate in St Stephens Church commemorates the reburial of the remains in 1847.

LOCATION: ON A685 26 MILES SOUTH-EAST OF PENRITH

Knaresborough NORTH YORKSHIRE

The secret of St Robert's Cave In February 1745 Eugene Aram, Richard Houseman and Daniel Clark walked across the fields to St Robert's Cave. Clark had obtained valuables from several local traders on a false promise; now the creditors were calling in their goods and he needed his friends' help. Without warning though, Aram bludgeoned Clark to death. Burying him in the cave, Aram and Houseman split his unpaid-for horde and separated. Thirteen years later a skeleton, thought to be Clark's, was found at Thistle Hill, and the subsequent enquiry called Houseman as a witness. Under pressure he turned King's Evidence and revealed the true location of the corpse. Aram was arrested in Kings Lynn and tried at York Assize in August 1758. He was convicted and sentenced to hang. Later his body was returned to Knaresborough, to swing from the town gibbet for another 20 years.

LOCATION: 1 MILE EAST OF TOWN CENTRE OFF B6164

Designed to intimidate: the main gate of Lancaster Castle

Lancaster LANCASHIRE

Hanging Corner Criminals from all over north-west England were brought to Lancaster for trial. Before 1800, those sentenced to death would be taken in a cart to the Gallows Hill, close to the modern Williamson Park. On the way they would stop at the Golden Lion pub on Brewery Lane for a last drink with friends and relations. The crowds would turn out in droves, treating the event as a carnival. From 1800 to 1856 executions were carried out at the Hanging Corner of Lancaster Castle, between the tower and the east wall. Stephen Burke was the last to die in front of the public here, in 1856, convicted for the murder of his wife.

Forced labour In 1822 treadmills were installed in the castle jail. Prisoners had to complete 96 steps per minute, and would walk for 15 minutes then get five minutes rest. Uniquely amongst prison treadmills, their energy was directed to a useful end: it was harnessed to power 23 calico looms and draw water from the castle well. Men and women were punished in this way, labouring ten hours a day in summer, four at a time and in strict silence. Children could be held here for relatively minor crimes, but teenagers were often transported to the Colonies.

Debt to society Debtors were also held in Lancaster Castle, until a change in the law in 1866. Sometimes as many as 400 at a time would be incarcerated for their inability to pay their creditors. Their conditions were less harsh than those experienced by the criminal inmates. They could buy and sell goods, pursue their professions and were allowed visitors between 8am and 8pm. Sometimes they would hold concerts or dances, the musicians drawn from amongst the prisoners.

LOCATION: 18 MILES NORTH OF PRESTON

Leeds WEST YORKSHIRE

Child labour In the early 19th century it was not unusual for children as young as five to be put to work in the mills. In 1832 a parliamentary committee recorded their harrowing tales.

Elizabeth Bentley worked at Busk's flax mill from the age of six. She was interviewed in the workhouse in Hunslet aged 23, unable to walk because the baskets she had been made to carry were so heavy they caused her spine to curve permanently. Her overseer in the mill would whip her with a strap if she flagged at all on her 13–16 hour shifts.

Samuel Downe also worked in a Leeds mill, and reported that one overlooker actually gagged him to silence his screams as he was whipped with a birch pole.

LOCATION: LEEDS INDUSTRIAL MUSEUM, ARMLEY MILLS, CANAL ROAD

Leeming Bar NORTH YORKSHIRE

Escape of the highwayman The Great North Road dropped down to Leeming Bridge before rising to the toll house at Leeming Bar. In 1812 this was still a dangerous place for travellers, the haunt of George Cutterman – the last gentleman highway robber. After he robbed an elderly Catterick couple of their £200 inheritance, a 100 guineas reward was offered for his capture. This was raised to 200 guineas after he politely held up the *High Flyer* stage coach on its way from London to Edinburgh. He was caught after robbing a butcher near Kirlington who recognised him. Constables found the inheritance money and his mask at his home and he was escorted to York for trial and inevitable execution. On the way he escaped by jumping into a passing haycart and was never seen again.

LOCATION: OFF A1 6 MILES SOUTH OF CATTERICK

PILGRIMAGE OF GRACE

In a bloody sub-plot to Henry VIII's dissolution of the monasteries in 1536, barrister Robert Aske succeeded in raising an army of over 30,000 to challenge the royal abolition of the Roman Catholic religion. Gaining popular support in Yorkshire and Cumbria, the rebellion, which took the name 'Pilgrimage of Grace', came to nothing as the loyal Duke of Norfolk headed off the rebels with a force of regular soldiers. Arriving in Cumbria he declared martial law, and acted on the King's instruction to 'cause suche dredfull exaction to be done upon a good nombre of th'inhabitauntes of every toune, village and hamlet that have offended in this rebellion'.

Throughout Cumberland and Westmorland 74 men were hanged from trees in villages. The abbots of the great monasteries at Fountains and Jervaulx, along with several others, were beheaded at Tyburn, and Aske himself was butchered at York and hung upon the city walls.

Liverpool MERSEYSIDE

Fire at sea The *Ocean Monarch* headed out into Liverpool Bay one morning in August 1848. By noon she was seen in distress off Great Orme, heading back to port. A fire had broken out, causing panic amongst the 322 steerage passengers, mostly poor Irish families heading for the New World. Other ships arrived to help, but many of the terrified passengers jumped into the sea trying to save themselves and drowned. A roll call back on the docks in Liverpool revealed 178 missing.

Panic at the music hall As Fred Coyne launched into his final rendition of 'You don't mean what I mean' on the stage of the Liverpool Colosseum one Friday night in October 1878, a fight broke out in the pits. As the scuffle grew, someone shouted 'Fire!' and the 4,000 strong audience was gripped by panic. As they fled the building, they surged into narrow stairwells, crushing those at the front who couldn't open the doors. Outside a crowd gathered and began to pull at bodies caught underneath the scrum, sometimes pulling off legs and arms. In all 37 people died, their bodies distinctive in the morgue with their open mouths, gasping for air.

Outside a crowd gathere
to pull at bodies caught u
scrum, sometimes pullin
arms. In all 37 people di
distinctive in the morgu
open mouths, gasping fo

Arsenic poisoners Patrick Higgins became suspicious when his brother Thomas's new wife, Margaret, took out a fifth life insurance policy on her husband. When Thomas died after a short illness in October 1883, Patrick went to the police. A post-mortem revealed it was arsenic poisoning, not bad whisky which had caused the poor man to have chronic diarrhoea. Three other people had since died whilst being nursed by Margaret Higgins and her sister, Catherine Flanagan, in their slum home in Ascot Street. All three had life insurance policies cashed in favour of the deadly pair. At their trial in February 1884 the jury spent less than an hour deciding their guilt. The two sisters were hanged side by side in Kirkdale jail.

Body-snatchers The trade in dead bodies for dissection, though illegal, was too lucrative for some to resist. Ireland was a good source of un-named corpses, and Liverpool was their usual port of entry. In 1826, dockers at St George's Dock complained of the acrid stench emanating from three casks marked 'bitter salts', which they were loading on a smack bound for Leith. When the casks were impounded they were found to contain

nd began
derneath the
ff legs and
, their bodies
vith their
ir.

11 naked corpses pickled in brine and packed in salt. The police followed a lead to a cellar beneath 11 Hope Street where they found 22 more corpses in various states of decomposition and a brass syringe, evidently used for injecting hot wax into the lifeless veins as a preservative. Three members of the Hope Street gang were imprisoned for 12 months each. At their trial, the revelation that dead babies had been discovered in a vat of brine caused the foreman of the jury to be physically sick.
LOCATION: OFF A562 UPPER PARLIAMENT STREET

Manchester GREATER MANCHESTER

Peterloo Massacre The area around the GMEX and the Free Trade Hall was once known as St Peter's Fields. In 1819 there was a huge rally here in support of electoral reform. It was a glorious summer day and as many as 50,000 men, women and children turned out from the city and surrounding mill towns. Local magistrates, who were then responsible for law and order, panicked at the size of the crowd and called in the army to disperse it.

Unfortuantely, the first troops on the scene were the inexperienced local mounted Yeomanry. They charged at the throng, swinging their sabres without mercy. Shortly afterwards a platoon of experienced Hussars arrived, and were more successful in scattering the scared protestors and tempering the Yeomanry. As the field cleared, nine men and two women lay dead, 400 more were injured, many with limbs severed by cavalry sabres. The infamous massacre became known as 'Peterloo', ironically echoing the army's triumph at Waterloo only four years before.
LOCATION: SOUTH OF PETER STREET

Fenians Sergeant Charles Brett was close to retiring from the Manchester police when he accompanied two Fenian suspects across town. Kelly and Deasey were high-ranking members of the Irish Republican Brotherhood, and their capture had been a major coup. As the prison wagon passed under a railway bridge on the Hyde Road, a mob surrounded it, forcing all but Brett, who was locked inside with his charges, to flee. Breaking open the van, the attackers demanded Brett's keys. He refused and was shot through the head. The prisoners escaped as officers armed with cutlasses arrived to control the mêlée. After a chase, William O'Mara Allen, Michael Larkin and William Gould were captured and later convicted of Brett's murder. They were executed in public at the New Bailey, Salford, in November 1867.
LOCATION: HYDE ROAD, A57 2 MILES FROM CITY CENTRE

Marsden Bay TYNE AND WEAR

Smuggling gang In the 18th and early 19th century the coast of north-east England was notorious for its smugglers. 'John the Jibber' was a member of a ruthless gang operating around Marsden Bay. One night while his comrades waited for a cargo ship to unload their illegal imports, he slipped away and tipped off the excisemen. A trap was laid, but a north-easterly gale blew the smugglers away from the authorities' grasp. Coming ashore down the coast near Souter Point the smugglers charged back over the cliffs to do battle with the officials. The excisemen fled in terror, and next morning John's body was found hanging from a rope over the cliff edge, his eyes pecked out by the wheeling gulls.

LOCATION: 2 MILES SOUTH-EAST OF SOUTH SHIELDS ON A163

Marston Moor NORTH YORKSHIRE

Defeat and death The Battle of Marston Moor was nearly a Royalist triumph. In July 1644 the Civil War was in full swing and the Scots, under Alexander Leslie, had just come in on Parliament's side. Despite being outnumbered by 10,000 men, Prince Rupert had engineered a situation where his cavalry was routing the Parliamentary right wing causing it to flee. But in the moment of victory, Cromwell arrived at the Royalist rear and put them to flight. Over 4,000 were killed in the subsequent scramble, leaving the north in Parliamentary hands. At Wilstrop Wood, to the north of the battle site, a servant girl opened a farm gate to help the Royalist retreat. Sadly the fleeing cavalry charge trampled her underfoot, leaving only a twisted corpse.

LOCATION: LONG MARSTON 6 MILES WEST OF YORK OFF B1224

Mirfield WEST YORKSHIRE

The Dumb Steeple This little mill town boasts a set of stocks and a pond which used to service a ducking stool, but its most interesting site is a mile or so out of town at a busy road junction. Here you will find the Dumb Steeple. In a field beyond this curious obelisk, George Mellor rallied his Luddites before their attack on Rawfolds in 1812. Five centuries before that, Robin Hood, the legendary outlaw, is believed to have been buried here, after he died at nearby Kirklees Priory.

LOCATION: JUNCTION OF A62 AND A644, WEST OF MIRFIELD

Morecambe LANCASHIRE

Morecambe's deadly sands Before the railway made light work of the journey between Ulverston and Lancaster, residents of Morecambe living beside the intervening shallow, quick-sand riddled bay were said to draw lots as to who would keep the belongings of the sands' next victim. Even after the railway's construction, tragedy was not a stranger. At Whitsuntide weekend in 1857 George Ashburner, a local carter from Flookburgh, led a party of nine across to Morecambe from Kent's Bank. Very drunk when they left, they never arrived in Morecambe. Their bodies were found near the rocks of Priest Skear the next day, face down in 8 inches (20cm) of water.

LOCATION: WEST OF A5105, HEST BANK NEAR MORECAMBE

Much Hoole LANCASHIRE

The Rose and Crown pub on the Old Liverpool Road was once the home of Albert Pierrepoint, Britain's last hangman. Albert famously also ran the 'Help the Poor Straggler' pub, now demolished, in Holinwood, Oldham. William Joyce (Lord Haw-Haw), several other notorious Nazis and Ruth Ellis were among over 400 despatched by Pierrepoint's hand. In 1944 he was flown to Dublin to execute Michael Manning, the last person in the Republic to go to the gallows. His father and uncle had also been executioners, though in his autobiography Albert revealed that he no longer considered the death penalty to have been an effective deterrent to serious crime.

LOCATION: 7 MILES SOUTH-WEST OF PRESTON OFF A59

Albert Pierrepoint, the last hangman in Britain, photographed in 1973

MP William Huskisson, the first victim of a railway accident

Newton-le-Willows MERSEYSIDE

First railway accident Little remains of Parkside station, but a monument commemorates the unfortunate death there of William Huskisson MP, the first man ever to be killed by a railway train. Huskisson was aboard the Duke of Wellington's carriage at the opening of the Liverpool and Manchester Railway, the first passenger railway, in September 1830. On its way to meet the crowds in Manchester, the train had stopped at Parkside to take on water. Huskisson stepped out of the carriage to admire the engine, *Dart*, then panicked when other trains in the convoy arrived. He fell back under *Dart*, and the engine and its carriage ran over his right leg. He died in excruciating pain several hours later.

LOCATION: 1 MILE EAST OF NEWTON-LE-WILLOWS

Northallerton NORTH YORKSHIRE

The Battle of the Standard A brief and bloody encounter, the Battle of the Standard, was fought outside Northallerton in August 1138. King David of Scotland led an impressive horde across the border which included Englishmen, Normans, Norwegians, Danes, Highlanders and Galwegians – the Pictish occupants of Galloway in south-west Scotland. It was the failure of the Galwegians' wild charge against the English line which decided the fight. Cut down by arrows, their retreat was halted against the pikes and shields of their own side. Annals claim 10,000 perished, to be buried where they were slain. Today you can still find Scotpit Lane bounding the field where they lie, whilst Standard Hill Farm crowns the ridge where the English, behind Bernard de Balliol, planted their banners.

LOCATION: 2½ MILES NORTH OF NORTHALLERTON OFF A167

Otley WEST YORKSHIRE

Tunnel hazards In the northern corner of the churchyard at All Saints stands a grand monument, not to a local family of worthies such as the Fawkes or the Fairfaxes, but to the 23 men who died whilst building the nearby Bramhope railway tunnel between 1845 and 1849. Over 1.5 billion gallons of water had to be pumped from the workings, and many of those killed in the building of the tunnel were, in fact, drowned. The monument is a scale model of the tunnel's grandiose northern portal.

LOCATION: OFF KIRKGATE

Otterburn NORTHUMBERLAND

Ill-met by moonlight Led by the two great opposing Border families, with the Scots under the Earl of Douglas, the English under Henry Percy (better known as Hotspur), the battle of Otterburn in August 1388 was a confusing affair, fought mainly in dim moonlight in dense woodland. Douglas's army was returning home after a successful pillaging raid in north-east England. They led the pursuing English into a trap which saw Percy's men butchering Scottish camp followers, while the main Scottish force of some 6,000 men moved in behind their right flank. The battle raged on well into the night. By dawn Douglas was dead, but Hotspur and Sir Ralph Percy had been captured and the English were in full flight. In victory the Scots claimed only 100 losses, but the true figure was probably nearer 1,000. The English may have lost as many as 1,500, with 500 prisoners ransomed and 500 more led back over the border.

LOCATION: ON A696 32 MILES NORTH-WEST OF NEWCASTLE-UPON-TYNE

Mystery still surrounds the violent death of Percy Topliss, on a Cumbrian roadside in June 1920.

Pannal NORTH YORKSHIRE

Resurrection Stone A large boulder in the churchyard at Pannal is known as the Resurrection Stone. In the early 19th century it was hired out to mourners at a cost of one guinea per fortnight to place over the fresh graves of their loved ones to deter grave robbers.

LOCATION: 2 MILES SOUTH OF HARROGATE ON A61

Penistone SOUTH YORKSHIRE

Train wrecks Once a busy trans-Pennine railway junction but now little more than a branch line halt, Penistone has seen many dramatic train wrecks. The most serious was in July 1884, when a passenger train from Manchester derailed at nearby Bullhouse Colliery. Five coaches were catapulted down an embankment and 19 people died in the wreckage, five more dying later in hospital. In 1916 the crew of a freight train made a lucky escape when the stone viaduct over the River Don began to crumble beneath their engine. As the fireman leapt to safety, his tender crashed 85 feet into the river below.

LOCATION: 7 MILES WEST OF BARNSLEY ON A628

Plumpton CUMBRIA

Mystery man Mystery still surrounds the violent death of Percy Topliss, on a Cumbrian roadside in June 1920. He was certainly on the run, accused of murdering a taxi driver in Hampshire and shooting a policeman and a farmer in north-east Scotland. But was Percy Topliss also the 'Monocled Mutineer', leader of a soldiers' rebellion at Etaples in northern France?

At Low Hesket he had been recognised by a policeman's wife. Armed officers in plain clothes were despatched from Penrith to apprehend him, and at Plumpton Topliss was shot dead in a struggle. In his pocket police found a gold monocle. He was buried in an unmarked grave at Penrith.

LOCATION: 4 MILES NORTH OF PENRITH ON A6

Pontefract WEST YORKSHIRE

Pontefract Castle Shakespeare had Richard II killed by his warders in Pontefract Castle shortly after Henry IV seized power in 1399. In reality, the unfortunate monarch may have died of starvation after languishing in the Gascoigne Tower here until 1409.

The castle was no stranger to bloodshed, for in 1322, Thomas Lancaster and 20 of his supporters had been beheaded within sight of its walls for treason against Edward II. During the Civil War the castle was fiercely besieged three times by Parliamentary troops. Prisoners carved their names on the cellar walls of the old Great Hall, which was used as a powder magazine. Finally the castle surrendered and was reduced to the shell you can see today.

LOCATION: OFF A645 NORTH-EAST OF TOWN CENTRE

Preston LANCASHIRE

Turning points The Lancashire town has provided a backdrop to two defining moments in Britain's internal wars. In August 1648, the second phase of the Civil War was brought to an end when Cromwell's troops routed the Royalist armies of Sir Marmaduke Langdale and the Duke of Hamilton. After fierce combat from hedgerow to hedgerow on Ribbleton Moor, Hamilton's Scots were pushed back to the old bridge which stood at Walton. The fighting was intense and over 5,000 Royalists were either killed or captured.

In November 1715, a Jacobite army led by Northumbrian MP Thomas Forster fortified the town and effectively resisted a large Hanoverian army for two days before surrendering. The defeat marked the end of the 1715 rising on English soil on the same day it fizzled out at the inconclusive battle of Sherifmuir, north of the border.

LOCATION: WALTON OLD BRIDGE WAS 50YDS DOWNSTREAM FROM THE CURRENT A6 BRIDGE OVER RIBBLE, SOUTH OF PRESTON

The Luddites tried to halt the mechanised path of progress

Rawfolds WEST YORKSHIRE

Luddite riot You can still drink in the Shears Inn in Hightown, where George Mellor and his Luddite accomplices planned their attack on a local mill. Of Cartwright's Mill, down the road at Rawfolds, little remains. On an April night in 1812, the insurrectionists had attacked the mill, intending to smash the newly installed shearing frames which threatened their livelihoods. Cartwright was prepared for trouble and had fortified his factory, with militia men keeping guard. In the fighting that ensued, Samuel Hartley and

John Booth were mortally wounded and died a few days later. One of the militia men who had been reluctant to fire on his fellow workers was court-martialled and publically whipped.
LOCATION: OFF A638 BETWEEN LIVERSEDGE AND CLECKHEATON

The building of the scenic Settle-to-Carlisle railway claimed many lives

Ribblehead

NORTH YORKSHIRE

Navvies die The Settle-to-Carlisle railway was the last in Britain to be built by spade power alone. In 1871 over 2,500 men, women and children lived in a shanty town on Batty Moss, beneath the arches of the viaduct they were constructing. In the three years it took to complete the section which included the viaduct and Blea Moor Tunnel, over 200 had been killed.

Five navvies were killed after falling asleep drunk on the constructor's tramway, seven were killed by falling masonry within Blea Moor Tunnel, two were murdered and the rest died through natural causes. The bodies of some 230 railway related victims are buried in the churchyard at Chapel-le-dale, 3 miles away.
LOCATION: 7 MILES NORTH-WEST OF INGLETON ON B6255

Riccal NORTH YORKSHIRE

Graveyard of the Scandinavians The confusing and bloody events of 1066 have never been objectively explained by historians. In 1956 a farmer digging a pit close to the River Ouse uncovered human remains. Local archaeologists discovered more skeletons and suggested there may be as many as 600 bodies buried in an 80ft (24m) grave. Icelandic sagas talk of a great battle here as Norwegians disembarked from their longships to support Tostig Godwinson's claim to the English throne. The Sagas claim victory for the invaders, but English chronicles suggest a different outcome. Research for the TV series 'Blood of the Vikings' in 2001 revealed that the remains were probably those of Scandinavians, and many had been hacked to death. Perhaps these are the last remnants of Harold Hardrada's great Norwegian army, defeated by Harold of England at Stamford Bridge (see page 180).
LOCATION: 5 MILES SOUTH OF YORK ON A19

Richmond NORTH YORKSHIRE

A prison for 'conchies' Richmond's fine Norman castle hides a disturbing secret from more recent conflicts. In World War I, detention cells in the shadow of the ancient keep were used to imprison men who refused to fight on moral grounds. Sixteen of these 'absolutist' conscientious objectors were taken to France, tortured then sentenced to death, though this was commuted to a prison sentence. Among the prisoners were Norman Gaudie, a railway worker and reserve team centre-forward for Sunderland, and Percy Goldsborough of Mirfield, who scrawled 'put in this cell for refusing to be made into a soldier' on the drab wall.
LOCATION: 12 MILES SOUTH-WEST OF DARLINGTON

Ripon Cathedral, scene of an unexpected trial

Ripon NORTH YORKSHIRE

Virginity test Ripon, which boasts two whole museums to crime and punishment, also hides an Anglo-Saxon fidelity test in the crypt of its lovely cathedral. St Wilfrid's Needle is a narrow passage through which young women had to squeeze to prove they were virgins.

LOCATION: 16 MILES NORTH OF HARROGATE ON A61

Rivington Moor (Horwich)

GREATER MANCHESTER

Sotsman's Stump High on the bleak West Pennine moorland, the television transmitter on Winter Hill, Rivington Moor can be seen for miles around. Less prominent is the cast-iron memorial known as the Sotsman's Stump near by. It commemorates the death of George Henderson, a 20-year-old travelling salesman from Annan in Dumfriesshire. On a grim day in November 1838, he was crossing the moors on his way to do business in Blackburn when he was attacked and shot. Crying out 'I am robbed, I am killed', he lay in a ditch, where his disfigured body was found by a local boy. James Whittle who lived close by was tried for the murder, but acquitted through lack of evidence. The real assailant was never identified.

LOCATION: ON WINTER HILL SUMMIT, 2 MILES NORTH-EAST OF HORWICH

Saddleworth Moor LANCASHIRE

Double murder-mystery Saddleworth Moor (part of Yorkshire until boundary changes in 1974) is synonymous with murder and tragedy. In 1832, 85-year-old inn keeper William Bradbury and his gamekeeper son Tom were brutally beaten to death with a spade and a poker in the Moorcock Inn, up on the Huddersfield road. The pair were notoriously curmudgeonly and had several local animosities which may have contributed to their fate. Despite making several arrests, the police never charged anyone for the atrocity and it

remains unsolved to this day.
LOCATION: GREENFIELD ON A635 NORTH OF MOSSLEY

Sandal Magna WEST YORKSHIRE

A bold highwayman John 'Swift Nicks' Nevison ran a successful protection racket on the Great North Road, robbing wealthy travellers and protecting poorer ones who paid his 'toll'. Arrested several times, the highwayman's daring escapes earned him a place in local legend, but in 1681 he shot and killed a publican who had tried to drug him and turn him in for the reward money.

In 1684 he was captured whilst sleeping at an inn in Sandal Magna, possibly where the Three Houses pub now stands. He was tried in York and hanged at Knavesmire after a girlfriend turned King's Evidence. His greatest feat was his epic ride from London to York in a day, which was later wrongly attributed to Dick Turpin.
LOCATION: OFF A61 BARNSLEY ROAD, 2 MILES SOUTH OF WAKEFIELD

Scafells CUMBRIA

Death of a young pilot The summits of the Scafells in the centre of the Lake District form England's highest mountains and a formidable prospect in bad weather. So found Flight Lieutenant J O Loudon of 603 Squadron in November 1947. Heading for Turnhouse, Edinburgh, the 25-year-old war hero became disorientated in appalling conditions. His Spitfire slammed into the fellside just 20 feet (6m) below the summit of Ill Crag. As it burst into flames he was catapulted out of his cockpit to land some 30yds (27m) away. So bad were the conditions that day, that the crash site could not be located. In fact it wasn't discovered until the following spring when a local shepherd happened on the grisly remains.
LOCATION: ¼ MILE EAST OF SUMMIT OF SCAFELL PIKE

Seaham CO DURHAM

Mining disasters Sometimes known as the 'Nicky Nack,' Seaham Colliery was one of the largest pits in the East Durham coalfield, opened in 1849. The mine's list of fatalities makes for grim reading. Little William Knox was only ten years old when he was crushed to death by coal tubs in 1861. Seventy-one year old Robert Clark must surely have been expecting to retire soon when he was caught in the disastrous explosion that blasted through the workings in 1880; 163 other miners lost their lives that day. Their sad memorial in the churchyard at Seaham is accompanied by one commemorating 26 men who perished in an explosion nine years before.
LOCATION: 5 MILES SOUTH-EAST OF SUNDERLAND

Sheffield SOUTH YORKSHIRE

Wartime devastation The Blitz came to Sheffield on a moonlit night in December 1940. Ten minutes after the eerie sirens had announced their presence, German bombers began dropping incendiary bombs in a rim around the city.

Over the next three days, 760 people were killed, including 18 when a public trench shelter in Porter Street took a direct hit. Three rescuers died when a second bomb fell on exactly the same spot in Westbrook Bank. The Moor, Sheffield's main shopping street, was reduced to rubble and over 85,000 homes were damaged.
LOCATION: CITYWIDE

The bleak tops of the Scafells, where a young airman met his death in 1947

Sowerby Bridge WEST YORKSHIRE

Runaway tram By the standards of the day, trams were a relatively safe form of transport. But when things did go wrong, the consequences were very public and very traumatic for passengers and on-lookers alike. Driving through Sowerby Bridge today, you can still see where a tram stalled on Pye Nest bend in 1898 and began to roll back down into town. At Bolton Brow it left the rails and smashed into a shop front. As the tram spun round and overturned, the upper deck was sliced off by the impact. In the devastation five people – including the conductor – lost their lives, and over 40 were injured.

LOCATION: ON A6142 JUNCTION WITH A58, EAST OF SOWERBY BRIDGE CENTRE

Stainmore CO DURHAM

Murder of Eric Bloodaxe The Rey Cross stands at the high point of Stainmore, just before the Cumbrian border. In a lay-by at the side of the busy A66, it marks where York's last independent king, Eric Bloodaxe, was murdered by Macca, an agent of Oswulf, Earl of Bamburgh, in AD 954.

LOCATION: 5 MILES WEST OF BOWES ON A66

Stamford Bridge NORTH YORKSHIRE

Norwegian defeat Harold's five day forced march with his army from the south of England to York in the autumn of 1066 is the stuff of legends. Just outside the city at a bridge over the River Derwent, he engaged in full battle with his brother Tostig and a huge army of Norwegians under their king, Harold Hardrada. After bitter hand-to-hand combat between small groups, the Norwegian monarch fell to an English bowman. Shortly afterwards Tostig, too, was felled, by an axe blow which split his skull to the jaw line. The remaining Norwegians fled and were cut down, though Hardrada's son Olaf was spared. (See also Riccall, page 177).

LOCATION: 8 MILES WEST OF YORK ON A166A

The Norwegians were soundly defeated at Stamford Bridge in 1066

Sunderland TYNE AND WEAR

Body-snatchers at work The old Holy Trinity Church near the docks in Sunderland proved a fertile hunting ground for body snatchers in the 1820s. Four days after Christmas in 1823, Captain Headley was visiting the grave of his 10-year-old daughter whom he had buried on Christmas Eve. To his horror he found her burial site had been disturbed and the child's body was missing. The corpse was found in the lodgings of Scots Thomas Thompson and John Weatherley, neatly packed in straw and addressed to a doctor in Edinburgh.

Another, less-skilled 'Resurrection man' earned the name 'Half-hanged Jack' while hauling the corpse of a young girl over the graveyard wall in a sack. He slipped and found himself garrotted by the chord around the top of the sack. Next morning, he was discovered hanging half-dead, and he died a few days later.

LOCATION: CHURCH STREET EAST, OFF B1293

Thornthwaite CUMBRIA

Bishop of Barf That the misfortune of the newly appointed Bishop of Derry was down to drink is perhaps why his story is still remembered. In 1793 the new incumbent was making his way to the port at Whitehaven, intending to sail to Ireland. He stopped at the Swan Inn, by the roadside just beyond Keswick and after several rounds began to boast of his riding prowess. His final boast was that he could take his horse directly up the fell behind the pub on to the hill known as Barf, before making a direct line across the fells and down to Cockermouth.

A crowd gathered to see him off and many bets were placed, but as his steed approached a rock pinnacle half-way up the scree, she stumbled and fell, and both rider and mount were killed. They were buried at the foot of the scree slope under a white-painted boulder known as the Clerk. The rock pinnacle too was painted white and has been known ever since as the Bishop of Barf.

LOCATION: OFF A66 3 MILES WEST OF KESWICK

Todmorden WEST YORKSHIRE

Vicarage murders Miles Weatherill broke into Todmorden vicarage in March 1868 with the intent of killing the Reverend Anthony John Plow, his wife Harriet and their maid Jane Smith. He blamed them for breaking up his relationship with their 17-year-old cook. Finding Plow at the front of the house, he attacked him with a hatchet and a pistol (which didn't go off). After a struggle Plow escaped, bleeding, to a neighbour's house. In the meantime Weatherill sought out Jane Smith, put the hatchet in her skull, and then shot her twice through the head. He lurched up the stairs to where Mrs Plow lay in bed and shot at her. The gun misfired, so he smashed her nose in with a poker, before giving himself up. The Reverend Plow died later of his injuries, and Weatherill was hanged to the sound of public cheering at Manchester's New Bailey.

LOCATION: ON A646 BETWEEN BURNLEY AND HALIFAX

Waiting for news at Maypole Colliery in 1908

Towton NORTH YORKSHIRE

Battle of Towton Palm Sunday, 1461, was one of the bloodiest days in British history. The Battle of Towton saw the timely death of Lord Dacre, the 'butcher of Wakefield' (see Wakefield, below) and the wholesale slaughter of many ordinary soldiers. Some 40,000 Lancastrians lined up against 36,000 Yorkists by the valley of the Cock Beck. After 10 hours of fighting, the Lancastrians retreated. At a little bridge on the Old London Road, it is said their bodies fell in such numbers as to allow the pursuing Yorkists to cross without getting their feet wet. Perhaps as many as 25,000 men in all were butchered or drowned on this cruel field. Dacre, hit by a Yorkist arrow whilst removing his helmet to drink, was only one of a dozen nobles slain; many more were captured and executed. The common dead lay unburied for many days. Today a cross marks the site and Dacre's grave can be seen in Saxton churchyard.

LOCATION: BETWEEN TOWTON AND SAXTON OFF A162, 5 MILES SOUTH OF TADCASTER

Wakefield WEST YORKSHIRE

Battlefield treachery When the Duke of York led his tiny army out of Sandal Castle to confront 12,000 Lancastrians in December 1460, he believed he had the support of Lord Neville to the Lancastrian's rear. Neville, however, stayed put and York and his men were quickly cut to pieces. Escaping north, his son Edmund was cornered by Lord Clifford in the Chantry Chapel on Wakefield Bridge. Clifford, whose father had been slain by York at St Albans, cut off the youth's head with relish, and earned the foul reputation which dogs his memory as the 'butcher of Wakefield'.

LOCATION: SANDAL CASTLE 1 MILE SOUTH OF WAKEFIELD

Whitehaven CUMBRIA

Mining tragedies Like every coal mining town, Whitehaven has had its share of tragedy. For the Cumbrian port however, two pit disasters stand out as being particularly horrific. An explosion and subsequent fire in Wellington Pit in May 1910 left 137 miners dead, their bodies only recovered months later when the fires finally burned out.

In August 1947, miners' families once more gathered at the pit head to hear the dreaded news. An explosion in William Pit caused roof collapses throughout the mine where 117 men were working at the time. Only three miners survived. The rest were found huddled in groups, poisoned by the carbon monoxide fumes.

LOCATION: 40 MILES SOUTH-WEST OF CARLISLE

Wigan GREATER MANCHESTER

Colliery disasters Wigan is at the centre of the Lancashire coalfield and was no stranger to the disasters which occasionally befell its collieries. Amongst these, the fate of the Moss Colliery at nearby Ince-in-Makerfield and that of the Maypole at Abram stand out. At Moss in 1871, an explosion ripped through the heart of the mine's Nine Feet seam, incinerating 70 men at a stroke. Explosions continued for several weeks afterwards, hampering rescue attempts and occasionally killing the rescuers. Finally the decision was taken to flood the mine, and it was another six months before many of the charred remains could be recovered. Maypole's turn came in 1908.

There were 75 pitmen working on the Four Feet seam when explosives used to loosen coal set alight a deadly pocket of methane gas. No one was saved from the ensuing fireball. Rescuers found one man on his knees in prayer, while others had their hands held up to their faces as if to shield their eyes from their inevitable fate.

LOCATION: ON A573 SOUTH OF WIGAN

Woodplumpton LANCASHIRE

Meg Shelton, witch A curious boulder in the graveyard of St Anne's Church marks the grave of Marjorie Hilton, better known as the witch 'Meg Shelton'. Local farmers believed she could transform herself into a stook of corn and turn their milk sour. After her death her restless corpse evidently scratched its way out of the grave three times to resume her reign of terror, before the ground was exorcised and she was re-buried face down. A heavy rock was laid across the tomb for good measure and she hasn't been seen since.

LOCATION: ON B5411, 5 MILES NORTH-WEST OF PRESTON

York NORTH YORKSHIRE

Dick Turpin's demise Dick Turpin, the Essex butcher's boy turned notorious highwayman, was hanged from the gallows at Knavesmire outside the city walls in April 1739. As the cart on which he stood began to pull away, he leapt off the back, the noose around his neck pulled tight, and he was killed instantly. But this was not quite the end for England's most wanted criminal. Soon after burial in St George's churchyard, onlookers witnessed the corpse being exhumed and carried off for dissection. A crowd gathered and made its way to the home of the city's leading surgeon. They retrieved Turpin's body from the garden and returned to St George's, reburying it with quicklime to finish the job.

Spiked at Micklegate Bar In the 1890s a tenant in the chambers under Micklegate Bar was scratching round for firewood when he came across a bundle of well-seasoned poles, each tipped with a spike. Unfortunately for history, the cold took priority and he broke them up for kindling. These were the spikes used to display the heads of enemies on the city gate.

In 1461 this would have meant the head of the unucky Duke of York, tricked into one-sided battle outside Sandal Castle near Wakefield (see page 182). In 1746 it was the heads of William Connolly and James Mayne, Jacobites captured at the battle of Culloden. The two heads remained here until January 1754, when they mysteriously disappeared. There was a public scandal and the corporation offered a £100 reward for information. Eventually William Arundel, a local tailor with Jacobite sympathies, was imprisoned for two years and fined £5 for their removal. After their defeat at the battle of Marston Moor in 1644, hundreds of Royalist troops fled this way, pursued by Parliamentary cavalry. Many were cut down before they reached the safety of the city. Those that made it to Micklegate Bar still had to prove to the

The Vikings now took on the captive king. H torn apart until they w out like wings and th poured on the open w

defenders that they should be allowed in. In the chaos, the streets before the Bar filled up with the wounded and the dying. Amongst those who did make it through was John Dolben, who became Archbishop of York in 1683.
LOCATION: WEST OF CITY CENTRE ON A1036

Saxon bloodbath In AD 867 a Viking army took advantage of the warring Northumbrian kingdoms of Deira and Bernicia and occupied York. On Palm Sunday, united in their adversity under their respective kings (Ella and Osbert), the Northumbrians swiftly advanced on the great city. Despite the attackers' superior numbers the Vikings held firm and Osbert was killed. Worse was to follow. As the Saxon army disintegrated, Ella was captured. The Viking leaders were the sons of Ragnar, another prominent Scandinavian who had been shipwrecked on the Yorkshire coast and captured. Ella had ordered his execution, allegedly by being put in a pit of snakes. The Vikings now took their revenge on the captive king. His ribs were torn apart until they were spread out like wings and then salt was poured on the open wounds.

eir revenge ribs were re spread salt was nds.

PRE-TABLOID TALES

In the days before tabloid newspapers and television, the popular taste for horror would be sated by printed sheets known as 'chap books' or broadsides. These gave lurid accounts of executions, crimes or accidents, and also served as advertising for the freak shows which made their living by touring the country. In 19th-century Yorkshire the giant Joseph Brice, 8ft (2.44m) and 30 stone (191kg) was threatened in a broadside by a competitor, Peto, the giant of Fychow. 'His height is stupendous, his strength Herculean, his weight is four tons', screamed the advert. Eager spectators were disappointed to find Peto was actually an elephant. Mermaids were also popular novelties. The flyers would suggest buxom beauties, half woman half fish. In reality they were often the torsos of dead monkeys sewn on to the back end of a small shark by Japanese fishermen.

Massacre York experienced many unsavoury events in its long history, but none compares with the nefarious destruction of its Jewish community in 1190. Anti-Semitic feeling ran high in the city, for this was the age of the Crusades, and there was considerable antagonism towards Jewish traders and money-lenders. They sought shelter in Clifford's Tower, the formidable castle keep, but the mobs outside demanded blood. To escape their fate many took their own lives. The tower was set alight and many more died in the blaze. Those that survived this onslaught were butchered by the angry townsmen, their homes were looted and the records of their transactions burnt.
LOCATION: CITY CENTRE

EDINBURGH

The noble, cultured façade of this favoured Royal Seat has always been betrayed by base, brutal, explosive passions. Barricading themselves within Edinburgh's original High School in 1595, pupils resisted all attempts by staff to end their occupation of that stately building. What began as a boyish prank ended in horror as Baillie MacMorran, summoned to bid the boys see reason, was shot and slain by unruly student William Sinclair of Caithness. This sorry tale says much of the character – the true nature – of the city itself.

The warlike Votadini first made a fortress of the Castle Rock – the remnant of a 325 million-year-old volcano – and held fast against the Roman camps at Cramond and Inverest. Since then Edinburgh has served as a spy-glass in which the wider prides and prejudices of the Scottish nation are reflected and enlarged.

Established as a Royal Burgh by David I (1084–1153), and assailed and occupied by English forces with alarming regularity during the Wars of Independence (1297–1304 and 1306–28), the city reached the height of its glory under the Royal House of Stuart. Its defining moment came in 1513, with the Scots defeat at Flodden and the death of James IV. The population of Edinburgh panicked: the ramshackle King's Wall, raised in 1450, offered little real defence, and some communities, including the then prosperous Cowgate, lay outside its protective boundaries. The Flodden Wall, 25 feet (7.6m) high and 5 feet (1.5m) thick, was raised, and 24 of the city's strongest men were recruited to watch its gates. The wall did nothing to deter the burning of the Burgh by English forces in 1544–45.

Riots and religion

In 1482 citizens had rescued James III from imprisonment within the Castle. By the 16th century the descendants of those brave souls, living in filthy and increasingly overcrowded conditions, had become a feared and fickle force to be reckoned with. They found full fury during the Reformation with the sacking of St Giles Cathedral, in 1557. The Holyroodhouse debates between the fiercely Catholic Mary, Queen of Scots, and her Calvinist critic, John Knox, encapsulated and encouraged the deadly divisions of faith which swept the country during her reign. The National Covenant (1638), which would set the Scots Kirk against the Episcopacy of Mary's grandson, Charles I, was signed at Greyfriars Kirk following further riots against the introduction of the English prayer-book. Citizens were set at odds

by Cromwell's occupation of the city in 1650, and again in 1715 and 1745 following Jacobite attempts to reclaim the city for the Stuarts.

By the dawn of the 18th century, the population of 'Auld Reekie' – so called because of its abundance of grimy and malodorous chimney-stacks – had risen to 21,000. Most people were housed in a huddled rash of 'lands' or tenements, spreading down from the ridge of the High Street. Rich and poor had little choice but to live side by side. One tenement, at Dixon's Close, was host to a fishmonger on the ground floor, a lodging-house on the first, the Dowager Countess of Balcarres on the second, and the cramped families of milliners, tailors and tradesmen in the floors and attics above. The poor and dispossessed were relegated to basements and cellars. Hewn from the volcanic rock beneath these early 'sky-scrapers', filthy warrens formed the foundation of both a literal and a figurative Underworld. With no sewage system, household waste was simply hurled into the street with a cry of 'Gardy-loo!' (a corruption of the French 'Gardez l'eau!' or 'Watch out for the water!'), providing ideal conditions for the spread of pestilence. The plague epidemic of 1644–5 had decimated the population, costing the city a staggering £10,792 6s 8d for the disposal of the dead. Some streets, like the notorious Mary King's Close, were simply sealed-up and built over, to limit the risk of contagion.

A New Town

During the 18th century the city finally got much needed new space. The Flodden Wall was knocked down; North and South Bridge were constructed over ruinous medieval wynds and alleys, as more prosperous citizens departed for spacious, regimented homes in the New Town. Yet all the while the dark, degraded heart of the old city beat on, the prettified façades of 'the Athens of the North' revealed to be just that by the lurking presence of Deacon William Brodie, and the black-hearted 'body-snatchers', Burke and Hare. These were constant reminders of the contrasts which define the town as William Hazlitt called it, 'a city of Palaces and of tombs'.

'Auld Reekie' or 'the Athens of the North' viewed from Calton Hill

Abbey Strand BY HOLYROODHOUSE

Haunt of criminals From the 16th century, wanted felons could still claim sanctuary within 'Houses of Refuge' along the road that led to the old abbey. Dismal, dangerous, and poorly policed by the Keeper of Holyroodhouse, or 'Baron Baillie', the Strand included several seedy taverns, and quickly became the popular haunt of local villains, who might easily vanish into this near-lawless hiding place at the first sign of trouble. It was also a favoured refuge for 'abbey lairds', rogues resisting incarceration in the Debtors Prison, who considered themselves above the common class of cutpurse. The debauched poet Thomas de Quincey (1785–1859) was a regular resident in the 1830s.

Arthur's Seat HOLYROOD PARK

Coffin mystery In 1836 children playing on this windy volcanic crag made a grotesque and puzzling discovery. Seventeen miniature coffins, no more than six inches long and each containing a carefully carved and clothed wooden doll, were found secreted in a cave-mouth. Many believe the sinister figures were *corp craidh* carvings hidden away as part of some long forgotten witches' curse. Another theory suggests they were a ragged memorial to those deprived of a proper burial by the murderous body-snatchers, Burke and Hare.

Blackfriars Street OFF HIGH STREET

Family feuds With Regent John Stewart, Duke of Albany, absent in France, feuding Douglas and Hamilton factions clashed here in April 1520, desperate for control of the city and custody of the eight-year-old King James V. After a prolonged and brutal battle, which extended up High Street, the beleaguered Hamiltons were finally forced to flee. Frightened locals were left to cleanse the bloodied causeway of bodies and debris.

The 13th-century Blackfriars' Monastery, miraculously spared from harm during this terrible 'tulsie', was wrecked by a Reformation mob in 1559.

Brodie's Close OFF HIGH STREET

The duplicitous deacon Few suspected, in August 1786, that respectable town councillor and Deacon of the Wrights, William Brodie, might have masterminded the theft of £800 from bankers at the Royal Exchange. For 20 months the city's merchants shuddered as the Deacon, who had personally fitted many of their locks and shutters, boldly continued his thieving spree.

Brodie's fantasy of invulnerability was shattered by the more practical villainy of his murderous cohort, John Brown. Wanted for capital crimes in London, Brown offered to turn King's

Evidence against his comrade in order to save his own neck. Brodie was duly caught and hanged at the Tolbooth (see page 190). The double-life of Edinburgh's most infamous felon is said to have inspired Robert Louis Stevenson's *The Strange Case of Dr Jeckyll and Mr Hyde* (1886).

Calton Hill BY CRAIGEND

A volunteer executioner In 1884 the so-called Gorebridge Murderers, a pair of feckless poachers, waited to be hanged at the former Calton Jail, but no executioner could be found to do the job.

Former policeman James Berry gleefully volunteered his services in despatching the cowardly duo, who had shot and killed a gamekeeper. He proudly proclaimed that what he lacked in experience, he more than made up for in enthusiasm: he even had his own ropes! Meanwhile, Berry's family petitioned the authorities, claiming that his appointment would ruin their good name. Despite their best efforts, he got the job.

LOCATION: OFF A8

Cannonball House LAWNMARKET

Defending the Castle In the weeks leading up to the Jacobite siege of Edinburgh Castle in 1745, countless local lives were lost as the fortress sought to defend itself, sheltered behind the dense huddle of High Street houses. Ominously, on 4 October the castle's commander, General Preston, ordered Lawnmarket residents to abandon their homes. Shortly after noon, Preston's artillery finally lashed out, firing on the now deserted tenements and killing a score of rebels in the process. The iron shot embedded in the gable of Cannonball House is believed to have been fired during this exchange.

Canonmills

Broken on the wheel In 1600 stable-boy Robert Weir strangled John Kincaid, adulterous laird of the now long demolished Warrison House. Weir, outraged by Kincaid's treatment of his mistress, escaped capture until 1604, when he was arrested, tried and broken on the wheel at the Mercat Cross. Lady Warrison, suspected of bewitching the boy, was strangled and burned at the stake on Castlehill in 1601.

LOCATION: ON B901, 1 MILE NORTH OF PRINCES STREET

Calton Hill is topped by the City Observatory (left) and Nelson's Monument (right)

Far right: The city at dusk

Castlehill BY CASTLE ESPLANADE

Burned at the stake The Witches' Well drinking fountain stands in memorial to those tortured and burned on this grim spot from the 16th–18th centuries.

Janet Douglas, Lady Glamis, fell victim of James V's feud with her brother Archibald, 6th Earl of Angus, and was accused of plotting to poison the King. Her servants were stretched on the rack to provide proof of her treason, and she was burnt on 17 July 1537. Her husband, forced to watch the awful spectacle, sought to escape his own confinement by leaping to his death on the jagged Castle Rock.

Protestant martyr Patrick Hamilton was burned here in 1528 by Cardinal David Beaton. Dean Thomas Forret was due to be executed here in February 1539 for the heresy of ministering the Sacraments in English rather than Latin. Accidentally strangled by his bonds, Forret was spared the blistering ordeal of death by fire.

Chessel's Court CANONGATE

The hanging of Deacon Brodie Betrayed, and captured after a bungled burglary of the Excise Office here on 8 March 1788, arch-villain Deacon William Brodie (see pages 188–89) stunned magistrates by his apparent good humour. Entertaining his Tolbooth guards with merry airs from Gay's *Beggars' Opera*, he marched to his death, gleefully unrepentant and garbed in his finest suit, cheered by a crowd of 40,000. As a former councillor, Brodie begged the Lord Provost to spare him the indignity of being left hanging after execution. The Provost granted this indulgence, and his corpse was hastily cut down.

A local tradition holds that Brodie had the last laugh: rushed by friends into the arms of a waiting surgeon, he was revived and secretly set off for a new life in America. This is unlikely. Ironically, the gallows, designed by Brodien himself, were the first in the city to employ a trap-door drop. He might have survived strangulation but the drop made sure that his neck would have been snapped, instantly.

City Chambers HIGH STREET

Secret wynd Beneath the 18th-century chambers are the still accessible sloping ruins of Mary King's Close, one of the many filthy and overpopulated wynds that were 'steekit', or sealed-up, during the plague epidemic of 1644–45. Tradition holds that diseased folk were walled up within their homes and left to starve in pain and misery as bulbous, bloody buboes spread through their flesh. The purple prose of George Sinclair's *Satan's Invisible World Discovered* (1685) catalogues apparitions of demons, severed limbs and strange spectral animals said to have plagued a later resident, Thomas Coltheart.

Corstorphine BY MURRAYFIELD

Penitent ghost The unfaithful James, Lord Forrester, was slain with his own sword in the grounds of Corstorphine Castle by his mistress, Christian Nimmo, in August 1679. Her eternally penitent phantom is still said to haunt the grounds.

LOCATION: OFF A8, 3 MILES SOUTH-WEST OF PRINCES STREET

Craigmillar

Fratricide In 1479 John Stewart, Earl of Mar, slowly bled to death in his bath, while imprisoned here by his brother, James III. The cause of Mar's bloody demise has long been a mystery. Simple mishap or a badly botched medical bloodletting have both been suggested. More likely, however, is fratricide.

Accused of consorting with known witches, the Earl was almost certainly killed because of the King's paranoia concerning a prophesy that he would be usurped or slain by his closest kin. The prophesy was fulfilled nevertheless by his 15-year-old heir at Sauchieburn, in 1488.

LOCATION: OFF A7, 3 MILES SOUTH OF CITY CENTRE

Edinburgh Castle

Forfeited to Richard II, frequently occupied by English forces during the Wars of Independence (1296–1328), burned by the Scots (1313) and twice besieged by Henry IV, Edinburgh Castle has a more turbulent history than most. Later occupations by Covenanters (1639), Royalists (1640), Roundheads (1650) and for James VII/II (1689) have confirmed its status as a symbolic and strategic stronghold for those who would dictate Scotland's destiny.

Siege and strife In April 1571, Sir William Kircaldy of Grange closed the castle gates and declared his allegiance to Mary, Queen of Scots, who was imprisoned at the time in England. It was the start of what became known as the Long Siege. Regent James Douglas, 4th Earl of Morton, lacking artillery to crush this rebellion, begged Elizabeth I for English arms. In March 1572, some 1,500 harquebusiers, 140 pikemen and a formidable train of artillery joined him. By 24 May, David's Tower and most of the castle's defences had been reduced to rubble. Five days later the weary rebels surrendered the castle – but to the English, not to Morton, hoping that they would be treated with greater mercy by agents of a foreign power.

They did not account for the fury of the city mob. Bitter at the barrage they had suffered under the castle guns during the siege, they pressed for the English to surrender their prisoners. Kircaldy was duly hanged and his head piked on the castle battlements. In 1581, James VI, suspecting that Morton had conspired to murder the king's father, Lord Darnley, had him beheaded at the Grassmarket in the 'Maiden'. It was a guillotine which Morton himself had introduced to the city.

Treason within On 8 September 1715, as Edinburgh made preparations for another long siege, treason was plotted within the castle itself. Sergeant Ainsley planned to permit the Jacobite supporters of James Stuart, the Old Pretender (1688–1766), secret entry to the fortress. Lingering too long in local taverns, however, the rebels missed their rendezvous and mislaid the rope ladder, which was to aid their entry. A militia lay in wait. Forced to flee, all but four of the Jacobite rebels escaped. Ainsley himslef was hanged, and his body draped over the Postern Gate.

Blockaded After his famous victory at Prestonpans 30 years later, James's heir, Charles Edward Stuart (the Young Pretender, or Bonnie Prince Charlie), paraded triumphantly into the city and blockaded the castle. The soldiers held back, unable to return fire without devastating the homes of innocent citizens. Equally unable to break the siege, the prince departed, condemning the redcoats for the death and debris his own presence had caused.

The Black Dinnour On 28 November 1440 the 15-year-old William, 6th Earl of Douglas, was invited with his younger brother to dine with the 9-year-old King James II at the Banqueting Hall, which once stood on the site of the Great Hall. The

Edinburgh Castle, high on its rock above the city, has withstood many a siege.

invitation to dine had been made by Sir William Crichton and castle's governor, Sir Alexander Livingston. Both were wary of William. His father, Archibald, had served as Regent until his death the previous year, and his family had power to rival even that of the ruling Stuarts. He commanded a formidable fighting force, had famously refused a summons to take his place in the Scottish Parliament, and was proving to be a wilful, proud young man: a possible future threat to Stuart authority, and to their own ambitions.

When the repast ended, a black bull's head – a traditional symbol of impending death – was set before the visitors, and a tearful James was forced to watch as his friends were brutally beaten, damned by their hosts as potential traitors, and dragged to Castlehill for beheading.

Cunning escape Like the Earl of Mar (see page 190), Alexander, Duke of Albany, was imprisoned here in 1479, subject to the fears of his elder brother, James III, that he would be betrayed by his closest kin. Alexander was held in David's Tower, where the palace now stands. A nobleman of rank, he was permitted luxuries including wine, which he used to intoxicate his guards. Stabbing them with their own swords, the Duke threw his armour-clad hosts into the hearth, roasting them in the flames before making his escape.

Below ground Scots, English, Jacobites, Royalists and Roundheads: all enjoyed the hospitality of the castle dungeons, as did the Frenchmen detained during the Napoleonic Wars in the cheerless chambers beneath the Great Hall.

An apocryphal 19th-century tale tells how a drummer-boy was lowered into a tunnel entrance too small to allow adult access, discovered beneath these vaults. Thumping his instrument heartily, the boy's muffled beats were followed down High Street, but by the Tron Kirk they stopped suddenly. The boy did not return. Rather than risk losing another child searching for him, it was decided to seal up the entrance. It's a fanciful tale, but not entirely implausible: ruins of long lost tunnels do exist beneath the fortress.

Right: The Covenanters' Memorial in the Grassmarket marks the spot of the common gibbet.

Empire Theatre

NICOLSON STREET

Trapped by fire Illusionist Sigismund Neuberger, 'The Great Lafayette', had drawn a crowd of over 3,000 to the Empire Theatre on 9 May 1911, when an electrical fire caused safety curtains to be dropped. Unsure if this was part of the act, the audience was led, amid a gaudy throng of harem-dancers and turbaned Turks, to the safety of the street. Outside, firemen faced a less obliging audience: spectators had gathered to gawp at the fire and were reluctant to be moved on. The stage doors had been locked to protect Neuberger's secrets, and the first Empire Theatre was soon consumed, along with the Great Lafayette, as firemen struggled with the crowd outside.

LOCATION: OFF A7

Gibb's Entry

Consorting with a body-snatcher Early in 1828, prostitutes Mary Paterson and Janet Brown innocently accompanied the body-snatcher William Burke to the Gibb's Close lodging of his brother, Constantine. Whether Burke planned to smother them and sell their corpses, or sought some more immediate reward, is unclear. Whatever the case, the arrival of his mistress, Helen McDougal, complicated matters. Well aware of her lover's murderous recreations, McDougal objected to Burke consorting with two such young and pretty harlots. As tempers flared, Janet escaped but Mary was not so lucky. Her corpse was sold to anatomist Robert Knox for £8.

LOCATION: OFF A7

Gogar House

Gogar Flashes In 1650, the reckless Covenanter Sir James Leslie, Lord Newark, led his men against Oliver Cromwell's vastly superior force as it attempted to traverse the marshy Gogar Burn. In a brief but bloody exchange, the 'Gogar Flashes' saw high-calibre field artillery used for the first time, and left many dead and injured on both sides

LOCATION: OFF A8, NORTH OF EDINBURGH INTERNATIONAL AIRPORT

Grassmarket

Officially dead In September 1742 Maggie Dickson was hanged for child-murder at the Common Gib, sited within this, the 17th-century marketplace. She was declared dead, and her body was ready for disposal when the corpse suddenly sat bolt upright. The authorities were unable to repeat 'Hauf Hingit' Maggie's sentence as she was officially deceased, and had a notarised death certificate to prove it. Her survival owed less to divine intervention, than to the inefficiency of the rickety gibbet favoured at the time – a tilting-frame, from which felons would be tipped and slowly strangled rather than dropped.

Burke's end Criminal corpses were customarily supplied to surgeons for study and dissection. In the case of body-snatcher William Burke evisceration occurred here, before a baying mob, on 28 January 1829. Bodily mementos of the event were later sold at public auction.

The 'Porteous Affair' In 1736 smuggler Andrew Wilson was taken to be hanged at the Grassmarket. Wilson was a popular rogue, and the Old Town Guard found themselves jeered and jostled by the mob. Captain John Porteous ordered the guards to fire on the crowd, leaving 30 dead or injured. Desperate to maintain order in the face of public outrage, magistrates then charged Porteous with murder. On 8 September crowds gathered again, eager to see the bully hang. When they learned that the execution was to be postponed, vengeful citizens attacked the Tolbooth Jail, burning down its doors and dragging Porteous from his cell. Taken to the Grassmarket, he was hanged as originally planned.

LOCATION: BETWEEN WEST PORT AND COWGATE

Criminal corpses were customarily supplied to surgeons for study and dissection. In the case of body-snatcher William Burke evisceration occurred here, before a baying mob, on 28 January 1829.

Greyfriars kirkyard made a secure enclosure for captured Covenanters

Greyfriars Kirk CANDLEMAKER ROW

A makeshift prison In the long months after the crushing defeat at Bothwell Bridge (1679) more than a thousand Covenanters were confined within a makeshift prison in this kirkyard – exposed to the elements, malnourished and open to public ridicule.

Protecting the corpses In the 1820s armed guards patrolled each night to protect against the Resurrection Men, or grave robbers. A fresh corpse for dissection practice could attract a handsome fee. Heavy iron mort-safes were clamped over new graves until the flesh beneath was too far rotted to interest the grave robbers or their surgeon customers.

Heave-Awa' House HIGH STREET

Cry for help Death came suddenly in the deep dark of a November night in 1862, as two long-neglected, tumbledown tenements collapsed in on one another, crushing 35 poor souls beneath a cascade of brick and rubble. Trapped amid the debris and the dead, survivor Joseph MacIvor is said to have called to his rescuers 'Heave awa', lads, I'm no' deid yet!'

MacIvor is remembered in effigy, engraved on an archway of this building, raised from the ruins the following year.

High Street (OR ROYAL MILE)

Busy street The Via Regia or Royal Mile has witnessed all manner of raid, riot and revenge, including a battle between rival Douglas and Hamilton factions during the 1520 'Cleanse the Causeway' riot, and burning by the English in 1544-45 during the 'Rough Wooing'. In 1689 respected advocate Sir George Lockhart ruled against the cruel and intemperate John Chiesly in an alimony dispute. Unwilling to accept this judgement, 'Mad John' lay in wait for Lockhart, shooting him dead as he left his house at Old Bank Street, once sited near the modern intersection with South Bridge.

Holyroodhouse BY HOLYROOD PARK

Rizzio's murder Many thought David Rizzio a far too 'familiar' presence within the court of Mary, Queen of Scots. The little Italian was with the monarch on 9 March 1566, when she was surprised by the sudden arrival of her estranged spouse, Henry Stuart, Lord Darnley. Bitter that his bride, then six months pregnant, would not permit him to reign as King beside her, Darnley was an

Mary, Queen of Scots, was never short of courtly admirers

infrequent visitor to the palace.

Close on his heels came the curious, agitated figure of Patrick, Lord Ruthven, a nightshirt carelessly pulled over his armour. Wild-eyed, Ruthven railed against Rizzio as a Papal spy and a seducer. The Italian grasped at Mary's skirts, but was dragged away, screaming. Pistols thrust into her gut, the tearful Queen was made to watch her friend suffer the first of sixty dagger blows, which left him a mess of bloody flesh and fabric. Mary and her unborn heir escaped harm. Though he struck no blow, Darnley's complicity in the murder was clear – his dagger left buried in the butchered body. If he had hoped to force Mary to grant what he wanted, Darnley was to be disappointed. Delivered of her child she is said to have warned: 'I have forgiven, but never will forget.'

Lochend House BY MEADOWBANK SPORTS CENTRE

Lover's revenge The remains of a holy well in the grounds celebrate the 4th-century St Triduana who, according to legend, spurned the advances of the Pictish King Nechthan. Besotted by her beauty, the chieftain plucked out her eyes, keeping them as a reminder of his unrequited ardour.

The nearby doocot of Lochend House was converted in 1645 for use as a kiln, to burn the contaminated chattels of plague victims.

LOCATION: OFF A1140, 1 MILE NORTH-EAST OF PRINCES STREET

The Meadows BRUNTSFIELD LINKS

Plague pits Few who stroll through this pleasant parkland realise that they tread over plague pits, dug for the disposal of corpses in the 17th century. Here, according to local tradition, the anatomist Robert Knox first realised that his association with the body-snatchers, Burke and Hare, had demonised him in the eyes of the population. Walking one morning, he came upon a little girl playing in the park. Presenting the urchin with a penny-piece, he joked that she would surely be his friend forever were he to give her such a token every day. 'No' me', replied the suspicious babe, 'ye wad maybe sell me tae Doctor Knox!'

LOCATION: OFF A700, SOUTH OF PRINCES STREET

For years visitors were shown the bloodstained floor at Holyrood Palace where Rizzio fell, until it was revealed as a fake.

The city's market cross was a public landmark for proclamations and punishment

Mercat Cross HIGH STREET

Public punishment A popular site for public proclamation and punishment, it was here that thieves might have their hands nailed, or be beaten the length of the High Street. Beggars would be whipped, or branded upon the cheek. In 1574 Robert Drummond, charged with the adulterous abandonment of his wife, was led to the Cross for 'chastisement'. Rather than face the humiliation of public scorn, Robert pulled a dagger from beneath his shirt, and plunged the blade deep into his breast. The more elaborate (and visceral) the 'entertainments', the larger the audience: tens of thousands gathered to watch murderer Robert Weir suffer as his battered body was slowly twisted and broken on the wheel here in 1604.

Robin Hood riots Pageant plays celebrating the exploits of English outlaw Robin Hood had long been a popular recreation for craftsmen in the 16th-century city. An Act of Parliament banned such entertainments in 1555, as a threat to public order. Defiance of this law, in 1561, resulted in the imprisonment of shoemaker James Gillon. Sentenced to be hanged at the Mercat Cross, Gillon was rescued, in the spirit of his historical hero, by the 'rascal multitude' that 'with stones, guns and other weapons, began to assault the Tolbooth.' The event was recorded by John Knox in his *History of the Reformation of the Church in Scotland* (1571).

In the mêlée, Councillor Robert Norwell shot craftsman John Tweedie, but with a citywide panic and the gates held by rioters, Gillon was released and all charges dropped.

Moray House CANONGATE

Condemned man attacked 1650 was not a good year for James Graham, 1st Marquis of Montrose. A former Covenanter, he had changed sides and led the King's army. In this year, having already been shipwrecked in Orkney and suffered a crushing defeat against Parliamentary forces at

Carbisdale, he was finally betrayed to his enemies for the huge sum of £25,000. Brought before the Scottish Parliament, Montrose was sentenced without trial to be hanged, disembowelled and have his head piked at the Tolbooth on 21 May.

Led in solemn procession to scaffold, he was spotted by friends of his former Covenanting ally Archibald Campbell, 1st Marquis of Argyll, who attacked the turncoat from the first floor balcony of Moray House.

Where Scotland died Battleground for rival Douglas and Hamilton factions during the 1520 'Cleanse the Causeway' riot, and burnt by the English in 1544–45 during the 'Rough Wooing', Moray House was assailed by an angry mob in 1707, as Lord Chancellor James Ogilvie, Earl of Seafield sought to sign the Treaty of Union with England here. The house was dubbed 'the place where Scotland died'.

Museum of Scotland CHAMBERS STREET

Many cruel and unusual mementos of Edinburgh's unpleasant past are housed within this modern museum, including the surviving 'Arthur's Seat Coffins', the 'Maiden' which beheaded Regent Moray, and the skeleton keys used by ebullient burglar, Deacon Brodie.

LOCATION: OFF A7

Niddry Street BY SOUTH BRIDGE

Pursuit of a warlock In 1591, troops commanded by the dangerously deranged Francis Stewart, 5th Earl of Bothwell, attacked James VI at Holyroodhouse. The King escaped and took shelter, cowering in the dungeons of the mansion of Provost Nicol Edward, deep beneath Niddry Wynd, as soldiers scoured the surrounding streets, wreaking bloody revenge upon his attackers. Bothwell, a suspected necromancer, had been imprisoned two years previously for his alleged dealings with the 'North Berwick Witches' (see right).

LOCATION: OFF A8

JAMES VI AND THE WITCHES

Servant Geillis Duncan was accused of witchcraft by her master, David Seaton of Tranent, and gave way under torture. It was a confession that was to shake Edinburgh society to its core.

Her fingers crushed in the pilniewinks, Geillis testified that she had taken part in a Witches' Sabbat at the Old Kirk, North Berwick, on Hallowe'en 1590. Its purpose: to raise storms and sink the ship that was bringing James VI home to Scotland with his new bride, Anne of Denmark; its host: none other than the troublesome Earl of Bothwell, in the guise of Satan himself. Treason and witchcraft wed, the King's curiosity was aroused. The unfortunate girl was encouraged to name names.

Soon Dr John Fian, the 'Devil's Clerk', was brought to Edinburgh for torture. He pleaded innocence, but his fingernails were torn out and needles driven into the bloodied quicks. A 'heid-rope' was then tied and tightened around his head, his feet crushed to pulp in the boot, and the flesh of his legs seared in the heated iron cage of the cashielaws. Agnes Sampson was brought to Holyrood, where James himself led her interrogation. She, in turn, implicated Barbara Napier and Euphame MacCalzean, respected Edinburgh citizens and relatives of Lord Cliftonhall. Napier was said to have used potions and enchantments to murder her first husband. MacCalzean, though cleared by a jury of all charges brought against her, had her judgement overturned by the King.

Accusation followed accusation, and by the end of 1591 almost 100 people had been tried, and many were strangled and burned at the stake. This least distinguished episode of James's reign resulted in the 1591 publication of his lurid study of witchcraft and magic, *Daemonology*.

Far right: Intricate carving on the 'Prentice Pillar', Rosslyn Chapel

Far right, below: The daunting bulk of St Giles Cathedral stands near the top of the Royal Mile

Parliament Square OFF HIGH STREET

The Tolbooth The decorative pavement slabs of the 'Heart of Midlothian' mark the former site of the Tolbooth, a prison and, from the 14th–18th centuries, a prime location for the punishment of those who had offended City and State.

Following the murder of James I in 1437, great pains were taken to ensure the even greater pains of those responsible. Walter, Earl of Athol was suspended by his feet from a wooden crane and dropped, jerking both legs from their sockets. Pilloried, he was branded with an iron circlet, scorching the legend 'King of Traitors' in fiery letters in his flesh. Dragged through the streets, he was finally hanged, drawn, quartered, and his severed head piked in the traditional manner for traitors. His ordeal lasted three days.

Princes Street Gardens

BY WAVERLY STATION

The Nor' Loch In 1460 this steep-sided valley was flooded to create the defensive Nor' Loch. It became a dumping ground for the detritus of the city; market waste, sewage and even the Old Town's dead were regularly despatched to its foetid depths. Witches were strapped to a ducking stool, and submerged in the noxious waters prior to strangulation and burning on Castlehill. Civil punishments were more common. During the 16th-century the 'branks', a form of scolds'-bridle, could be placed over the heads of troublesome wives. Wearing this heavy iron helmet, locked at the chin, and with a sharp metal spike thrust in the mouth, the beldams were dragged the length of the town, at risk of losing their tongues if they called out.

Prestonfield House

Presbyterian revenge The friendship of James, Duke of York, Catholic governor of Scotland, cost the household of Edinburgh Provost James Dick dearly. In 1681, Presbyterian students, their faith marginalized under York's rule, razed his home, Priestfield, to ashes. While Dick escaped harm, several servants were fatally injured in the blaze.

LOCATION: OFF A7, SOUTH-EAST OF CITY CENTRE.

Queensberry House CANONGATE

Act of a lunatic James Douglas, lunatic son of James, 2nd Duke of Queensberry, was hidden from sight, confined to a wing of this fine 17th-century mansion. In 1707, as his father celebrated the signing of the Treaty of Union, the troubled teenager escaped from his chambers. He was later discovered, having spit-roasted and partially eaten an unfortunate kitchen-boy. Disdainful locals deemed this a timely judgement on the 'Union Duke' for his support of the unpopular Treaty.

Ratho

Last public hanging in the village With no less than 11 taverns, it's no surprise that spirited passions in this otherwise unremarkable 19th-century quarrying community occasionally got out of hand. The Bridge Inn here was home to George Bryce, who in 1864 murdered local nursemaid Jane Seaton. The 'Ratho Murderer' achieved unwarranted fame as the last man to be publicly hanged at Edinburgh's Lawnmarket; subsequent executions occurred within the grim walls of the Calton Jail.

LOCATION: OFF M8, 3 MILES SOUTH-WEST OF CITY CENTRE.

Rosslyn Chapel

Chapel murder Many curious traditions surround this 15th-century chapel. It has (probably apocryphal) associations with the mysterious Knights Templar, and its extensively engraved carvings and corbels are said by some to be a sophisticated code, revealing the last resting place of the Holy Grail.

Of these decorations the 'Prentice Pillar' is the most interesting. A spiral column of intertwining dragons, wreaths and flowering foliage, it is said to have been the earnest endeavour of a humble apprentice, who laboured long and hard to create

the work in the absence of his master. On his return the stonemason was so impressed by the boy's efforts that he jealously smashed the lad's brains out with a mallet.

LOCATION: OFF A701, 6 MILES SOUTH OF CITY CENTRE.

St Andrews Square

BY WAVERLEY CENTRE

On the long lost Gabriel's Road, tutor Robert Irvine, for reasons unknown, strangled two children in his care. Hanged in 1717, he first had both hands reduced to bloody stumps by the executioner's axe.

St Giles Cathedral HIGH STREET

The National Covenant In 1528 the Presbyterian passions of Edinburgh's congregations were sparked by Cardinal Beaton's brutal burning of the 'heretic' Protestant preacher, Patrick Hamilton. By 1557 this Reformation blaze threatened to consume the 'High Kirk' itself, as priests were attacked, altars smashed, and idols 'drowned' in the murky depths of the Nor' Loch. Charles I's attempts to foist his faith on his Scots subjects did nothing to calm the discontent. On hearing the first words spoken from the new Episcopalian prayer book, in 1637, fish-wife Jenny Geddes violently hurled her stool at the startled preacher. Within hours the revolt had spread throughout the city, leading to the signing of the National Covenant, which abolished Episcopacy in Scotland, set Protestant against Protestant, and laid down dogmatic battle-lines which led to thousands of deaths in the years which followed.

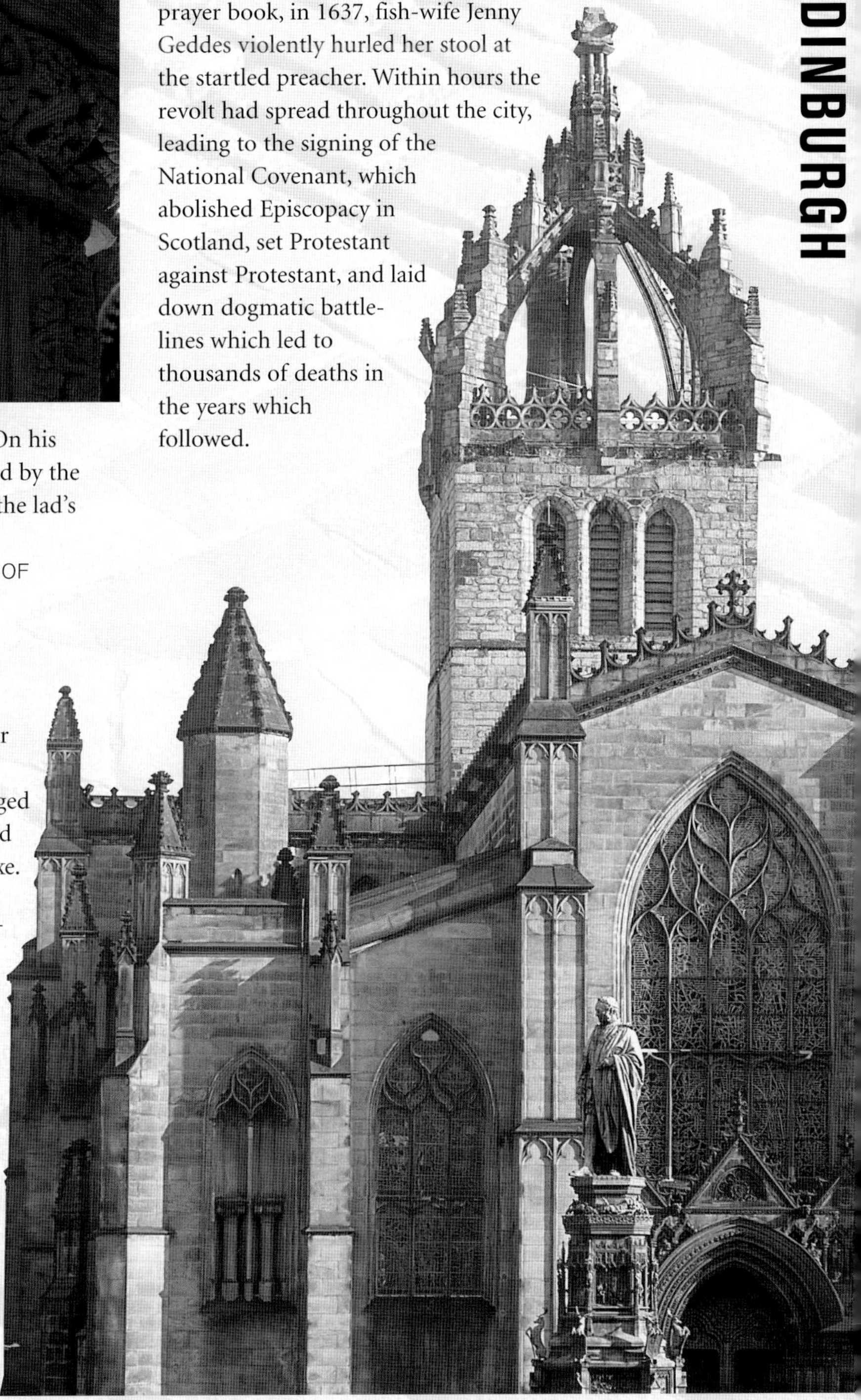

The Underground City

The filthy cellars beneath the High Street tenements, or 'lands', had long been the overcrowded city's only shelter for its poorest, most desperate inhabitants. The late 18th-century construction of the North and South Bridges created a new network of vaults, hidden from respectable view, and home to all forms of degraded humanity.

Out of sight, out of mind If the condition of poverty-stricken adults living in these dismal warrens was unfortunate, then that of their children was tragic. Many were simply 'sold-on' to the Lothian Mines, to nail-makers, who might pin their ears to workshop doors if they produced too many bent nails, or to the army of sweeps eternally occupied in cleansing 'Auld Reekie's' thousands of twisted 'lums' (chimneys). A four-year-old entering this unpleasant profession might expect to survive for six months. Two early 19th-century master sweeps were prosecuted for the fatal 'keel-hauling' of their apprentices through chimneys, their arms and legs tied tight to their bodies with ropes.

The 'loiterers' The cloistered cellars and closes of the Cowgate became a natural home for vice and villainy. Deacon Brodie frequented cock-pits and gambling dens here; Edinburgh's own 'Hell Fire Club', a focus for refined debauchery, was rumoured to meet in chambers beneath South Bridge; and Burke and Hare chose their victims from this damned population. Most, like Mary Paterson, the prostitute murdered by Burke at Gibb's Close (see page 194), might live and die without ever ascending to the upper streets.

Robert Louis Stevenson (1850–94), a prosperous son of the New Town, spoke

Children aged fast in the underground stews of the city

despairingly of his encounters with these 'loiterers': a grim faceless muddle of lost humanity.

The Great Fire In 1584, an urchin set a stack of heather smouldering at the Mercat Cross. Panicked, stallholders seized the tyke and burned him alive. Over centuries of raid and riot the population lived in fear of such conflagrations.

The blaze which swept out of Old Assembly Close on 5 November 1824 surpassed them all. Tearing through the Royal Mile from Parliament Square to Hunter Close, and toppling the spire of the Tron Kirk, it reduced the towering huddle of wooden tenements to ashes. Many pitiful residents of the cramped cellars beneath the 'lands' died as the floors above collapsed in on them. The cellars of the Cowgate and Grassmarket and the vaults beneath South Bridge were unaffected, but the city was changing. The old 'Underground City' was no more.

Under South Bridge Parts of the Underground City, including sections of the medieval Niddry Wynd, beneath South Bridge, are still accessible. Here, in 1742, an angry mob stormed the surgery of physician Martin Eccles, discovering the hastily concealed corpse of Alexander Baxter, lifted from the West Kirk by 'Resurrection Men' the previous night. Many Christians believed that if a body was spliced and cut on the dissecting table, then it would be literally unable to rise on the sounding of the Last Trump, and would be deprived all hope of ultimate resurrection. It was not simply dead flesh that was stolen by grave robbers; it was the promise of eternal life. Brought before the bench, Eccles, like many respectable surgeons, was cleared of complicity in the raising of the dead.

In 1822, Mary McKinnon attempted to expel ruffians from her vaulted tavern beneath South Bridge by brandishing a kitchen knife and accidentally skewered city clerk William Mowatt. The landlady was hanged for his murder on 16 April 1822.

University of Edinburgh

The 'Kirk o' Fields' The University stands on the site of the Old Provost's House, which was itself built in the grounds of the 12th-century Church of St Mary of the Field: the 'Kirk o' Fields'. Here Lord Darnley, estranged husband of Mary, Queen of Scots, was killed by an explosion on 19 February 1567, his body hurled into fields beyond the Flodden Wall. Some accounts argue that Darnley's slumbers were disturbed by the assassins' arrival. Assisted by servant William Taylor, he lowered himself from a window and attempted an escape. The murderers pursued the panicked pair, smothering them with their own nightgowns. This would certainly explain why Darnley's body bore no marks from the explosion. The obvious suspect for the murder was Mary's lover James Hepburn, 4th Earl of Bothwell. He was quickly cleared of the crime, though this was perhaps due to the

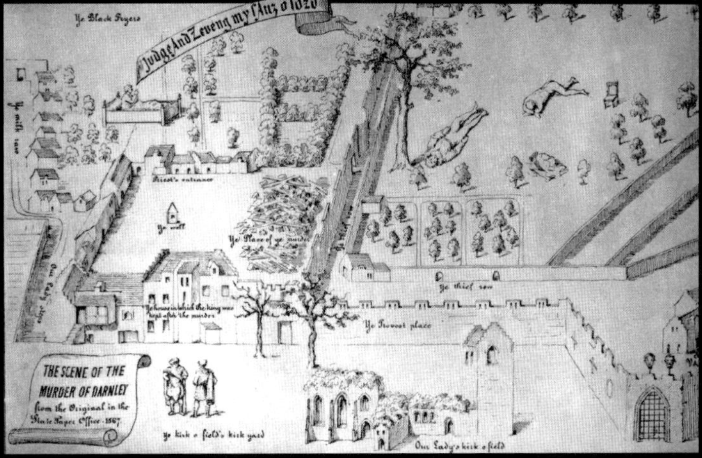

A contemporary 'scene of crime' map for the botched murder of Lord Darnley

threatening presence at the tribunal of his own heavily armed guard.

Snowball rioters In 1870, police were warned of rowdy scholars pelting pedestrians with snowballs. The response of the constabulary was to corral the youngsters within University grounds and beat them senseless. The Victorian mob, outraged by this brutal overreaction, joined the students in a renewed assault on the police.

University of Edinburgh (CONTD)

A familiar corpse Charged with the task of teaching anatomy, the Royal College of Surgeons, based from 1694 at Surgeon's Hall, was provided with corpses from Edinburgh's poor houses and public gib. The irregular nature of these sources prompted some surgeons to employ grave-robbers to seek out specimens. By the early 19th century, public outrage and increased vigilance limited even this supply. Anatomist Robert Knox sought other sources, engaging two Irish labourers, William Burke and William Hare, to procure bodies for his classes in Surgeon's Square (see opposite). How these were obtained did not concern him.

In 1828, his students, recognising a young prostitute set before them for study, refused to dissect her not because they feared foul play but because they considered her too 'pretty' to cut up. Knox responded by pickling the alluring 'specimen' in alcohol, and employing a local artist to produce sketches of her, which were then offered for sale to his pupils.

West Bow BY GRASSMARKET

Wizard of the West Bow Major Thomas Weir had been a distinguished Covenanter and Commander of the City Guard, and lived with his sister, Grizel, at the West Bow. A member of the 'Bowhead Saints', a strict Presbyterian sect, he gained respect as a powerful preacher. In 1670, in his seventy-second year, the 'Angelic Thomas' surprised his brethren by calmly announcing that both he and his aged sibling were, in fact, servants of Satan. Surprisingly in this superstitious age, every effort was made to prove that Weir was little more than a sick old man. After an examination by physicians and clerics, it was concluded that he was physically sound, but clearly suffered the pangs of a guilty conscience.

Both Weirs were duly arrested. Grizel, as deranged as her brother, warned guards to remove Thomas's staff: a gift from Satan, and the source of his powers. Both freely confessed to incest, bestiality and necromancy, and told how an enchanted root, given to Grizel by the Queen of the Fairies, had allowed her to become a skilled spinner.

Condemned, the 'Wizard of the West Bow' was burnt, with his staff, on 14 April. His sister, distraught and clearly insane, was hanged shortly afterwards at the Grassmarket.

Whiteford House CANONGATE

Inspiring crime Favoured for furtive meetings of the city's Jacobites, the original Jenny Ha's Changehouse once occupied part of this site It was a haunt, too, of the 18th century's greatest celebrant of murder, villainy and vice, John Gay (1685–1732), author of *The Beggar's Opera*, whose fictional highwayman-hero, Captain Macheath, was claimed by Deacon Brodie as the inspiration for his crimes.

World's End Close OFF HIGH STREET

Ordeal by blood Originally known as Stansfield Close, this was home to melancholy merchant Sir James Stansfield. When Stansfield was found drowned on 2 November 1587, suicide was thought the most likely cause, and he was buried without incident. However, the death became a topic of surmise and suspicion among the Old Town gossips, who thought the prodigal, and recently disinherited, son, Philip Stansfield, a credible culprit. The Lord Advocate, too, was suspicious and ordered the corpse to be exhumed. According to the tradition that a murdered man would bleed if touched by his killer, Philip Stansfield was subjected to 'Ordeal by blood', as reported by an anonymous wordsmith of the day:

'Young Stansfield touched his father's corpse
Where rose a fearful wail;
For blood gush'd through the burial sheet,
And every face grew pale.'

After a botched hanging at the Mercat Cross, Philip was strangled, his tongue and right hand severed, and his head piked.

THE 'BODY-SNATCHERS'

Left to right: William Blake, William Hare and Robert Knox

It is a popular misconception that Burke and Hare were grave-robbers. In fact, they conceived a much more grisly and efficient method of supplying the city's anatomists with a steady stream of fresh corpses.

They got the idea after being paid £7 by Robert Knox for the body of an army pensioner, who had died owing rent to Hare's mistress. Feigning friendship, the pair sought out the beggarly and the infirm – those like prostitute Mary Paterson who would not be missed (see page 194). Rendered senseless with alcohol, the victims would be slowly smothered. An unmarked corpse commanded a price as high as £12, and, bearing no mark of violence, was unlikely to rouse suspicions of murder.

As many as 16 victims fell to the 'body-snatchers', but they were charged with only one murder, that of an old Irishwoman whose belongings had been found in their possession. Any evidence of murder had been long since washed from the surgeons' slab, and so Lord Advocate Sir William Rae was forced to take drastic measures to guarantee a conviction and calm public passions. Hare was eventually persuaded to turn King's Evidence. Burke, still complaining that Knox owed him £5, was hanged and publicly dissected at the Grassmarket on 28 January 1828. Hare was never charged and is believed to have died a pauper on the streets of London, around 1860. Edinburgh's most enduring 'bogey-men' are remembered, still, in a popular skipping rhyme:

'Up the close, an' doon the stair,
But an' ben wae Burke an' Hare.
Burke's the Butcher; Hare's the Thief,
Knox the boy that buys the beef.'

Burke, still complaining that Knox owed him £5, was hanged and publicly dissected at the Grassmarket on 28 January 1828.

SCOTLAND

Its turbulent relationship with neighbouring England and an unfortunate tendency to in-fighting has ensured that Scottish history is liberally scattered with incidents of bloody mayhem. Thanks to its relative proximity to Scandinavia, there were early skirmishes with Danes and Norwegians, some of whom came to fight, others to settle and farm. Whole sections of land changed hands regularly, and the islands of Shetland and Orkney only reverted to Scottish rule in the mid-13th century.

Culloden, where the Hghlanders made their last stand under Bonnie Prince Charlie

The Romans and after

Roman soldiers reached Scotland in AD 80. Their most famous battle against the native Picts was described by Tacitus as a bloody affair: '10,000 of the enemy were slain; on our side there fell 360 men.' Despite this apparent omen of success, the Romans retreated south to the safety of England. Their lasting memorial is the great wall which they built to keep the Scots out. The isolation suited later arrivals such as St Columba, who hoped the remote island of Iona would prove a secure refuge from marauding Vikings (he was mistaken).

By the 7th century Scotland was occupied by an uneasy mix of Picts, Celts and Scots (who invaded, confusingly, from Ireland). Picts and Scots united against the threat of a Norse invasion, and so the first Scottish kingdom was formed north of the Forth in AD 843, under Kenneth MacAlpin. It was not until 1018 that the Northumbrian King Canute was thrown out of the southern lands, and Scotland as we know it became an entity.

Scottish Wars of Independence

Unfortunate events in 1286 precipitated years of unrest and bloodshed. King Alexander III was killed in a riding accident and guardians were appointed to run the country while arrangements were made to bring his three-year-old grand-daughter from Norway to succeed him. However the 'Maid of Norway' was a sickly child and died on the boat, leaving Scotland with several claimants to the vacant throne.

The guardians asked Edward I of England to adjudicate, but he made his own claim as overall sovereign and demanded that all contenders for the throne swear an oath of fealty to him. In the final choice between Robert the Bruce and John Balliol, Edward chose the latter and installed him as his puppet on the throne. Known as 'Toom Tabard' (empty jacket), Balliol eventually displayed some resistance and was removed by Edward, who then invaded Scotland in 1296.

During the ensuing wars, patriot William Wallace mounted a guerrilla war, but was eventually betrayed and executed in London. Bruce advanced his own claim to the throne by murdering his main rival, the Red Comyn, and launching an attack on occupying forces in the south-west. Crowned king at Scone, he continued his campaign against the English until his decisive win at Bannockburn in 1314. With the English out of the way, Bruce tightened his grip on Scotland by ruthlessly exterminating all who opposed him.

The Rough Wooing

In 1544 Henry VIII instigated a series of border raids and besieged Haddington, planning to unite the kingdoms by forcing the betrothal of his young son to the infant Mary, Queen of Scots. The Scots invoked the 'Auld Alliance' with France, and hastily arranged her betrothal to the French dauphin instead. Raised in the French court, she did not return to Scotland until after his death. By then the Reformation had taken place, and Catholic Mary soon fell foul of the Protestant reformer John Knox. Implicated in the murder of her husband, Lord Darnley, she fled to England, where her cousin Elizabeth I had her imprisoned and finally beheaded.

The Stuarts

In 1603 Mary's son, James VI, succeeded Elizabeth as James I of England and the crowns of both countries were indeed united. During his reign, the king found time to join in the active persecution of witches.

Through the reigns of Charles I and Charles II, the Scots were preoccupied with the persecution of the religious outlaws known as Covenanters (see pages 214–15). The Stuart dynasty was finally deposed when the unpopular James II fled the country, and the crown was offered to William of Orange. Recalcitrant clan chiefs, slow to display loyalty, were given a sharp lesson with the bloody massacre at Glencoe.

In 1715 the accession of the German George I resulted in a revival of support for the Stuart claimant, James VII, and an unsuccessful armed rebellion by the Jacobites. James's son, Charles Edward, raised an army in the Highlands and led a second rebellion in 1745. Although his forces reached as far south as Derby, poor advice and an ill-provisioned retreat led to ignominious and final defeat in the mire at Culloden.

Highland Clearances

After Culloden, the British government determined to destroy the old, feudal clan system. The wearing of the kilt was proscribed, the bearing of arms forbidden. A shift in agricultural practices decimated the population as landlords removed entire tenant communities to clear the land for sheep, and resettlement in hostile coastal environments was the alternative to mass emigration.

Aberdeen CITY OF ABERDEEN

Burning of Alexander Geddes Banffshire farmer Alexander Geddes was found guilty of having committed, 'reiterated acts of the monstrous crime of bestiality with a mare.' He was sentenced to death and on 25 June 1751 he was taken to Hangman's Brae, Aberdeen's place of execution. He was slowly strangled on the gibbet, cut down while still alive and then burned to ashes. He was the last person in Scotland to suffer for this crime and was also the last to be burned alive following hanging. A steep flight of steps at Castlehill now marks Hangman's Brae.

Arsenic murder George Thom was an avaricious villain. He was 61 when he married Jean Mitchell. Shortly before the marriage she, her two brothers and two sisters, had inherited the estate of another brother. Thom planned to wipe out the family and get the money himself. During a stay at the family farm at Burnside, Thom slept in the kitchen. In the night he mixed arsenic with the salt, and next morning excused himself from breakfast on the pretext of visiting a neighbour. The family sat down to share a pot of porridge, sprinkled with the deadly salt. They were all violently sick, although only one brother, William, died.

The family sat down to share a pot of porridge, sprinkled with the deadly salt. They were all violently sick, although only one brother, William, died.

Thom and his wife were arrested but she was released and her husband faced trial alone. He went to the gallows on 16 November 1821, a pitiful sight, in a state of collapse as his shroud was fitted. When the trap was sprung, he died a quicker death than his poor brother-in-law had done. His body was taken to the College to be the subject of a series of electrical experiments.

Throat slitting Robert McKintosh was a 21-year-old farm servant, engaged to a 40-year-old called Elizabeth Anderson, whom he had got pregnant. But he fell for another girl, and got rid of his fiancée by the simple expedient of cutting her throat from ear to ear. He was sentenced to death by hanging. Joining him on the gallows on 31 May 1822 was William Gordon, a maker of fishing-tackle who had killed his wife with a sharpened poker. This was Aberdeen's first double public hanging of the 19th century and both men were dressed in black for the occasion instead of the customary shroud.

LOCATION: 14 MILES NORTH OF STONEHAVEN ON A90

Airds Moss AYRSHIRE

Battle of Airds Moss Just north of where the A70 meets a disused railway line is a monument and 'Cameron's Stane', marking the spot where the Reverand Richard Cameron was killed in 1680.

On 22 July a group of Covenanters was crossing this inhospitable moorland, when they were surprised by a party of government troops led by David Bruce of Earlshall. The Covenanters were outnumbered and although they fought fiercely the battle was soon over. Nine of their number, including the Reverend Cameron, were killed, and five taken prisoner, while the rest managed to escape. Cameron's head and hands were cut off so that the troops could verify that they had slain him and claim the reward. The prisoners were taken to Edinburgh, where four of them were hanged and the fifth, David Hackston of Rathillet, had his hands chopped off before being hanged, drawn and quartered. His head was displayed at the Netherbow, while his limbs were dispersed, to be put on public display around the country.

LOCATION: 2 MILES SOUTH-WEST OF MUIRKIRK ON A70

THE ABERDEEN MAIDEN

The crude-looking blade in Aberdeen's Tolbooth Museum belonged to the burgh guillotine, fondly referred to as the 'Maiden'.

The Maiden consisted of a heavy axe blade, mounted on a wooden block and raised by a rope and pulley to the top of a wooden frame. The blade was kept sharp, and its weight combined with the velocity produced by the drop caused the instant severing of head from trunk. Prior to the invention of the Maiden the condemned were beheaded using a 'heiding sword'. In 1574 John Ewen, a burgess of Aberdeen who was convicted of coining, was hanged, cut down while still alive and ' heidit' with a sword. Although the Maiden was more efficient and humane than the 'heiding sword', it was a gory spectacle, as blood would spout from the headless trunk, covering the surrounding area.

The Aberdeen Maiden was referred to in account books in 1594–95, at least ten years before any similar reference to the Edinburgh Maiden. It was stored in a walled passageway in the Earl Marischal's house in the Castlegate. The burgh accounts record payments to George Annand for transporting the apparatus to the Heading Hill and for carrying out necessary repairs. It was last called into service in Aberdeen in 1615, when Francis Hay was decapitated for murdering Adam Gordon, a brother of the Laird of Gight.

Appin ARGYLL & BUTE

Falsley accused In 1752, Colin Campbell of Glenure was shot in Lettermore Wood on his way to evict some farm tenants in Ardsheal. The Campbells falsely accused James Stewart of Acharn. Found guilty by a jury of Campbells on the flimsiest of circumstantial evidence, he was sentenced to death by hanging. His body was hung in chains and guarded by soldiers for 18 months. In January 1755 the remains were blown from the gibbet but were wired together and re-hung. The Stewart Monument near the Ballachulish Bridge marks the spot where James was hanged. The incident inspired Robert Louis Stevenson to write *Kidnapped* (1886) and *Catriona* (1893).

LOCATION: 3 MILES WEST OF GLENCOE ON A82

Arran NORTH AYRSHIRE

Murder on Goatfell During the Glasgow Fair of 1889 two young men with a common interest in hill walking met in Rothesay. Londoner Edwin Rose agreed to join John Annandale and two others on a steamer trip to Arran. Annandale and Rose stayed on after the others departed and set off to climb Goatfell. Annandale returned alone, spent the night at his lodgings but disappeared next morning, leaving the bill unpaid. Rose's body was eventually found hidden in a cairn, his head and face beaten almost to a pulp by repeated blows from a stone. Annandale, whose real name was Laurie, led police a merry chase, sending letters to the press from Aberdeen and Liverpool. He was eventually arrested near Hamilton. He was sentenced to be hanged at Greenock, but was reprieved and imprisoned in Perth, where he died in the Criminal Asylum in 1930.

LOCATION: 14 MILES WEST OF ARDROSSAN BY FERRY

Ayr SOUTH AYRSHIRE

Burning of Maggie Osborne Maggie was the illegitimate daughter of the Lord of Fail, who was known as 'the Warlock'. She was accused of witchcraft by the Presbytery of Ayr, and confessed after being made to dance, bare-foot, on a red-hot metal plate. In 1698 she was burned alive at the stake. According to local legend she asked for two new plates that had never been washed. The messenger bringing the plates dropped one in a stream but retrieved it, dried it and handed them over to Maggie. As the flames started to consume her body she put the plates behind her back and they changed into wings. Unfortunately the one that had been wet didn't fully develop, and a guard hooked her by the skirt and forced her back into the fire.

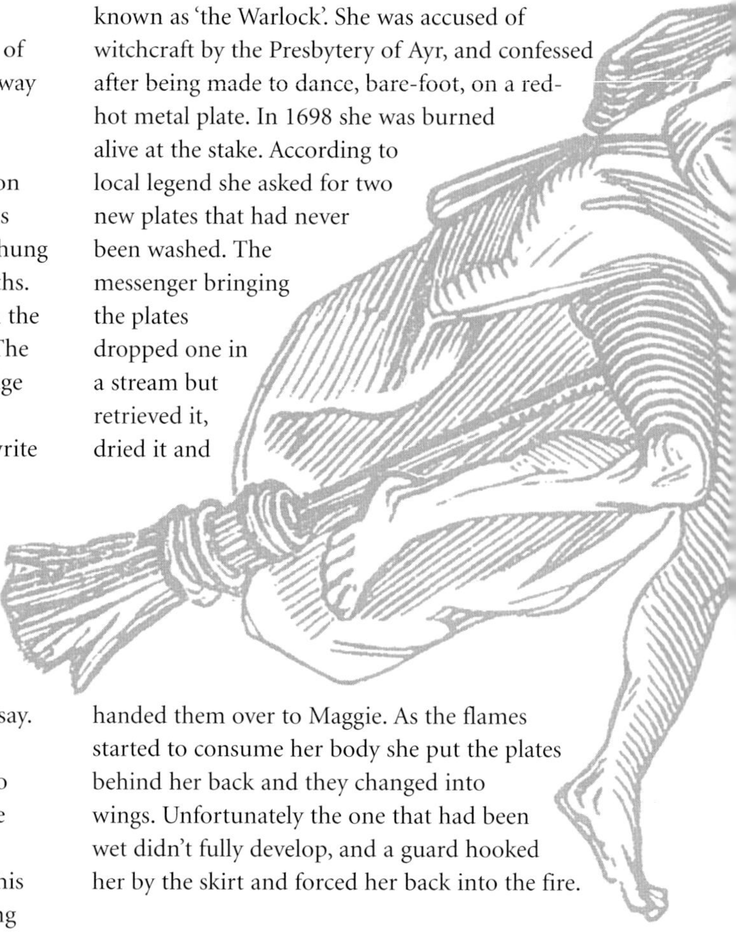

Disappearing corpse Matthew Hay, a farmer from Dundonald, near Ayr, was a smuggler and counterfeiter. Aspiring to higher social standing through the marriage of his daughter to Sir William Cunningham, he was dismayed when his overseer's daughter, Lizzie Wilson, told him that she was pregnant by him. In desperation he laced the Wilsons' food with arsenic. Lizzie's father died an agonising death, but she escaped unharmed. Hay was sentenced to hang on Ayr Common, and to be anatomically dissected by Dr George Charles. He was duly executed on 13 October 1780. When Hay's grave was opened in 1812 the coffin contained nothing but sand. It remains a mystery whether the doctor sold the body or disposed of it in some other way.

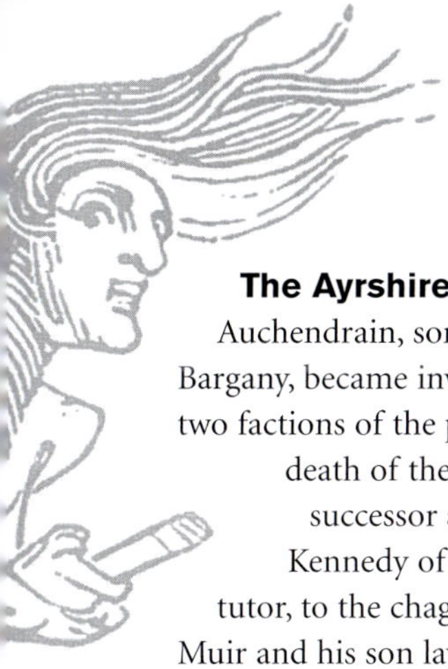

The Ayrshire tragedy John Muir of Auchendrain, son-in-law to Kennedy of Bargany, became involved in a feud between the two factions of the powerful Kennedy family. The death of the 4th Earl of Cassillis left his successor a minor, and Sir Thomas Kennedy of Culzean was appointed his tutor, to the chagrin of Kennedy of Bargany. Muir and his son lay in wait for Sir Thomas one night when he was returning from Maybole. Although he escaped the first time, they ambushed him again and butchered him. Father and son were executed at the Mercat Cross of Edinburgh in 1611.

LOCATION: 37 MILES SOUTH OF GLASGOW ON A77

Ballantrae SOUTH AYRSHIRE

Sawney Bean, cannibal Half way between Girvan and Ballantrae, at Bennane, a massive cave on the shore once harboured Scotland's foulest family. Sawney Bean and his wife raised a huge incestuous family, who lived entirely on human flesh. Undetected for 25 years, they stalked and ambushed travellers over this remote hill.

One evening they set upon a farmer and his wife, returning from a fair in Ballantrae. The man fought them off but his horse reared and his wife fell off. Instantly they cut her throat, and as some fell on her to drink the blood, others disembowelled her. Horrified at this sight the farmer fled, to be met by a party of others from the same fair.

A detachment of troops and several bloodhounds eventually discovered the cannibals deep in a dark cave, with human limbs hanging from hooks and other body parts preserved in barrels of salted water. They were taken to Edinburgh, imprisoned in the Tolbooth overnight and executed without trial the following day, cursing to their last breath.

LOCATION: 13 MILES SOUTH OF GIRVAN ON A77

**Instantly they cut her throat, and as some fell on her to drink the blood, others disembowelled her. Horrified at this sight the farmer fled, to be met by a party of others from the same fair.
A detachment of troops and several bloodhounds eventually discovered the cannibals deep in a dark cave, with human limbs hanging from hooks and other body parts preserved in barrels...**

Banff ABERDEENSHIRE

MacPherson's lament Immortalised in song by the poet Robert Burns, this notorious rascal appears to have been innocent of the crime for which he was executed at the Mercat Cross on 17 November 1700. He had apparently been in pursuit of a gypsy girl he had taken a fancy to, when he was apprehended along with her group.

A notable fiddler, James MacPherson played the famous rant that bears his name before mounting the scaffold. He then asked if anyone would take his fiddle and play on it. Anyone who did would have been branded an accomplice, so no-one came forward. He broke the instrument into two, declaiming 'Nae other hand shall play on thee when I am dead and gane.' According to legend, a reprieve was expected at any moment, but the magistrates put the clock forward to make sure MacPherson was already dead when it arrived. Indeed, the records show that although he was due to be executed in the afternoon he was hanged in the morning.

LOCATION: 32 MILES EAST OF ELGIN ON A98

Bannockburn STIRLING

Battle of Bannockburn Just north-west of the village of Bannockburn on 23-24 June 1314, the decisive battle in the Scottish Wars of Independence was fought. King Robert the Bruce with 6,000 spearmen, some archers and about 500 light horse faced the superior forces of Edward II. Bruce formed his troops into schiltrons (flexible squares of spearmen) and drove the English infantry back into the Bannock Burn, where they were set upon and butchered. Edward's cavalry stumbled into spear-filled pits and they, too, perished. Most of the English army's leaders were either killed or captured. Scotland became self-governing, but it would be another 14 years before Edward's successors recognised this in the Treaty of Edinburgh.

LOCATION: SOUTH OF STIRLING ON A9

Bathgate WEST LOTHIAN

Murderous encounter A Bathgate miner, Thomas Maxwell, met with Peter McLean, his wife and a companion. An argument broke out and as it grew more heated, they started throwing stones at each other. McLean then produced a knife and stabbed the unfortunate Maxwell to death. He was hanged at Linlithgow on 2 February 1857 on a scaffold borrowed from Edinburgh, with the London hangman, William Calcraft, hired to carry out the execution. It was apparently a jolly affair, like a holiday in the town, as a large crowd watched McLean go down in history as the last man hanged in West Lothian.

LOCATION: 18 MILES WEST OF EDINBURGH ON M8

Bishopbriggs EAST DUMBARTONSHIRE

Railway murder When the railway line from Glasgow to Edinburgh was being built in 1841, fighting was common among the navvies. During one incident John Green suffered a fatal blow to the head. Three men were arrested and charged with his murder. Two of them, Dennis Doolan and Patrick Reeding, were sentenced to death by hanging. A vast crowd of over 75,000 lined the route from the jail at Glasgow Green to Crosshill, Bishopbriggs, where the gallows had been erected. The condemned men

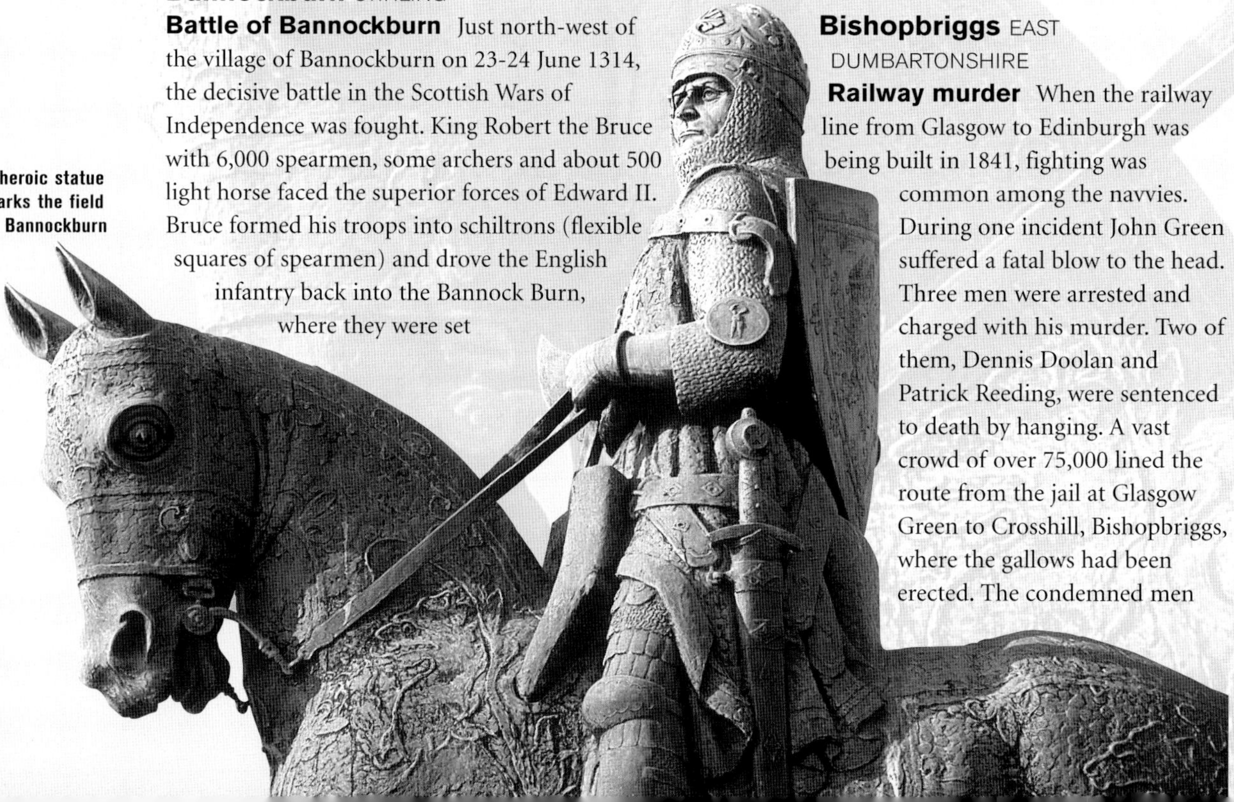

A heroic statue marks the field at Bannockburn

rode in an open cart, accompanied by priests. Militia and police formed part of the procession, and heavy guns were mounted at the gallows site in case of trouble. In the event, the crowd was silent as the trapdoor opened and the two men dropped into oblivion.

LOCATION: 6 MILES NORTH OF GLASGOW ON A803

Bothwell SOUTH LANARKSHIRE

Battle of Bothwell Bridge Following the rout of government forces under John Graham of Claverhouse at Drumclog in 1679 (see page 214), the Covenanters advanced to a camp near Bothwell Brig, where some 6,000 more recruits joined them. However, as they argued about the best way forward, the government force of 10,000 men advanced over the narrow bridge and soon defeated them. Few men actually died in the battle, but some 200 Covenanters were executed afterwards..

LOCATION: 14 MILES SOUTH OF GLASGOW ON M74

Braemar ABERDEENSHIRE

The Gallows Tree o' Mar
This famous gallows tree stands on the south side of the twisty road from Braemar to the Linn of Dee. It is a rare example of a primitive gallows dating from a time when local lairds had total power over their lands. Hangings were crude and painful. A rope would be thrown over the limb of the tree, and a noose placed around the neck of the victim, who was then hoisted into the air. Death was slow, with victims struggling and kicking until they died from strangulation.

LOCATION: 6 MILES WEST OF BRAEMAR ON THE ROAD TO LINN OF DEE

Culloden HIGHLAND

Battle of Culloden Fought on Drummossie Moor on 16 April 1746, this was the last battle on British soil. Government forces led by the Duke of Cumberland defeated the exhausted Jacobite army of Charles Edward Stuart. The Prince had landed at Eriskay in July 1745, and on 19 August he raised his father's standard at Glenfinnan to rally his supporters in an attempt to regain the thrones of Scotland and England. The Highlanders flocked in support and he moved forward rapidly, capturing Perth, Edinburgh and continuing as far south as Derby. However, instead of advancing on London, the Jacobite army retreated until, tired and hungry, they faced their enemy at Culloden. Cut to ribbons by Cumberland's artillery, they made one last famous 'Highland charge', rushing headlong towards the enemy. It was a brave but futile gesture, destined to fail on such terrain and against such opposition. Hundreds died and were buried where they fell. Following the battle, Cumberland lived up to his nickname, 'the Butcher': the wounded were slaughtered, and those fleeing the battle were hunted down and killed.

LOCATION: 7 MILES EAST OF INVERNESS ON B9006

Prince Charlie's Highland army met its match at Culloden in 1746

Donibristle FIFE

Slaying of the Bonnie Earl O' Moray

The murder of James Stewart, the second Earl of Moray, in 1592, has been the subject of many songs and stories and the truth of the matter may never be known.

The alleged murderer was George Gordon, Earl of Huntly, who was involved in a long running family feud with Moray. The King reputedly sent Huntly to arrest Moray. According to legend, Huntly laid siege to the house, set it on fire and slew the Earl when he rushed out to fight. However a painting commissioned by Moray's mother shows several lead ball wounds on his chest and numerous cuts and slashes about his body, supporting a contemporary ballad account that he was murdered in his bed.

Little remains of the old Donibristle House, which is 3 miles north of Aberdour.

LOCATION: 4½ MILES EAST OF DUNFERMLINE ON A92/B925

Drumclog SOUTH LANARKSHIRE

Battle of Drumclog On 3 May 1679 a party of Covenanters murdered James Sharp, Archbishop of St Andrews, at Magus Muir outside the town. After they had hacked him to death, they headed south to join up with an armed and well trained conventicle at Drumclog.

Meanwhile John Graham of Claverhouse, who was hunting another group of Covenanters, reached Strathaven on 1 June. Receiving information about the group at Drumclog, he moved to engage them. In a brief but bloody battle, Claverhouse led his troops into a bog, where they were defeated by the Covenanters.

LOCATION: 14 MILES EAST OF KILMARNOCK ON A71

THE COVENANTERS

The Killing Time refers to the indiscriminate slaughter of Scottish Presbyterians during the 1680s. In all some 18,000 Scots died for their religious beliefs.

At the Reformation in 1569, the Scottish parliament abolished papal jurisdiction, banned the mass, accepted John Knox's 'Confession of Faith' and established the Protestant Church of Scotland. The monarch was not the head of the church and there were to be no appointments of bishops or ministers. The entire structure from Kirk Session to the General Assembly was elected.

Then Charles I introduced a *Book of Common Prayer* in 1637, without even consulting the General Assembly. At its first use in St Giles Cathedral, Edinburgh, the congregation rioted and the service was abandoned (see page 201). In the following year, the National Covenant was produced. This was an anti-papist declaration which asserted the Church of Scotland's right to a direct relationship with God – without royal interference. Some 60,000 people signed this document in Greyfriars Kirkyard in Edinburgh and further signatures were collected throughout the country. Charles I's execution by the English Parliamentarians and their agreement to a 'Solemn League and Covenant' seemed to put an end to the dispute. Charles II signed the Covenant and was crowned king at Scone in 1651 before fleeing abroad.

However, when he was restored to the monarchy in 1660 Charles reneged, restored episcopacy and appointed bishops and curates to govern Scottish churches. Ministers who refused to conform were ejected from their parishes. The people defected from the church and attended services, called conventicles, in private houses or outdoors. The government tried to stop these services, and by 1670 attendance at a conventicle was treasonable and preaching at them a capital offence.

Government forces were given lists of non-attenders at church services and there was widespread intimidation. Resentment boiled over in the Galloway village of Dalry, when soldiers were torturing an old man with branding irons. The local people overcame the soldiers, then marched towards Edinburgh, their numbers swelling en route. In what became known as the Pentland Rising, the Covenanters were defeated at the battle of Rullion Green (1666) by a superior force under General Tam Dalyell ('Bluidy Tam'). One hundred were killed in battle, others cut down in retreat and 120 hanged, ten at a time on the Mercat Cross in Edinburgh. Further skirmishes occurred in the south-west at Drumclog (see page 214) and Bothwell Brig (see page 213).

When Catholic James II ascended the throne he was determined to eradicate the Presbyterians. In what has become known as the Killing Time, he pursued a policy of genocide, giving soldiers the authority to kill anyone who refused to swear an oath of allegiance to the Crown. Troops scoured the countryside murdering men, women and children.

In 1688 James II fled before the advance of Protestant William of Orange, and the persecution of Scottish Protestants came to an end.

Some 18,000 Covenanters lost their lives in the persecutions of 1661–88

The nine women were each bound to a stake by the executioner and strangled until they lost consciousness. He then lit the fires. Some regained consciousness and struggled and screamed as the flames burned them alive.

Dumfries DUMFRIES & GALLOWAY

Witch burning In the summer of 1658, members of the Presbytery of Dumfries were searching for evidence against anyone suspected of 'the heinous and abominable sin of witchcraft'. The following year they tried and sentenced to death nine witches charged with 'divers acts of witchcraft'. Nine stakes were driven into the ground at the Whitesands, on the banks of the Nith. The nine women were each bound to a stake by the executioner and strangled until they lost consciousness. He then lit the fires. Some regained consciousness and struggled and screamed as the flames burned them alive.

Murder of the Red Comyn Robert the Bruce and John Comyn, Lord of Badenoch, known as the Red Comyn, were rival claimants to the Scottish throne. At this time English soldiers garrisoned all the castles and towns, and the rule of law was enforced by English sheriffs. Bruce was planning to overthrow the English and offered Comyn land in return for his support. Comyn agreed to support Bruce, and then betrayed him to the English king.

Bruce discovered Comyn's treachery and summoned him to a meeting in Greyfriars Church on 10 February 1306. The exchange became heated, and Bruce stabbed Comyn with his dagger in front of the altar. When he confessed what he had done to his companions, one of them, Sir Roger Kirkpatrick, said 'I'll mak' siccur.' Rushing into the church, he ran Comyn through with his sword to ensure that he was dead.

Last public execution There's a death mask in Dumfries museum of the last man to be publicly hanged in Scotland. Robert Smith raped and strangled 11-year-old Thomasina Scott in Croftshead Wood, near Annan. To conceal his crime he tried to shoot a witness who had seen him earlier with the girl. When that failed, he attempted to cut his victim's throat with a blunt knife and then to break her neck, but he was disturbed and fled, leaving his second victim alive to tell the tale. He was convicted of murder, rape and theft and sentenced to hang. On the morning of 12 May 1868 he mounted the scaffold with the Yorkshire hangman, Thomas Askern, a man with a reputation for bungled executions. This was to be no exception. Askern had put the knot in front of Smith's ear instead of behind it and he took fifteen minutes to die, his body shaking the whole time.

LOCATION: 78 MILES SOUTH OF GLASGOW ON A74/A701

INFAMOUS HANGMEN

The public hangman has been both feared and despised throughout the ages. The stereotype of a tall, muscular man, bare from the waist up but for a black hood and mask, is far removed from reality.

Stature and build had little to do with choosing a hangman. He was often a criminal, who took the post in order to escape the gallows himself. The appointment was for life, and magistrates had the power to execute any hangman who deserted his post. Payment could include a tied house, food, clothes and even a salary. Hangmen were also entitled to the effects of their victims, and there was more than one incident where a condemned man received a reprieve and then had to walk home naked as the hangman kept his clothes.

By the middle of the 19th century it was no longer necessary to press condemned criminals into the post as there was no shortage of volunteers. By then it was a salaried position, and remained so until the celebrated hangman, William Calcraft, retired in 1874; thereafter a fee was paid for each execution. Hanging was abolished in the 1960s.

William Calcraft was one of the longest serving public executioners. He was famed for his 'short drops' which resulted in his victims being slowly strangled and taking some three to five minutes to die. Although officially the hangman at Newgate, London, he travelled extensively and was well known throughout Scotland.

One of his victims was the notorious Dr Edward William Pritchard, whom he dispatched in front of a crowd of around 100,000 in Jail Square, Glasgow, on 28 July 1865. As well as his salary, Calcraft received a fee for each execution. He also sold the victim's clothes to Madam Tussaud's for use in the 'Chamber of Horrors', and sold pieces of the rope as souvenirs.

Calcraft was responsible for the last public hangings in England, but the Yorkshire hangman, Thomas Askern earned that dubious honour north of the border. Askern miscalculated the drop for George Bryce, the last man to be publicly hanged in Edinburgh, who wriggled and twisted on the end of the rope for five minutes before he was still. When Askern carried out the last public hanging in Scotland, a Dumfriesshire journalist described him as '... more an automaton than an intelligent human being.'

Dundee

The last witch The last witch burned to death in Dundee was an unfortunate woman called Grissel Jaffrey. Her crime appears to have been an ability to predict whether a course of action would bring ill fortune or good luck. Imprisoned in the Tolbooth, she was tortured by having her flesh ripped by red hot pincers, finger nails torn off and her leg crushed until the marrow spurted from her bones. Found guilty and sentenced to death, she was burned at the stake near the Mercat Cross.

Roasting of the Ab
he was stripped, b
roasted over a fire
and consumed to th

According to legend, a young sailor had that morning returned to Dundee to see his elderly parents – only to find his mother being publicly burned. He cursed Dundee and left, never to return.

The Dundee Ripper On Sunday 10 February 1889, an Englishman by the name of William Henry Bury walked into the police office in Bell Street claiming to be the notorious murderer Jack the Ripper. He also mentioned that his wife had committed suicide.

At his home, officers found the dead body of his wife in a wooden packing case. One leg had been twisted right across her body, with the foot on the opposite shoulder. The other had been broken below the knee in order to squeeze the body into the packing case. Her belly had been slashed and her entrails had spilled out into the box and across the floor. The officers also found two messages scrawled in chalk outside the building, claiming that Jack the Ripper was within.

Bury had lived in London, next to Whitechapel, during the period of the Ripper murders, but the police investigating those crimes never considered him as a serious suspect. Nevertheless, convicted for the murder of his wife, Bury was the last man to be hanged in Dundee.

LOCATION: 22 MILES WEST OF PERTH ON A90

Dunscore DUMFRIES & GALLOWAY

Bloody Grierson of Lag A large monument towards the rear of the ancient burial ground at Dunscore marks the last resting place of Sir Robert

Grierson of Lag (1655–1733). As a Justice of the Peace, he was instrumental in the persecution of the Covenanters, who knew of him as 'the worst villain Scotland ever gave birth to', and demonised the man. He was responsible for the deaths of the Wigtown Martyrs (see page 237) and various other bloody atrocities. In later years he was fined and imprisoned as a Jacobite.

Local legend tells how on the night of his death, a ghostly coach driven by three hellish drivers and drawn by six black horses was seen on the Solway. When asked where they were bound the driver answered 'From Lag to Hell.'

LOCATION: 5 MILES NORTH OF DUMFRIES ON A76

Dunure SOUTH AYRSHIRE

Roasting of the Abbot of Crossraguel

In 1570, in the black vault of the castle of Dunure occurred an act of torture so terrible that it is a wonder the victim survived. But he did so, to stand before the court in Edinburgh and accuse his persecutor, Gilbert Kennedy, 4th Earl of Cassillis.

Described as a very greedy man, Kennedy had designs on the lands of Crossraguel Abbey, near Maybole. He confined the abbot, Allan Stewart, in Dunure Castle, where he was stripped, bound to a spit and roasted over a fire until his 'flesh burnt and consumed to the bones'. Stewart, crippled for life, eventually signed the papers. Cassillis was fined by the Privy Council and forced to pay Stewart a pension – but he was allowed to keep the lands.

LOCATION: 7 MILES SOUTH OF AYR ON A71

ot of Crossraguel –
ınd to a spit and
ntil his 'flesh burnt
e bones'.

Eday ORKNEY ISLANDS

Torture of Pirate Gow The bloodstains on the wooden floor of the 17th century Carrick House are supposedly those of the notorious pirate John Gow, captured here in 1725. Gow had run away to sea and ended up on a ship called the *Caroline*. Conditions were harsh and the food rotten. In November 1724 Gow led the crew in a mutiny, slitting the throats of the officers and shooting the captain. Renaming the ship *Revenge*, he led his crew on a murderous, piratical journey around Spain, France and Portugal. Gow sailed home to Orkney, hoping to lie low, but ran aground opposite Carrick House. After a fight, Gow was taken and held prisoner in Carrick House, before being taken to London for trial. He was tortured and hanged at Wapping on 11 June 1725.

Crows picking over the corpse on a gallows tree

Fochabers MORAY

Alexander Gillan's gallows Alexander Gillan was only 19 when he was sentenced to death, in 1810, for the rape and murder of 11-year-old Elspeth Lamb, whose sister had rejected his advances. Part of his sentence was that he should be 'hung until the fowls of the air pick the flesh off your body, and your bones bleach and whiten in the winds of heaven'. On 18 November he was hanged on a gibbet, which had been erected on the Moor of Stynie, near Fochabers. After death he was cut down, bound in irons and suspended again. His corpse vanished, but for years afterwards the eerie clank and rattle of the chains on the gibbet made many folk wary of travelling that way at night. In 1911, when estate workmen dismantled the gibbet, they discovered Gillan's skeleton buried beside it.

LOCATION: 9 MILES EAST OF ELGIN ON A96

Forfar ANGUS

Witchburning Helen Guthrie, a Forfar witch, described to her local court how she and her companions exhumed the body of an unchristened child and made a pie from flesh obtained from the head, buttock, feet and hands. It is not recorded whether she confessed to this voluntarily or under torture. She was sentenced to death by burning.

Witches were either 'worriet' (strangled) and then burned at the stake or else burned 'quick' – a more terrifying death. The condemned would be placed, alive, into a tar barrel, tied to a stake and then set alight. Sometimes the poor creatures would break free and though horribly burned would try to escape from the flames only to be pushed back by the executioner.

LOCATION: 13 MILES NORTH OF DUNDEE ON A90

Fortrose HIGHLAND

Burning of the Brahan Seer Coinneach Odhar, the Brahan Seer, is a shadowy 16th-century figure who could be described as a Gaelic Nostrudamus. He made many predictions including one which foretold a terrible end to the Seaforth family. According to one tradition he also insulted Lady Seaforth, who determined to be rid of him forever. Convicted of witchcraft, he was taken to Chanory Point, east of Fortrose, and there burned alive in a blazing barrel of tar. There's a stone slab, buried under the sand a couple of hundred yards north-west of the lighthouse, which locals still point out as the spot of his execution.

LOCATION: 16 MILES NORTH-EAST OF INVERNESS ON A9/A82

Glencoe HIGHLAND

Massacre of Glencoe Clan Campbell was the most cunning and political of all the Scottish clans, and the first to become Protestant. The newly appointed King William of Orange offered rebel clan chiefs an amnesty if they would swear allegiance to him by 1 January 1692. All complied, with the exception of MacIain, Chieftain of the

The massacre in the narrow defile of Glencoe was designed to make a grim example of a recalcitrant Highland clan

MacDonalds of Glencoe. He intended making the declaration but put it off until the last moment, when a snowstorm delayed him and he did not finally make his oath until 6 January.

Sir John Dalrymple of Stair, the Secretary of State, obtained an order from the King to exterminate the MacDonalds as an example, neglecting to inform him that MacIain had made the pledge, albeit late. On 1 February Captain Robert Campbell of Glenlyon led two companies into Glencoe and asked for hospitality. Despite their age-old enmity, the MacDonalds fed and sheltered them for almost two weeks. At midnight on 12 February the government troops struck, attempting to kill all MacDonald males under the age of 70. They butchered women and children as well, but managed to kill only 38 of the clan, while the rest escaped. Campbells are reviled to this day in parts of the Highlands for this act of treachery.
LOCATION: 16 MILES SOUTH OF FORT WILLIAM ON A82

Glasgow

Battle of the Butts Following his defeat by the Covenanters at the Battle of Drumclog (see page 214), John Graham of Claverhouse retreated to Glasgow and roused the garrison to bolster his depleted force. He faced the advancing Covenanters at the Butts in the Gallowgate, but was obliged to retreat after suffering further heavy losses. The dead bodies lay around for days, and were eventually consumed by packs of local dogs.

The butcher Glasgow butcher John Buchanan stabbed Anne Duff, a young woman who was the chief witness in the prosecution of some of his friends for theft. Although dreadfully injured, Anne managed to drag herself outside to get help and was able to confirm Buchanan as her attacker before she died. He was tried in 1819, and although the Glasgow butchers had raised a subscription to hire the best defence available, he was found guilty and hanged a year later.

Glasgow (CONT)

The diabolical doctor The last man publicly hanged in Glasgow was Dr Edward William Pritchard, who killed for the fun of it. He arrived in Glasgow in 1860 from Yorkshire, where it was rumoured he had poisoned patients.

In 1863 a fire broke out in his home, and the body of a young servant girl was burnt beyond recognition. There was a suspicion that he had drugged her, and started the fire to cover the fact that she was pregnant by him. Pritchard turned his advances towards his next servant, Mary McLeod. She also became pregnant, but he silenced her by promising to marry her if his wife died.

He started to poison his wife in October 1864 using a potion of tartarised antimony, aconite and opium. His mother-in-law, concerned about her daughter's health, visited from Edinburgh. Pritchard poisoned her, too, and she died 11 days later. Three weeks after that, Pritchard's wife died. Post mortems on both women revealed the poison, and Pritchard was at last arrested.

He confessed his guilt from the scaffold to a crowd of some 100,000 people, before London hangman, William Calcraft (see page 217), pulled the lever that ended his reign of terror.

Execution of radical weavers John Baird, Andrew Hardie and James Wilson were three radical weavers, found guilty of publishing a 'wicked, revolutionary and treasonable address' on 1 April 1820. It called on the people to take up arms to regenerate their country. James Wilson was executed by hanging in Glasgow, the task being performed by local executioner, Thomas Young. His body was cut down and his head was severed. Wilson's bloody head was then raised aloft by Young who declared to the crowd, 'This is the head of a traitor.' Andrew Baird and John Hardie received similar treatment in Stirling. It took three strokes to sever Hardie's head and two for Baird's. Afterwards the executioner was heard to mutter that he wished he had not had to do it.

THE ANATOMISTS

Scientists have built a detailed knowledge of the workings of the human body by dissecting the dead. However the religious belief that dissected bodies could not be resurrected in heaven made it almost impossible at one time to get bodies.

Parliament permitted the dissection of one hanged felon each year, but that was not enough – so surgeons took to grave-robbing to get a supply of cadavers. Overcoming their superstitious fears of being in cemeteries at night, church elders and concerned relatives took to organising graveyard watches. The reputation of the medical profession was at an all time low. The trial of body-snatchers Burke and Hare in Edinburgh in 1828 led to the passing of the Anatomy Act of 1833, which allowed the dissection of bodies provided the executor agreed and the deceased had made no objection known while alive. The Act also provided the judiciary with dissection as a further grisly sentence on criminals, to be imposed in addition to the death sentence.

Granville Sharp Pattison, a teacher of anatomy at Glasgow University Medical School, primed his students to do their utmost to obtain corpses. Following a raid on the Ramshorn Kirkyard in 1813, police discovered several cadavers and the remains of others in the basement of Pattison's home. The teacher was tried in Edinburgh, but the jury returned a 'not proven' verdict.

At the dissection of Matthew Clydesdale (see below), Dr Ure attempted to revive the

The 'Glasgow Frankenstein' James Jeffrey, Professor of Anatomy at Glasgow University, conducted a series of gruesome electrical experiments on executed criminals in the year that Mary Shelley's novel, *Frankenstein*, was published,

corpse. He was convinced that the best hope of achieving success would be to place 'two moistened, brass knobs, connected to the battery ... on the skin over the phrenic nerve and the diaphragm.' This crude device was very similar to the modern electrical defibrillator, which now brings many back from death.

Ure recorded that 'several spectators were forced to leave the apartment from terror and sickness, and one gentleman fainted.'

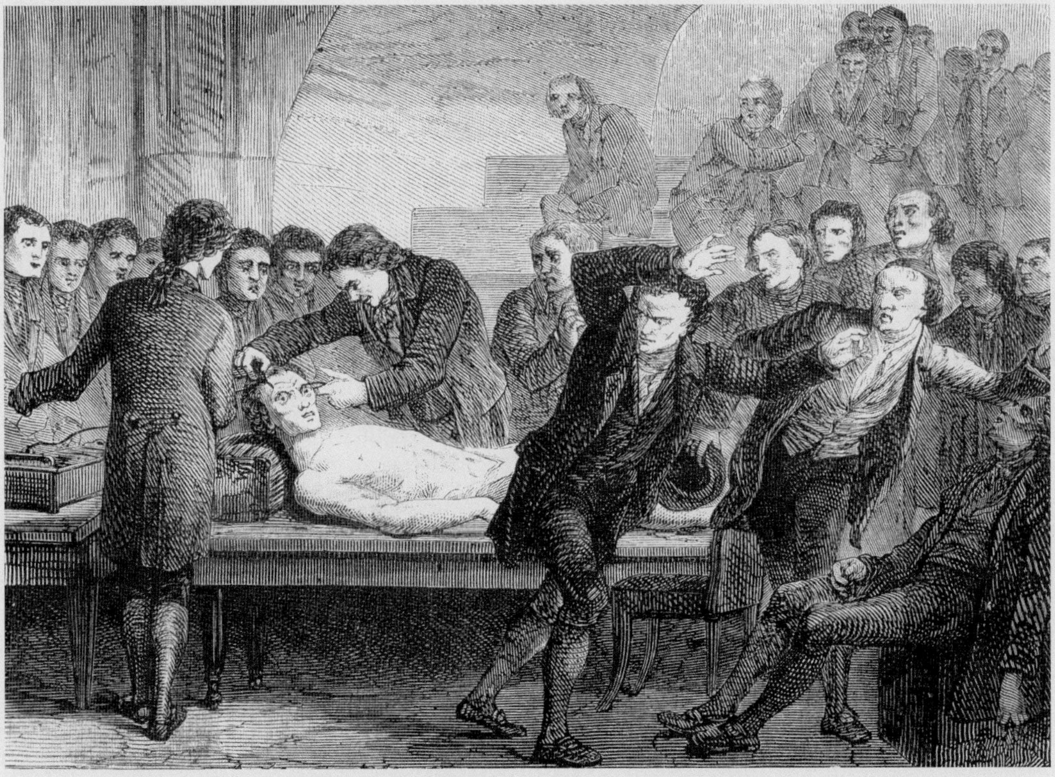

Left: experiments on corpses by anatomists such as Andrew Ure (left, above), although terrifying in their day, were the forerunners of modern scientific research.

1818. The body of murderer Matthew Clydesdale was attached to a primitive form of battery by Dr Andrew Ure, assisted by Professor Jeffrey. By touching electrical wires to various parts of the body the two men produced a series of unsettling reactions. Clydesdale's chest heaved, his leg struck out and kicked a student and his face alternately grinned, scowled and appeared anguished and distressed. However unlike Dr Frankenstein, they were unable to bring Clydesdale back to life.

Glasgow (CONT)

Jessie McLachlan The body of Jessie MacPherson, was discovered by her employer, John Fleming, in the basement of his home. She had been decapitated with a meat cleaver. Her friend Jessie McLachlan was charged with the murder. McLachlan claimed that she had been drinking with her friend and Fleming's father, when they ran out of whisky. She had gone for more supplies, and when she returned, found her friend's body lying in her room. Fleming senior had threatened to accuse her of murder unless she made the incident look like a robbery by pawning the dead woman's clothes. She also claimed her friend had complained in the past of unwelcome advances from Fleming senior.

Despite the fact that the old man had been reported to the Kirk Session on previous occasions, Jessie McLachlan was sentenced to death. Her sentence was later commuted to life imprisonment in Perth.

A Victorian poisoner The daughter of a wealthy Victorian architect, Madeleine Smith lived at 7 Blythswood Square. She started seeing an impoverished clerk called Pierre l'Angelier, although her father forbade it. Eventually she tried to end the affair with l'Angelier and asked for the return of her love letters. When he refused and threatened to show them to her father, she determined to poison him with mugs of cocoa, laced with arsenic. L'Angelier was violently ill, and died at the third attempt.

Despite the evidence against her, including damning extracts from l'Angelier's diary, the charges against Madaleine Smith were found not proven. This is a peculiarly Scottish verdict that is usually interpreted as, 'We know you did it but we can't prove it'. Smith's family was ostracised as a result of the case. She herself moved to England, and eventually died in New York, aged 95.

Miscarriage of justice A notorious miscarriage of justice occurred in 1908 when Miss Marion Gilchrist was battered to death with the back legs of a chair. A male assailant was seen rushing from the house, and circumstantial evidence pointed to Oscar Slater, a local dentist. Slater was sentenced to death at the High Court in Edinburgh, but on the day of execution – 6 May 1909 – it was commuted to penal servitude for life.

The procurator fiscal was a close friend of one of Miss Gilchrist's relatives, and there was a suggestion that Slater had been set up in order to draw the heat from the real killer. Slater was eventually released in November 1927, and the conviction was quashed the next year, after two anonymous letters were received by the Secretary of State.

LOCATION: 46 MILES WEST OF EDINBURGH ON M8

Greenock INVERCLYDE

Rape and robbery Robert Morrison of Everton Farm was breakfasting with his sister-in-law, Janet Crawford, and his servant, Mary Black, on 23 March 1817, when three men burst in on them. They beat Morris up, robbed him of all the money in the house and then raped the two women.

But the evil trio –Bernard McIlvogue, his brother, Hugh, and friend, Patrick McCrystal – didn't get far. They were apprehended, tried and sentenced to death for their crimes. They were hanged in Glasgow in front of a crowd of 10,000 at the New Church in the Square.

LOCATION: 24 MILES EAST OF GLASGOW ON M8/E5

GIBBETING

Victorian hangmen developed a scientific approach to execution. The measured drop, taking into account the culprit's weight, together with a strategic positioning of the hangman's knot, would snap the neck causing instant and – allegedly – painless death.

Before this, death on the scaffold was a long and painful business. Gallows were crude but effective. A rope was thrown over the limb of a tree and a noose fastened round the felon's neck. He was then obliged to climb a ladder before being pushed off by the hangman. Alternatively, he was hoisted from the ground and suspended in mid air.

The first advance on these methods was the introduction of a horse and cart. When the horse was driven away the prisoner would be left suspended. Death was slow and agonizing as the criminal strangled. The face became purple, the eyes popped from the sockets and the tongue protruded.

Gibbets were familiar landmarks on the outskirts of towns and cities, on lonely moorlands or at a crossroads. Gibbeting, or the hanging of the corpse from the gibbet after death, was a common practice. The body, bound in chains or sealed in a metal cage, was suspended as a deterrent to crime. This was viewed by many as a punishment greater than death itself.

Greenyards HIGHLAND

The village of Greenyards was cleared of its inhabitants with much bloodshed in 1843. Sheriff Taylor and a force of drunken policemen marched from Tain to serve eviction notices on the tenants. They were met by resistance from 200 or so women. Taylor addressed them in the alien tongue of English (although he could speak Gaelic), then he ordered the police to proceed. They used their truncheons to brutally bludgeon the women, breaking their arms, and then tying them up before dragging them by the hair to carts, which took them to jail.

LOCATION: 5 MILES WEST OF BONAR BRIDGE IN STRATHCARRON

Gretna DUMFRIES & GALLOWAY

Troop train disaster On 22 May 1915 at Quintinshill, near Gretna, a train full of soldiers was heading southwards at full speed when it hit a stationary local train. The second train had been on the southward line to await the passing of the northern express, which minutes later ploughed into the wreckage. The gas-lit carriages of the troop train caught fire, creating an inferno so intense that many of the bodies were burned beyond recognition. In total 227 people died, all but 9 of them from the troop train.

LOCATION: 23 MILES EAST OF DUMFRIES ON A75

Iona ARGYLL & BUTE

The sacking of Iona St Columba landed here in AD 563, and his early church became a centre of pilgrimage and Christian learning. Norsemen attacked in 795 and razed the buildings. They struck again in 798 and 802, pillaged all they could carry and destroyed everything else. The monks rebuilt a fourth time. The Vikings returned in 806, but this time the monks had hidden their treasures. When they refused to reveal their whereabouts, the Vikings slaughtered 68 monks at Martyrs Bay, just south of the ferry jetty.

LOCATION: 35 MILES SOUTH-WEST OF OBAN VIA FERRY AND A849

Iona's cathedral, now owned by the National Trust for Scotland

THE HIGHLAND CLEARANCES

In one of the blackest episodes in Scottish history, tens of thousands of people were removed from land their families had occupied for centuries to make way for sheep.

The clearances were a result of a period of agricultural improvement between 1785 and 1850, and a shift from communal land tenure to individual ownership. Prior to the Jacobite Rebellion of 1745, Highland chiefs held the land on behalf of their clansmen. They allocated parcels of land and in return received rents. In times of trouble their kinsman tenants would provide the muscle for their armies. In the aftermath of the failed rebellion, the government was determined to dismantle the clan system and many chiefs were encouraged to move south, becoming absentee landlords. Their new lifestyles required greater incomes than their rents could generate, so many turned to new schemes to increase the revenue from their estates. Sheep were profitable but were incompatible with small-scale subsistence farming. Whole communities were given notice to quit. If they refused to move on, they could be forcibly evicted, their homes torn down and the roof timber burnt to prevent them re-building.

The most notorious clearances took place on the estate of the Countess of Sutherland under the supervision of her factor, Patrick Sellar. Sellar had a vested interest in the clearances, for in many instances he had obtained the lease of the cleared land for sheep. During the now infamous Strathnaver Clearances of 1814–15, Sellar acted so abominably that he was arrested and charged with culpable homicide. It was alleged that he deliberately set fire to the house of an old, bedridden woman called Margaret MacKay. Sellar had been warned that to move the old woman would result in her death, but he torched the house anyway. As the flames were licking about her bed she started screaming and was pulled from the flames by her daughter. With no shelter and suffering from shock, she died a few days later without uttering another sound. Sellar committed many more atrocities in the name of progress, and was tried in Inverness. Despite the weight of evidence against him he was acquitted, and the clearances continued unabated.

Many of those evicted chose to emigrate. Others were re-settled on harsh, barren land along the coast, where they were given crofts (small parcels of land) on which to live and sustain their families. However the size of the parcel of land was often too small to sustain a family, and landowners needed labour for the harvesting of kelp, which was then a lucrative crop. With few other resources or options, the crofters were forced to work for slave wages. When the kelp industry collapsed, the crofters were destitute and many more sought refuge in emigration.

The Clearances highlighted the problems of a rural population at the mercy of a patriarchal feudal system.

Inverkeithing FIFE

Jealousy and revenge The wealthy young Master of Burley, Robert Balfour, became infatuated with his sister's governess, Miss Robertson. To discourage any liaison, his father sacked the unfortunate woman, and dispatched young Robert on a tour of the Continent. However Robert swore to kill her should she marry anyone else. She did marry and moved to Inverkeithing, where Balfour surprised them in 1707 and shot the couple dead. He was sentenced to death, and because of his noble status was beheaded rather than hanged.

LOCATION: 4 MILES SOUTH OF DUNFERMLINE ON M90

Inverness HIGHLAND

Longman's Grave Longman's Grave was the site of a famous gallows on the east shore of the Moray Firth, a mile east of Inverness. Hugh Macleod, convicted of the murder of a pedlar, Murdoch Grant, was hanged there on 24 October 1831. He was dressed in a long black cloak and a white nightcap and walked to the spot, reading from his bible, a rope looped round his neck.

The last public execution at this gallows was in October 1835, when John Adam was hanged for the brutal murder of his wife. He wore the same clothes as Macleod, but was driven there in a cart as the large crowd made it impossible for him to walk. After this, the gallows was dismantled; the ground is now covered by an industrial estate.

LOCATION: 112 MILES NORTH OF PERTH ON A9

Kelso SCOTTISH BORDERS

Death at Sharpitlaw Anna In 1831 a young Irishman was murdered on Sharpitlaw Anna, a small island near the north bank of the River Tweed, opposite Hendersyde Lodge. Like many other Scots at the time, Thomas Rogers, a carter from Coldstream, held deep prejudices against Irish immigrants. He was drunk when he encountered Neil McKiernon and his friends at Sharpitlaw and pursued them to the river. Crossing to the small island, he caught McKiernon and bludgeoned him to death with a heavy stick. Rogers was duly sentenced to death and hanged in front of a crowd of thousands in Jedburgh Square.

LOCATION: 1 MILE NORTH-EAST OF KELSO ON A698.

THUMBIKINS AND TAM DALYELL

General Tam Dalyell was a Royalist general who persecuted the Covenanters during the 17th century. Known to the Covenanters as 'Bloody Tam' or the 'Muscovy Brute', he was reputed to be in league with the Devil. Other legends had him playing cards with the Devil at the House of Binns, his West Lothian seat, or burning holes in the ground with his spittle. Dalyell was imprisoned in the Tower of London following the death of Charles I, but escaped to Russia in 1652 and for ten years commanded armies of the Tsar. When the monarchy was restored in Britain, Dalyell returned to Scotland bringing with him the torture device known as 'thumbikins'. This was a bar of metal a few inches long, with three legs. Another bar with three holes was fitted to the metal legs and a nut added to the centre. A special key would be used to move the top bar down onto the bottom one by tightening the screw. The victim's thumbs would be firmly gripped between the bars until crushed. Some thumbikins had a length of chain attached, to enable the executioner to drag his victim about and increase the level of pain.

The Jacobite victory in the narrow pass of Killiekrankie was a highlight of the rebellion

Killiecrankie PERTH & KINROSS

Battle of Killiecrankie This was a decisive battle during the first Jacobite rebellion. John Graham of Claverhouse ('Bonnie Dundee') received intelligence reports at Glen Roy that government forces, commanded by General Hugh MacKay, were heading from Stirling to recapture Blair Castle. Claverhouse moved quickly and, on 26 July 1689, reached Blair with an army of 2,500 Highlanders.

MacKay meanwhile had arrived at Dunkeld with a vastly superior force, numbering over 4,000 soldiers. Next day, ignoring reports of Graham's approach, he entered the narrow pass of Killiecrankie. A Highland sniper kept Mackay's advance guard at bay while Claverhouse led his men to higher ground. At 7pm the order was given to charge and the entire Highland army charged downhill, brandishing their broadswords and howling like banshees.

Nothing could resist the famous Highland charge in terrain like this, and Mackay's forces were overwhelmed. Fatalities were enormous on both sides. Although the Jacobites won the day, Claverhouse himself was killed in the battle.

It is difficult to imagine such bloodshed in this beautiful wooded gorge, now in the care of the National Trust for Scotland.

LOCATION: 29 MILES NORTH OF PERTH ON A9

DEPRIVED OF SLEEP

During the Scottish witch persecutions, one of the torture techniques employed to extract a confession was sleep deprivation. Men called 'wakers' worked in shifts to ensure the suspected witch was kept alert and wide awake. They did this by holding lighted candles to the soles of her feet, or burning between her toes or even inside her mouth.

So effective were they that one accused woman complained to the Privy Council that she had been kept awake for 20 days and nights.

Far right: The tower at Largs, known as ' the Pencil', recalls the Scots' victory over the Norwegians in 1263.

Kirk Yetholm SCOTTISH BORDERS

Gypsy murders In August 1829 a famous riot took place at Maxwellheugh Cottage, the former toll house just outside Kelso. The toll house, which was also an inn, was busy with folk returning from the St James Fair in Kelso. When a drunken party of gypsies was evicted, fighting broke out between the gypsies, locals and the police. The gypsies retreated, but later attacked three young couples returning from the fair. John Hall was so badly beaten that he died the following morning. Three gypsies were taken for trial to Jedburgh, but served a mere nine months in jail for riot and assault.

LOCATION: 8 MILES SOUTH EAST OF KELSO ON B6352/B6350

Largs NORTH AYRSHIRE

Battle of Largs In 1098 Norway took possession of the Hebrides. In 1263 Alexander III of Scotland set about getting them back. Following a raid by the Scots on Skye, King Haakon IV of Norway set sail intent on battle. He arrived at Arran with 200 galleys, and on 30 September he anchored off the coast at Largs. Unfortunately equinoctial gales hit his fleet for the next four days, wrecking vessels or driving them onto the beach. Fierce fighting ensued, with the Scots gaining a decisive victory. Only an improvement in the weather allowed Haakon and the remains of his fleet to escape total annihilation.

LOCATION: 14 MILES SOUTH OF GREENOCK ON A78

Lauder SCOTTISH BORDERS

The Cleekhimin killer On 4 December 1852 Andrew Mather, the toll keeper at Cleekhimin, went to the Cleekhimin Inn for a drink. At around 1am his daughters found his body lying on the road in front of the row of cottages at Lylestone. As the girls drew near, a bloodstained man rose from beside the body. The girls' screaming alerted nearby cottagers who came out and grabbed the assailant, John Williams, a local labourer with a bad reputation and wicked temper, who had been ejected from the inn earlier that evening. Evidence revealed that Mather had been savagely kicked about the head. His hairs were found on Williams' boots and on a large stone discovered near by. Williams denied the murder, but was found guilty and hanged in front of the Castle Hotel, Greenlaw.

LOCATION: 11 MILES NORTH OF MELROSE ON A699

Lendalfoot SOUTH AYRSHIRE

The Ayrshire Bluebeard The ancient ballad 'Fause Sir John' tells of the laird of the castle of Carleton, now an imposing ruin above the village of Lendalfoot. Sir John met an appropriate end after disposing of seven young heiresses whom he had married for their fortunes. He took his brides to Bennane Hill, a mile or so south of the castle, and threw them into the sea from a rocky crag known as Gamesloup. His eighth intended victim, May Culzean, was a match to his trickery. When he asked her to take off her clothes, she demanded that he face away while she did so. When his back was turned she pushed him over the edge instead.

LOCATION: 6 MILES SOUTH OF GIRVAN ON A77

Loch Ness INVERNESSSHIRE

The Beast of Boleskine Boleskine House, set on the southern shore of Loch Ness and opposite a very creepy cemetery, is infamous as the former home of Aleister Crowley, the self-styled 'Beast 666'. Crowley bought Boleskine in 1900 when he was 25 years old, and continued his training as a black magician. He was a controversial man who loved to shock. His attempt to raise demons, using the complicated occult ritual of Abramelin the Mage, was followed by a series of unexplained deaths and disasters. His housemaid mysteriously vanished, and a workman went insane and tried to kill him. Crowley also claimed responsibility for the death of a local butcher, who bled to death from a severed artery after Crowley had written the names of demons on a bill from his shop.

LOCATION: BETWEEN FOYERS AND INVERFARIGAIG ON B852

An uncomfortable public shaming was popular sport

Lady Cassillis was forced to watch while the 'gypsies' were hanged in turn on the Dule Tree of Cassillis. Her former lover was killed last, suffering a slow and tortured death before her eyes.

Maybole SOUTH AYRSHIRE

Lady Cassillis and the gypsies At Maybole Castle, a window surrounded by nine carved stone heads depicts a particularly grisly event in the history of the Kennedy family. While John Kennedy, 6th Earl of Cassillis, was away, his wife's former lover arrived at Cassillis House, a few miles from Maybole. Disguised as gypsies, he and his companions spirited Lady Cassillis away with them. By chance, the Earl returned early; he soon overtook and captured the party. Lady Cassillis was forced to watch while the 'gypsies' were hanged in turn on the Dule Tree of Cassillis. Her former lover was killed last, suffering a slow and tortured death before her eyes.

Afterwards Lady Cassillis was taken to Maybole Castle, where she was incarcerated for the rest of her life. As a constant reminder reminder of what had happened, the heads of her dead lover and his

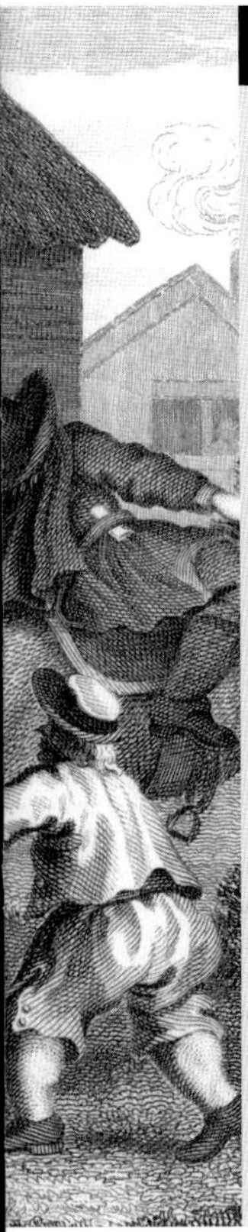

RIDING THE STANG

This was an ancient form of punishment found under different names in many parts of Britain.

It was a punishment reserved almost exclusively for men who were guilty of infidelity, or who beat or assaulted their wives.

The culprit was forced to mount a piece of timber known as the 'stang' – either a rough beam or the trunk of a tree. The stang was then lifted onto the shoulders of a team of men, who proceeded to march around the community. Meanwhile, the onlookers would shout and bang on any implement that would make a noise. Periodically the party would stop to allow the spokesman to shout aloud the guilty party's crime.

Needless to add, serious injury could result from a bumpy ride on rough timber.

companions were carved around her window.
LOCATION: 9 MILES SOUTH OF AYR ON THE A77

Moniaive DUMFRIES & GALLOWAY

Glencairn martyrs In the ruins of the 13th century church of Glencairn an inscription on the gate reads: ' Halt passenger, tell if thou ever saw Men shot to death without process of law…' This refers to four Moniaive Covenanters who were murdered in 1685 and interred at Glencairn. A stone at Ingleston Mains marks the spot where they were shot by soldiers on 28 April 1685.

The James Renwick Monument is a tribute to a young minister who preached throughout the troubles until he was captured. He was just 26 years old, when he was hanged in Edinburgh in 1688, the last Covenanter to be so despatched.
LOCATION: 18 MILES NORTH-WEST OF DUMFRIES ON B729

Montrose ANGUS

Husband battering With her husband, Henry Shuttleworth, Margaret Tindal ran a small shop selling spirits. She was prone to drunkenness and while inebriated often abused her husband by hitting him and throwing objects at him.

On 28 April 1821 he was found dead with a fractured skull and badly cut scalp. Margaret claimed he had fallen down the stairs, but Shuttleworth's doctor declared the injuries could not have been caused by a fall. Margaret was found guilty of murder and taken to Aberdeen where she was publicly hanged in front of the jail in September. Her body was taken first to Dundee, and then to Edinburgh to be dissected.
LOCATION: 35 MILES NORTH-EAST OF DUNDEE ON A92

Orkney ORKNEY ISLANDS

Torture and death Orkney witch Alison Balfour was tortured for 48 hours by having her legs encased in irons that were then heated. All this, while watching her husband being stretched, her son flogged mercilessly and her seven-year-old daughter tortured with thumbscrews, extracted a confession. She was then killed by having her body covered by a door and heavy stones piled on top until she was crushed to death.

Torture for a plotter Thomas Papley was arrested and accused of involvement in a plot to murder the Earl of Orkney by witchcraft and poison. Subjected to the full force of judicial torture to extract a confession, he was kept in 'cashielaws' for 11 days. These were iron frames that were put round the legs and then tightened. During interrogation the cashielaws would be first put into a fire or portable furnace to increase the agony. He was also stripped naked and scourged daily with ropes until there was no skin left on his body.
LOCATION: 26 MILES NORTH OF SCRABSTER BY FERRY

The bleak walls of Hermitage, one of the most imposing and complete of the border castles

Paisley RENFREWSHIRE

A jealous husband William Pirrie was an insanely jealous man. In October 1837, he heard tales that a man had been eyeing up his wife and rushed back from work in a fit of rage. Ejecting his children from their home he locked the door and went for his wife, hacking her into pieces. The police were called and Pirrie was charged with her murder. Found guilty, he was publicly hanged in Paisley.
LOCATION: 9 MILES WEST OF GLASGOW ON M8

Perth PERTH & KINROSS

The Gowrie Conspiracy According to King James VI, he encountered Alexander Ruthven, brother of the Earl of Gowrie, as he was leaving Falkland Palace on 5 August 1600. Gowrie told him that he had arrested a man with a pot of gold and requested that the king return with him to Perth to deal with the matter.

In Perth, Alexander locked the king in a room but James managed to attract the attention of his retinue, who broke down the door to find him struggling with Ruthven. One of the king's men, John Ramsay, plunged his dagger into Ruthven, and in the ensuing battle many more were killed including the Earl of Gowrie.

The corpses of Gowrie and his brother were carted back to Edinburgh, tried for treason and convicted. As a result their lands and property were seized and their name proscribed by act of parliament. Was the whole affair engineered by the King to get rid of the Ruthvens?

Regicide James I, the second son of Robert III of Scotland, was born in Dunfermline in 1394. He was held by the English in the Tower of London for 18 years. On returning to Scotland in 1425, he set about reducing the power of his nobles and had several of them, including his own cousin, beheaded at Stirling. The nobles were not prepared to accept this and Sir Robert Graham, the Earl of Athole, and the King's Chamberlain, Robert Stewart, plotted his downfall. The end came at the Dominican Friary in Perth, where the royal household was staying. Armed men rushed the friary and James, seeking to keep them out, ordered the door barred. Finding that the Chamberlain

had removed all the bars, a brave lady-in-waiting, Catherine Douglas, used her own arm as a bar and held the door until her arm was smashed to pieces. Meanwhile the King fled to a vault below the floorboards seeking escape. Finding the exit blocked, he was trapped. His assailants discovered him in the vault and stabbed and slashed him to death. There were 16 gashes on his chest and a further 12 wounds on other parts of his body.

Within weeks the assassins were rounded up and sent to a traitor's death.

LOCATION: 42 MILES NORTH-WEST OF EDINBURGH ON M90

Pittenweem FIFE

Evil eye Fisherman Alexander McGregor accused Janet Cornfoot of causing him harm in 1704. She was banished from the parish, but the minister ordered two men to return her to Pittenweem, where she was seized by a mob and paraded through the streets. They next suspended her from a rope tied between a fishing boat and the harbour wall and stoned her. Finally she was brought ashore, beaten with sticks, then covered with an old door and the mob stood on it until she was crushed under their weight.

LOCATION: 20 MILES NORTH EAST OF KIRKCALDY ON A915

Roxburgh SCOTTISH BORDERS

Hermitage Castle At a 13th century keep on the site of this castle, Lord de Soulis met a horrible end. Locals, enraged by his excesses and considering him to be a warlock, captured him, dragged him to the nearby stone circle of Nine Stane Ring and boiled him alive in a cauldron.

A cramped and narrow pit dungeon in the current building is where Sir William Douglas incarcerated Sir Alexander Ramsay and slowly starved him to death. Ramsay hung on longer than was expected by eating grains of corn that slipped between the cracks in the floorboards of an overhead granary.

LOCATION: 4 MILES SOUTH OF KELSO ON A699

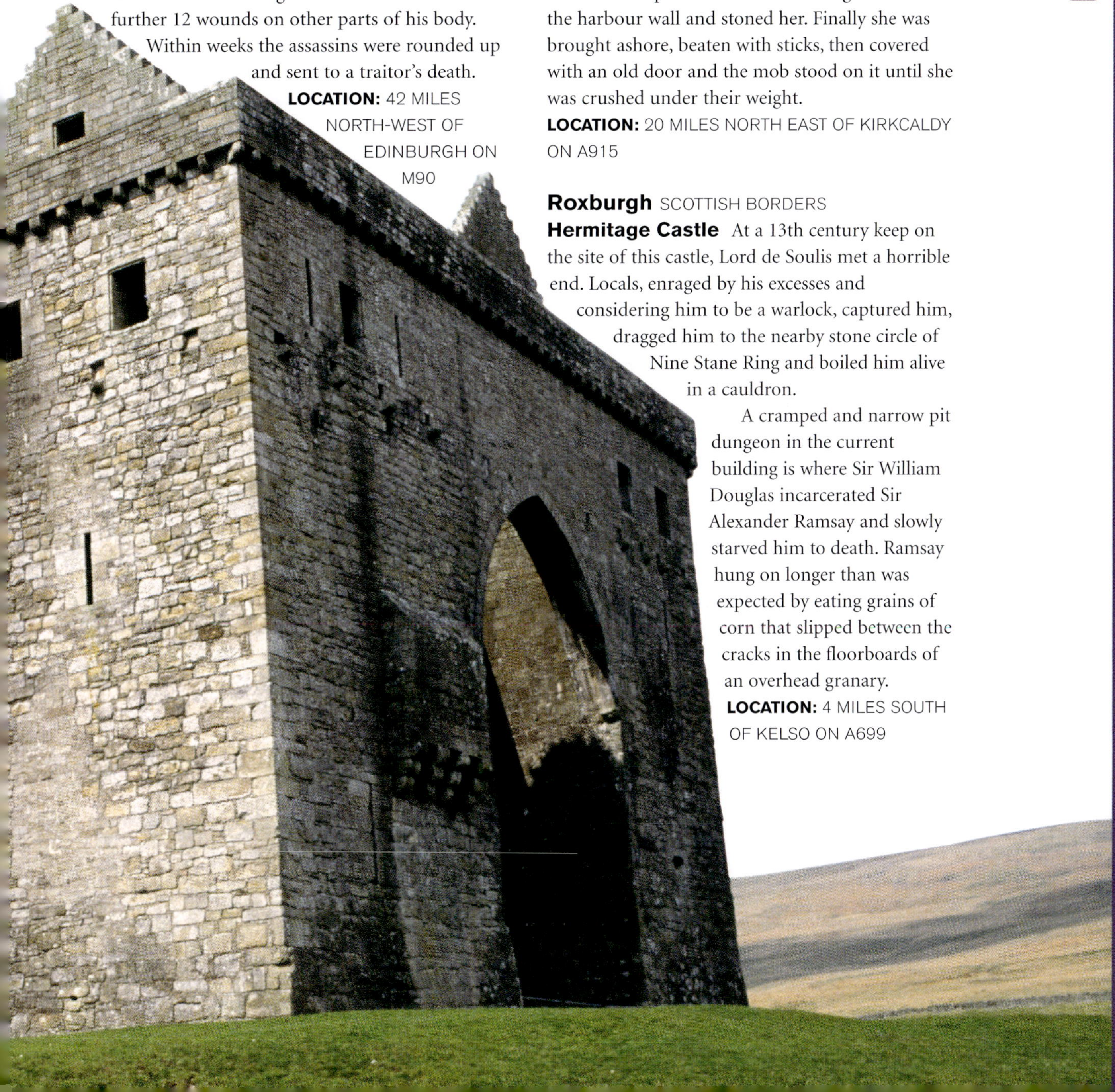

Smailholm SCOTTISH BORDERS

Mary Watson's last walk William Murray came to work on the turnpike road at Smailholm and lodged with the Watson family. He married Mary, the daughter, and in February 1845 the pair walked to Kelso, where they ended up drinking in a tavern. Later in the day they had an altercation and Murray struck his wife.

The couple started home at 10pm. Four hours later Murray knocked on the door of the Hendersons' cottage 2 miles along the road. He asked for assistance with his wife, who he said was lying drunk on the road. They found Mary covered in blood and carried her to the cottage. Murray left and went home, while Mrs Henderson sat up all night with Mary until she died. The police were called and discovered blood tracks on the road, indicating that Mary had been dragged for some distance, bleeding heavily. Murray was charged with murdering her by beating her with a stick, kicking her, trampling on her and strangling her. Despite the overwhelming evidence the jury returned a verdict of not proven, and William Murray got away with it.

LOCATION: 6 MILES WEST OF KELSO ON B6397

St Andrews FIFE

Martyrdom of Patrick Hamilton Educated on the Continent and influenced by the theology of Luther, Hamilton returned to his native Scotland in 1528 to preach the gospel. His success alarmed the Catholic clergy, who lured him to St Andrews. There he was arrested and condemned to death for heresy.

Archbishop Beaton (see below) had him burned at the stake, but the fire burned too slowly, and so gunpowder was added. This exploded, scorching Hamilton's face. He died slowly and very painfully, still refusing to recant.

Murder of Cardinal Beaton David Beaton succeeded his uncle, James Beaton, as Archbishop of St Andrews and was made a cardinal in 1538. He was deeply involved in politics, and kept a

Beaton protested that they could not kill him as he was a priest, but they slew him on the spot and hung his bloody corpse from the window, suspended by his own bed sheets.

mistress by whom he had several children. In March 1546 he had the Protestant preacher, George Wishart, apprehended, and then sentenced him to be burned before the castle walls without a trial. From a window overlooking the execution site, Beaton watched, while Wishart died in the flames.

On the morning of 29 May, he was surprised in bed by a group of Fife lairds, their swords drawn. Beaton protested that they could not kill him as he was a priest, but they slew him on the spot and hung his bloody corpse from the window, suspended by his own bed sheets.

LOCATION: 12 MILES SOUTH OF DUNDEE ON A914

Tighnabruaich ARGYLL & BUTE

Alfred Monson, a confidence trickster, portrayed himself as a gentleman and set himself up as Laird of Ardlamont using borrowed money. He arranged insurance on the life of a young friend, Cecil Hamborough, and then attempted to drown him by staging a boating accident.

When this failed, he took Hamborough shooting and then claimed that his friend had died when his gun discharged accidentally. However all the evidence pointed to Monson having fired the shot and he was arrested and charged with murder. The jury returned the peculiar Scottish verdict of 'not proven' and Monson got away with the crime.

LOCATION: 23 MILES WEST OF DUNOON ON A8003

Wigtown DUMFRIES & GALLOWAY

Drowning of the martyrs Two women, Margaret MacLachlan, aged 60 and 18-year-old Margaret Wilson, were tried as Covenanters in Wigtown in April 1685. The justices, including Bloody Grierson of Lag, found them guilty and sentenced them to death by drowning. On the day of execution they were taken on to the sands at Wigtown and tied to stakes below the high water mark. The old woman's stake was placed furthest from the shore in the mistaken belief that seeing her die would lead to the younger one renouncing her faith. MacLachlan fainted from the cold of the water and was unconscious as she drowned. Meanwhile the large crowd on the bank were entreating Wilson to recant and save herself, but she answered by singing verses of psalms, quoting from the Bible and finally praying before the water covered her mouth and nose. A stake on the sands marks the spot of the execution.

LOCATION: 7 MILES SOUTH OF NEWTON STEWART ON A714

Cardinal Beaton was a key figure in the 'Rough Wooing' of 1543

JOUGS AND BRANKS

The 'jougs' was a commonplace form of punishment in Scottish towns and villages from the 16th century. It was a hinged iron collar closed round the culprit's neck, and locked by a padlock. Fastened by a length of chain to public places like market crosses, the parish church, tollbooth or even the gallows, it was a humiliating punishment devised by the all-powerful kirk session.

The 'branks' were reserved almost exclusively for women. This cruel device had a framework of iron, which fastened round the victim's head and was held in place by an iron gag of spiked or sharpened iron on the culprit's tongue. Women sentenced to this punishment would have the branks placed on their heads and then be led through the streets by a chain or rope.

INDEX

ACKNOWLEDGEMENTS

The Automobile Association would like to thank the following libraries, photographers and establishments for their assistance in the preparation of this book.

BRIDGEMAN ART LIBRARY 227 The Last of the Clan, 1865 (oil on canvas) by Thomas Faed (1825–1900), The Fleming-Wyford Art Foundation; BRISTOL CITY MUSEUMS AND ART GALLERY 19; www.britainonview.com 24/25, 82, 114, 146; DORSET COUNTY MUSEUM 30; HULTON ARCHIVE 10/11 (background), 35, 41, 48, 49 (background), 49 (main), 50, 52/53 (background), 52l, 54, 55, 61, 71, 76, 77, 140/141 (background), 140 (main), 173, 174 (background), 182/183 (background), 182/183 (main), 205l, 205c, 205r, 226/227 (background); THE KOBAL COLLECTION/ICON/LADD CO/PARAMOUNT/COOPER, ANDREW 157; MARY EVANS PICTURE LIBRARY 26, 37, 39, 57c, 62/63 (background), 65, 72r, 73, 75, 94/95 (background), 98/99 (background), 99 (main), 102, 104 (background), 104 (main), 115, 131 (background), 131 (main), 135, 137 (background), 137 (main), 150/151 (background), 150 (main), 154/155 (background), 160/161 (background), 160 (main), 169, 174, 176/177 (background) (Tom Morgan), 176 (main) (Tom Morgan), 180/181, 196b, 202, 203, 215, 221, 223t, 223c, 225, 232/233, 237; © NATIONAL MARITIME MUSEUM, LONDON 32; NATIONAL WESTMINSTER BANK, STEVENAGE 91; ROTHWELL HOLY TRINITY CHURCH – www.Rothwellholytrinity.freeserve.co.uk 8/9 (background), 116/117 (background), 116 (main); TUC/TOLPUDDLE MARTYS MUSEUM 21.

The remaining pictures are held in the Association's own library (AA PHOTO LIBRARY) with contributions from the following:
PAT AITHIE 128/129 (background); M ALEXANDER 201t; M ALLWOOD-COPPIN 129; PETER BAKER 28 (background), 28 (main); VIC & STEWART BATES 151; JEFF BEAZLEY 162, 234/235; PETE BENNETT 158; M BIRKITT 12/13 (background), 94; E A BOWNESS 165, 178/179; IAN BURGUM 126/127 (background), 130, 148; MICHAEL BUSSELLE 62; DOUGLAS CORRANCE 192/193, 196t; STEVE DAY 212/213 (background), 212 (main), 228/229 (background), 228 (main); RICHARD G ELLIOT 191 (background), 197; DEREK FORSS 68, 80/81; STEPHEN GIBSON 231; T GRIFFITHS 168; ANTHONY HOPKINS 92/93, 105; RICHARD IRELAND 20; CAROLINE JONES 110/111, 124; ANDREW LAWSON 10; CAMERON LEES 154, 156/157, 162/163; S&O MATHEWS 86/87; GRAHAM MATTHEWS 132/133 (background), 134 (background); ERIC MEACHER 12; COLIN MOLYNEUX 128, 148/149; ROGER MOSS 29; RICH NEWTON 120 (background), 120 (main); HUGH PALMER 122/123; KEN PATERSON 188/189, 194, 198, 200/201 (background); PETER SHARPE 220/221 (background); TONY SOUTER 18, 84; DAVID TARN 158l, 166/167, 177, 178; RUPERT TENISON 30/31; JAMES TIMS 43b, 56; WYN VOYSEY 56/57 (background), 74, 88/89, 107; RONNIE WEIR 206; JONATHON WELSH 121t.